Professional Learning and Development in Schools and Higher Education

Volume 4

For further volumes:
http://www.springer.com/series/7908

Lily Orland-Barak

Learning to Mentor-as-Praxis

Foundations for a Curriculum in Teacher
Education

 Springer

Lily Orland-Barak
Faculty of Education
University of Haifa
7a/3 Hardoff St.
34747 Haifa
Israel
lilyb@construct.haifa.ac.il

ISBN 978-1-4419-0581-9   e-ISBN 978-1-4419-0582-6
DOI 10.1007/978-1-4419-0582-6
Springer New York Dordrecht Heidelberg London

Library of Congress Control Number: 2009943911

Printed on acid-free paper

Springer is part of Springer Science+Business Media (www.springer.com)

To Mika, my first grandchild who has granted me access into new meanings of being and creating.

Foreword

Lily Orland-Barak offers us a breathtaking work of science fiction. Or perhaps I should say 'science *and* fiction.' The science side of the equation employs sophisticated technique for observing and describing interpersonal and intrapersonal dynamics among professionals in education. Both dramatic and seemingly ordinary episodes in the lives of teachers in relational tension with one another are analyzed with scientific care, precision, and insight. The scientific study of mentoring is like the scientific study of soap bubbles – their formation, growth, and sudden exit from the visible world with a nearly soundless 'pop!' Scientific and intellectual tools can be used to describe and predict the behavior of soap bubbles, to study their colors, shapes, surface tension, and tiny mass. The same is true of the study of mentoring. But in both cases, the greatest care must be taken to avoid popping the almost magically elegant form – to avoid destroying the delicate relationship by rushing in, by heavy attempts at control, or by premature dissection, or even by paying attention too intensely to a private, personal relationship. Mentoring is best studied by being still, by listening with authentic interest, and by using our peripheral vision. The science and the scientist have done their best work here.

The fiction side of this fine book gives life to telling examples of mentoring in action. Lily Orland-Barak is a gifted storyteller who, with a few deft brush strokes, fires our imagination. We feel like we are right there in the room: happy but worn out from an intense conversation; delighted by a teacher's breakthrough insight; worried; and in love with a novice teacher's idealism and innocence. This is fiction writing in the best sense of the term: stories composed from the clay of facts observed, artfully arranged to evoke powerful feelings and to help us see invisible phenomena at play in the world.

In this book, science and fiction have been brought together to generate powerful, memorable story lines about mentoring. These story lines lead us to theory – a theory of action and interaction, of learning at the highest levels of professional and personal transformation, which we call 'mentoring.' The lasting contribution of this book will be to take readers to places we have never visited before, yet are as near as our neighborhood school or kitchen table. Lily Orland-Barak takes us to a high hill from which we can see the colors and contours of mentoring laid out at our feet.

Most importantly, she gives us new vision with which to appreciate and encourage the delicate dance of mentoring as the 50-year long extension of a journey that begins when a child first says, 'I want to be a teacher.'

Bryn Athyn, Pennsylvania, USA   Dr. Christopher M. Clark
                                                    President of Bryn Athyn College

Acknowledgements

The personal and intellectual journey that I underwent in the writing of this book owes a lot to a circle of critical friends, colleagues, students, teachers, mentors, and family who have supported and encouraged me in the various phases of the process: From the conception of the idea, toward its possible translation into a book, and finally into its actual writing and publication.

I am greatly indebted to Chris Clark who encouraged me to disseminate my ideas and pursue new intellectual challenges and creative paths to understanding mentoring and mentored learning.

I am especially grateful to two graduate students and mentees whose contribution has been invaluable for the creation of this book. Dalit Wilheim, whose wisdom of practice, dedication, enthusiasm, and creative thinking have been a great source of inspiration and support throughout the entire process.

A very special gratitude goes to Ayelet Becher, my most critical mentee and challenging cothinker and reader of the various versions of the manuscript. Ayelet has accompanied me as an insightful 'mentor' in the interpretation, representation, and editing processes, reminding me of the true meaning of reciprocity in a mentor–mentee relationship.

Special thanks to the blind reviewers of the manuscript for their insightful and constructive comments.

I am grateful to Sarah Williams, Editorial Assistant of Springer, who has been particularly supportive and kind, always willing to respond to any queries.

Finally, my deepest appreciation and love go to my husband and close friend, Ami Barak, and to my two beloved children, Alon and Dafi.

I owe to my parents, Gina and Yaacov Orland, who passed away a few years ago, and who taught me to never give up on my dreams and ideals.

Contents

Chapter 1
Introduction: Learning to Mentor-as-Praxis Foundations for a Curriculum in Teacher Education

1.1 Introduction

Consider the following story written by Fatin, an Arab mentor working with novice and experienced teachers in an Arab school in Israel:

As a result of the latest upheavals I sense a strong national awakening in the Arab sector which is also strengthened by feelings of anger. I have been working in the Arab villages as a mentor to promote the series 'Sesame Street' which is a program designed by national television to promote coexistence between Arab and Jews. However, in light of recent tensions and events, the teachers in the villages do not want to hear about the program. They are resistant to implementing it in their classes because they claim that the program conveys hidden messages against Arabs and that it conveys the message that the Arab will always give in to the Jew. The teachers explained to me that their identification with the Palestinian people stops them ideologically from connecting to anything that is related to the Jewish people: they don't want to learn about them, they don't want to work with them, they don't want to cooperate or collaborate and that is the message that should be passed on to the children. I was confronted with an extremely difficult conflict: I want to educate for coexistence and serve as a bridge for communication between the two peoples. But I couldn't say that to the teachers because being an Arab they would interpret it as if I was betraying my own people. Although I tried to talk to them about it, I gave up fairly quickly and avoided the issue. We are now working together on other issues ... but I still think it is a worthwhile program implementing and I think that we missed a lot by avoiding it in our sessions ....

Fatin's story is compelling. Although written at the background of one of the most unresolved political conflicts, the Israeli–Palestinian conflict, the tensions and contradictions that she shares with us as a mentor might speak to any kind of mentoring context where issues of political, social, and cultural tensions are at stake (e.g., amongst Hispanics, Chicanos, African Americans, and Anglo Americans in the United States; Maoris, New Zealanders, and Europeans in New Zealand; Irish, Pakistanis, and British in the United Kingdom; and many more). In fact, as Berger and Luckmann (1966) remind us in their treatise on the social construction of meaning, 'any kind of practice must be understood in the cultural, social, political context

L. Orland-Barak, *Learning to Mentor-as-Praxis*, Professional Learning and Development in Schools and Higher Education 4, DOI 10.1007/978-1-4419-0582-6_1, © Springer Science+Business Media, LLC 2010

within which it occurs,' urging us to attend to how the particular social, cultural, and political features of any given practice shape the way in which its participants make sense of and learn to perform in that practice. In an era of globalization and individualism vis-à-vis a search for local religious, ethnic, and cultural identity (Giddens, 2000; Giroux, 2005), Fatin's conflict seems to cross cultural and geographical borders.

In the context of teacher education, these issues have become a major concern for thinking and implementing a practice which is culturally responsive (Cochran-Smith, 2004; Villegas & Lucas, 2002), and for thinking about practice as embedded in multicultural realities at the intersection between ideologies, values, belief systems, and behaviors. Already in the early eighties, Zeichner (1983) called for being more concerned in teacher education with the question of which educational, moral, and political commitments ought to guide our work in the field rather than with the practice of nearly dwelling on procedures and organizational arrangements. Indeed, the past three decades of educational research have contributed with important insights to our understanding of how issues related to ideological, moral, and political agendas play out to shape the realities of teacher education (Cochran-Smith, 2004; Clark, 1995; Fenstermacher, 1990; Lickona, 1980; Loughran, 2002; Sleeter, 1998; Tirri, 1999; Tom, 1984; Valli, 1990; Villegas & Lucas, 2002). This was especially pronounced in the overall orientation of the recent annual American Educational Research conference theme (AERA, 2006), which stressed the importance of attending to how contextual conditions and commitments guide educational research in the public interest.

1.2 Learning to Mentor: Extended Meanings

Mentoring, as an integral component of teacher education, aligns with the above concerns and orientations. Rooted in Homer's Odyssey, the term Mentor was traditionally equated with expertise, reflected in the mentor's capacity to guide, instruct, protect, and challenge the novice protégé (Anderson & Shannon, 1988). In tune with the above shifts, however, the clear-cut boundaries that used to define the one-to-one relationship between an expert and a novice envisioned in the role of Mentor toward Telemachus have now been expanded to include both formal and informal mentoring relationships (Evans, 2000) between teachers and pupils, teachers and teachers, supervisors and teachers, and so on (McIntyre, Hagger, & Wilkin, 1993; Roberts, 2000; Rust & Dreifus, 2001). To date, mentors' roles, both at preservice and in-service levels, range from modeling and instructing to information sources, cothinkers and inquirers, evaluators, supervisors, and learning companions (Zanting, Verloop, Vermunt, & Van Driel, 1998). These extended roles also address the importance of being tolerant to and of acknowledging the voices and cultural practices of the various ethnic and minority groups of student teachers and mentees.

Learning to mentor in this extended sense should then entail learning about how ideologies, rituals, values, belief systems, and behaviors play out in mentoring interactions amongst various participants (mentors and student teachers, mentors and experienced teachers, mentors and school principals, inspectors and mentors and other colleagues), from different cultural, ethnic religious backgrounds and educational orientations. Only recently, however, has mentoring begun to consider these agendas as inherent to the practice (Kochan & Pascarelli, 2003; Miller-Marsh, 2002; Mullen & Lick, 1999; Mullen, Cox, Boettcher, & Adoue, 1997; Orland-Barak, 2003a, 2003b; Roberts, 2000; Wang, 2001). There is a growing recognition of the role of the mentor as a professional role that develops within complex interpersonal and social professional webs (Achinstein & Athanases, 2006; Little, 1990), challenging mentors into functioning in critical and moral ways, considering their decisions and subsequent actions in terms of dilemmas that carry moral values (Benner, 1982; Van Manen, 1991; Eisner & Powell, 2002; Feiman-Nemser, 2001).

1.3 Characterizing the Landscape of Mentoring: A Portrayal of the Literature

The intertextual understanding of literature requires the establishment of a two-way relationship. The first one faces the literary text in relationship to other texts ... The second, however, is the one which places the literary text in relationship to a separate sign system from the sphere of culture, history and reality (Kulavkova, 2004)

Kulavkova's conceptualization of the intertextual nature of literary texts calls for examining the evolving literature of mentoring from an historic perspective of the textual positionings undergone by the practice – as related to broader theoretical texts and ideological orientations to professional learning. Indeed, a survey of the literature on mentoring in teacher education, spanning from the last two decades of the twentieth century and into the sprouts of the twenty-first century, suggests a portrayal of the practice which reflects the emergent 'bigger picture' of clinical practices striving to become recognized as professional practices (Glazer, 2008). Such a shift is reflected in the extension of structural and organizational dimensions which predominated in the late eighties and early nineties (Wilkin, 1992; Yeomans & Sampson, 1994; McIntyre et al., 1993; Tomlinson, 1995; Kerry & Mayes, 1995; Mullen & Lick, 1999), toward the acknowledgement of supportive, collaborative, and ethical aspects that are integral to practices that define themselves as professional.

For example, the range of published books and articles on mentoring in the early nineties stress topics such as strategic planning, training on practical skills, development of professional competencies, matching processes to desired outcomes, designing induction programs, summative and formative assessment of mentored learning, monitoring teaching activities, scaffolding subject matter teaching and learning, formal and informal aspects of assistance, and collaboration that occurs in dyadic interactions (Daloz, 1983; Tomlinson, 1995; Yeomans & Sampson, 1994; Wilkin, 1992). From the mid-nineties, we see a surge of publications that emphasize the value of collaborative professional learning for the enhancement of reflective practice, for developing interpersonal sensitivity, for engaging in team and coteaching, for creating partnerships, and for developing common ground through shared activity (Tomlinson, 1995; Kerry & Mayes, 1995; Mullen, 1997; Mullen & Lick, 1999; Shulman & Sato, 2006; Achinstein & Anasthases, 2006). Important articles have also contributed to understanding how subject matter dialogue can assist prospective teachers in scaffolding their learning (Athanases & Achinstein, 2003; Ball, 2000; Edwards & Collison, 1996; Grossman, 1991; Rodgers, 2001; Norman & Feiman-Nemser, 2005). The last decade of scholarship and research on mentoring has gradually become more attentive to dimensions of the practice that pertain to issues of diversity, cultural sensitivity, context, and power relations (Kochan & Pascarelli, 2003; Mullen, 1997). Recently, there is small but growing body of publications that attend to ethical and moral considerations and dilemmas, tensions between individual needs and the needs of the system, the place of advanced technology and its ethical implications, and inherent complexities within communities of practice (Bardram, 1998; Craig & Deretchin, 2009).

Taken together, the various developmental shifts to the practice suggest important ideological, methodological, and conceptual directions:

(1) Methodologically and conceptually, we witness a shift toward a view of the practice along the following continua (Fig. 1.1):
(2) A recognition of political, ethical, and moral dimensions intrinsic to the practice of mentoring suggests its gradual shift toward becoming *a professional practice* connoting 'a universal system for solving a set of problems underscored by a set of norms and skills among the community ... [and shaped by] the mechanisms by which the practice is managed and controlled' (Glazer, 2008). In this extended sense, mentoring as an emergent profession begins to attend to various measurements of professionalism such as cultural authority, control of entry into the profession, state protection, control over working conditions, congruency between technical dimensions of the practice and the social environment in which the practice is interpreted and understood, and consistency in identifying, interpreting, and acting on a set of problems (Glazer, 2008).
(3) Studies on exemplary mentoring and leadership across professions (Miles, Saxl, & Lieberman, 1988; Orland-Barak & Hasin, 2009; Popper, Mayseless, & Castelnovo, 2000) draw our attention to a number of general qualities that are displayed in 'good mentoring practices across contexts.' For example, exemplary mentors hold an articulated educational ideology. There is also a strong correspondence between what mentors say they believe in and their enacted roles in practice. Most of all, exemplary mentors exhibit highly developed organizational skills, interpersonal relationships, reflexivity, ability to integrate theory and practice, subject matter expertise, professionalism, leadership roles and the right combination of challenge, modeling, and support. These attributes connote with Miles et al.'s study (1988) of teacher leaders who had taken or changed agent roles in their schools. Their study and others suggest that leaders come to their work as knowledgeable and experienced in demonstrative and organizational skills, have a strong disposition to

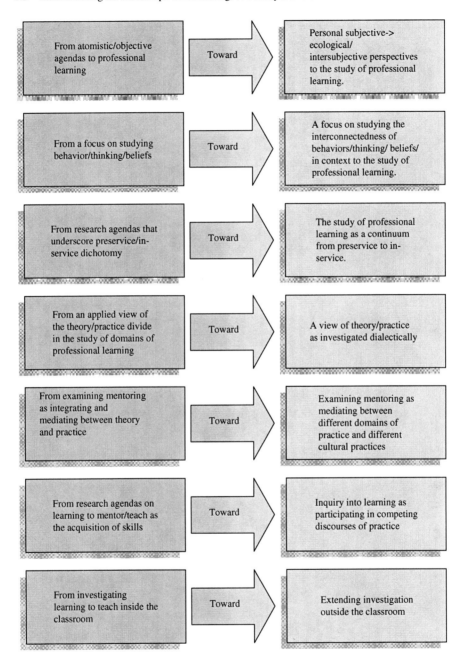

Fig. 1.1 Shifts in orientation to the practice of mentoring

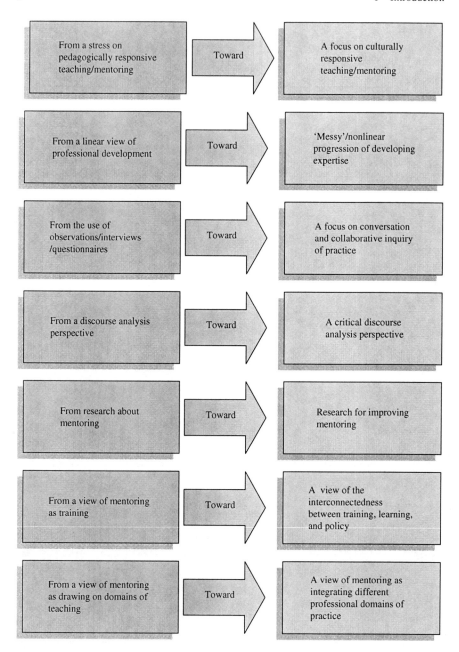

Fig. 1.1 (continued)

learn about the complexity of the workplace culture, are risk takers willing to promote new ideas that might seem difficult or threatening to their colleagues, and hold strong interpersonal skills (Burns, 1978; Bass, 1985; Popper, 2001; Popper et al., 2000). These characteristics speak to those of exemplary mentors, who display an ability to empower, promote autonomy, raise motivation, and encourage reflection. Star mentors mentioned leading the mentees toward autonomy, empowering them and developing them professionally by focusing on developing their thinking through questions that encourage reflection. They also stressed the importance of building supportive relationships in a mentoring conversation that is empathetic, respectful, and accepting (Orland-Barak & Hassin, in press).

(4) The accumulated knowledge grounded in the various studies foreground a platform of *generic attributes* that seem to cross mentoring practices. From a phenomenological reading of the literature, Andy Roberts collated the essential attributes of mentoring. In his survey *Mentoring Revisited* (Roberts, 2000, p. 51), he suggests similar dispositions and features of good mentoring practices: a process form; an active relationship; a helping process; a teaching–learning process; reflective practice; a career and personal development process; a formalized process; and a role constructed by and for a mentor. Drawing on Roberts' characterization, and extending it to my own research and synthesis of the literature, I propose the following basic, generic practices, phrased as speech acts (Austin, 1962; Searle, 1995), to stress their illocutionary force, that is, that 'by saying something, one *does* something.' As Austin contends, an utterance is an action, that is, it is intentional and meant as something. It becomes a speech act when it is taken up by the others to whom it has been addressed. Each speech act has an illocutionary force, that is, its social power as uttered in a certain context (Harre & Gillett, 1994). A focus on acts rather than on traditional 'roles' underscores the praxical, action-oriented character of mentoring and mentored learning.

- Reading a mentoring situation
- Appraising pedagogical practices
- Observing pedagogical practices
- Recording appropriate modes of support
- Mediating persons, context, and content
- Assuming diverse supportive roles
- Managing accountabilities
- Establishing and sustaining professional relationships
- Tuning In
- Articulating teaching, learning, and subject matter
- Responding in the 'spot' by connecting experience, beliefs, and knowledge.

1.4 The Discursive Character of Generic Attributes

> Discourse involves both symbolic interactions and the conventions and relationships in
> which those interactions are constrained by informal rules and interconnected with each
> other in ways that reflect the order of things . . . I inhabit many discourses, each of which
> has its own cluster of significations . . . . An individual person in discourse with others is
> a meeting point of many discourses and must, to some extent, integrate the multifaceted
> subjectivity that arises from the intersection of influences . . . (Foucault, in Harre & Gillett,
> 1994, pp. 25–26)

The generic attributes elaborated above draw on sound theoretical propositions
and research findings. Said that, they are still represented through a rather encapsu-
lated and fragmented conglomerate of research agendas – much like separate rather
than coherent islands of connected studies to inform guidelines for the development
of a curriculum. Like the problem of fragmentation in preservice preparation, induction, and professional development, mentoring agendas lack "connective tissue . . .
holding things together within and across the different phases. . ." (Feiman-Nemser,
2001, p. 1049).

This book attempts to stand to the challenge of suggesting a coherent portrayal of
the generic dimensions of the practice, extending them to their *discursive attributes*.
In discursive terms, discursive attributes speak to the *actions and the acts they
accomplish* [that] *make up discursive practices . . . which is the repeated and orderly
use of some signification system, where these uses are intentional, that is directed at
or to something . . .* (Harre & Gillett, 1994, p. 28).

In doing so, I hope to contribute to our understanding of mentoring as an emergent profession – characterized by an ethics of practice and shaped by moral,
political, and social agendas which underlie particular forms of practice.

1.5 Back to Fatin's story. . .

Fatin's story, as many other cases that are considered in the various chapters of
this book, stems from a large pool of stories, cases, and critical incidents in my
own research on learning to mentor. These data sources shed light on how cultural,
ideological, and political dispositions play out to shape mentors' attributions, reasoning, and actions. Fatin's story, for example, reflects some of the dilemmas and
conflicts that Arab mentors experienced as they participated in mentoring interactions in their own regional schools. These were rooted in emergent contradictions
between what they regarded as western, educational ideologies, as opposed to eastern authoritative orientations to teaching and learning. In many cases, mentors were
concerned that they would be seen by their Arab fellow teachers as betraying their
faith and commitment to the traditions that spoke to eastern modes of thinking and
acting. Fatin's case depicts this conflict: Although we might expect that being an
Arab mentor working with Arab teachers, Fatin would not have to participate in
conflicts of loyalty and national identity; she is, nevertheless, caught in the political–
ideological tensions brought about by the Israeli–Palestinian conflict. These tensions
yield educational and pedagogical encounters which are extremely problematic and

grounded in competing and often clashing educational agendas and power relations. As a resolution to her conflict, and similarly to other cases of mentors, she opts for responding in a way that is receptive to the cultural codes and political sensitivities of her mentees. As a result, she finds herself putting aside her initial agenda, in fear that she would be seen as betraying her own people. Although she states that she *want[s] to educate for co-existence and serve as a bridge for communication between the two peoples* and that her mandate to implement the Sesame Street program in her school would help to achieve her vision, she opts for not endangering her Arab identity in the eyes of the teachers. She gives up on her professional and ideological sense of agency so as not to jeopardize her image as a Palestinian Arab and her commitment to the Arab cause in the eyes of the teachers *because being an Arab they would interpret it as if I am betraying my own people* .

What makes this case compelling, as many other cases, is the fact that even in situations in which the mentor shares the same ethnic and religious background with her mentees, the political friction embedded in her context of mentoring often shapes the way in which she appreciates, records, and responds to the situation. In doing so, he/she might opt for a mode of participation that might eventually contradict her own ideologies and educational agendas, when these are in political clash with the mentoring context within which she works.

1.6 Unfolding Mentor's Dialogical Journey: Beyond Homer

Besides Homer's mandate to guide, instruct, and protect his protégé Telemachus, the dialogical character of mentoring practices is (if only) implied in Homer's allusion to the role of Mentor as fluctuating between two poles of social representations. One is the matriarchal function, including roles of caring, emotional support, nurturing, and maintaining the home. The other, the journey of Telemachus, with the accompanying and guidance of Mentor, produces a narrative of maturing into manhood and reinforces the ethos of the patriarchic public sphere. In this implied representation, we find that the function of balancing power relations between competing agendas of the different social agents (the competitors for inheriting Odysseus home and public role, during his absence) becomes a central task in mentoring. Thus, already at the origins of western culture, we are indirectly introduced to the image of the mentor as navigating between opposing (yet complementing) competing voices. This book explicitly foregrounds this image, by critically exposing the multicultural realities, ideologies, values, belief systems, and behaviors that shape the practice. As such, it engages in a comprehensive reading beyond Mentor's implied discursive roles in the Odyssey.

1.7 Learning to Mentor: Domains of Praxis

Attending to how mentors' ideological, political, and moral stances intersect with pedagogical action to shape curricular reasoning calls for a perspective, as the title of this book suggests, to learning to mentor as 'praxis.' Praxis, in this sense, constitutes

an encounter between participants (in our case mentors and mentees) at the intersection between theory and practice. Such an encounter takes place in action and is
inherently complex and stranded in ethical, moral, cultural, and political conflicts,
dilemmas, and tensions.

Learning to mentor-as-praxis would, then, attend to questions such as which
'texts' are being responded to in mentoring interactions; how participation and communication is reciprocated, legitimated, improvised, and sustained; what roles are
assumed and valued; what is recorded, listened for, and for what purposes; and how
various cultural and organizational codes and rituals of practice are represented
and appreciated. This calls for extending the contents of a curriculum for learning to mentor from the acquisition of skills in practice toward the acquisition of
professional competence and performance within *domains of praxis*.

Theoretically, learning to mentor-as-praxis calls on social-constructivist and
cultural theories of professional learning that attend to these commitments in educational thought and practice. As such, they emphasize learning from experience
(Dewey, 1933), and knowledge as dialectically constituted through reasoned inquiry,
observation, experience, participation, and practice (Clark, 2001; Engeström, 1994;
Engeström, 2001; Lave & Wenger, 1991; Loughran, 2003; Tillema, 2005).

Programmatically, mentoring as praxis calls for replacing traditional 'theory as
informing practice' curriculum paradigms for a curriculum which validates theory and practice as existing in reciprocal relationship (Gore & Zeichner,1991;
Korthagen & Kessels, 1999; Kwo, 1996; Laboskey, 1994; Rodgers, 2002; Schon,
1987), to guide its design and implementation procedures. The latter also implies a
shift from a 'mentor training' curriculum perspective (focusing on techniques and
skills) to a 'mentor education' curriculum perspective, beyond the acquisition of
skills, emphasizing the systematic process by which prospective mentors develop
their own critical subjective educational theories (Kelchtermans & Vandenberghe,
1994) alongside the acquisition of mentoring skills. As such, it views learning to
mentor as *the acquisition of competencies* that transcend technical thinking about
'what to do' and 'what strategies to adopt' in the work of mentors. This implies
endorsing a curriculum that is attentive to *appreciation* of underlying codes, rituals, contradictions, and interests represented in particular cultures of teaching and
mentoring; to modes and modalities of *participation*; and to developing strategies
for informed *improvisation*. It also speaks to a curriculum that endorses a view of
learning that spans throughout a continuum of time and experiences (as opposed
to condensed 'one-shot' meetings) whereby learning is collaboratively construed,
distributed, and disseminated both locally and publicly.

Specifically, and drawing on the past decade of studies that I conducted in
mentoring, *learning to mentor-as-praxis* would entail the following dimensions of
knowledge competence and performance: Appreciating and recording the underlying codes, rituals, contradictions, and interests represented in particular cultures
of teaching and mentoring [appreciation]; becoming aware of modes and modalities of participation [participation]; responding to a variety of discourses of practice
[response]; and, as a result, developing strategies for engaging in informed improvisation [improvisation]. Taken together, these dimensions of knowledge competence

and performance call for attending to three interrelated 'domains of praxis' in a curriculum for learning to mentor, explored throughout the book:

- *Appreciation*
- *Participation*
- *Improvisation*

1.8   Foundations for a Curriculum

Domains in a curriculum can be defined as content areas that provide a means for structuring the 'knowledge base' of a curriculum within a particular field of study or professional discipline (Behar, 1994). Whether viewed in philosophical and/or operational terms, domains suggest broad conceptualizations of content areas or classical topics which, in turn, guide specific curriculum practices (Ibid.). Curriculum practices are the behaviors and activities in which curriculum workers engage while planning, implementing, or evaluating curriculum in educational settings. The integral character of domains and practices in a curriculum knowledge base calls for delineating concrete forms of practice within each domain, to guide specific designs and forms of implementation of the curriculum.

Taken to our context and espousing a curriculum for learning to mentor *as praxis*, the above implies endorsing a conception of domains that integrates dimensions of knowledge competence as well as performance. In this vein, each chapter is organized around a case or cases that provide a scenario or 'instance of action' which 'zooms in' to particular domain in learning to mentor. These scenarios provide authentic, situated illustrations of how ideological, political, and moral considerations might shape modes of participation, appreciation, record, response, and improvisation in mentoring (i.e., the domains of praxis). The presentation of the scenarios is followed by a discussion grounded in theoretical, empirical, and experiential sources. These sources draw on evidence from empirical research (my own and other), alongside reflections on my own experience as a mentor of mentors, as a course professor in numerous academic and professional courses for the preparation of mentors, and as a mentor of new faculty members at the university. The analysis and interpretation of the cases presented in each chapter provide the basis for the curriculum guidelines and practices, developed in the last two chapters of the book.

Specifically, Chapter 2 and Chapter 3 situate the empirically rooted conceptual framework for thinking about a curriculum in learning to mentor as 'domains of praxis' within theories of professional learning and knowledge development. Chapter 2 presents an overview of prevalent orientations to mentoring and professional learning, situating mentoring-as-praxis within sociocultural approaches and reflective, critical views of professional learning.

Chapter 3 expands on the conceptual framework of 'learning to mentor-as-praxis,' presenting the concept of praxis and situating it in the philosophical discourse of dialectics and phronesis. Chapter 4, Chapter 5, and Chapter 6 each focuses on a specific domain of learning to mentor-as-praxis, explored through illustrative scenarios of action. Chapter 4 explores 'Appreciation,' Chapter 5 discusses 'Participation,' and Chapter 6 presents 'Improvisation.' Chapter 7 describes and interprets the concrete and dynamic meanings that improvisation, informed by appreciation and participation, takes in the discourse of two dyadic mentoring conversations. Chapter 8 introduces two contrastive examples of group conversations, showing how appreciation, participation, and improvisation can be either successfully or unsuccessfully constituted in the public space of group mentoring conversations to enhance participants' learning. Chapter 9 presents the foundations underlying a curriculum on learning to mentor-as-praxis, with a focus on principles underlying the design of appropriate settings, conditions, and tasks – as grounded in the three domains of praxis developed throughout the chapters. Chapter 10 offers concrete examples of working methodologies for accomplishing these principles. Chapter 11 considers paradoxes, ambivalences, challenges, and difficulties that might emerge while implementing and appropriating such methodologies.

1.9 Focus and Audience

The book is intended for educational researchers and teacher educators in the area of mentoring, mentored learning, faculty development, and curriculum development. The book can inform curriculum developers and policy makers in preservice and in-service teacher education, and in the area of faculty development in higher education. The book can also contribute to researchers and curriculum developers in the area of mentoring across disciplines (nursing, social work, etc.)

Endorsing an inclusive perspective to understanding and practicing mentoring, the book offers the following distinctive angles:

It suggests a conceptual framework for understanding learning to mentor that is rooted in *ideological, political, and moral dimensions* that play out in mentors' pedagogical reasoning and action. Adopting a sociocultural perspective to *learning to mentor-as-praxis*, it attends to recent calls for considering social, cultural, and contextual aspects of mentoring. Methodologically, the book offers a theoretical framework which combines insights from empirical findings with insights informed by personal experience, attending to complementary modes of inquiry and reflection on lived experiences.Informed by the above conceptual framework, the book presents *concrete guidelines* for the design and procedures of *a curriculum for learning to mentor.*The proposed curriculum is organized around the notion of *domains of knowledge competence and performance in mentoring.* This classification *extends* traditional views of learning to mentor as the acquisition of skills toward a view of learning to mentor as the acquisition of *interrelated knowledge areas* of professional competence and performance.

The book *focuses on learning to mentor prospective teachers in preservice education, experienced teachers in in-service education, and in higher education.* As such, it suggests a view of preservice, in-service, and higher education as one continuum of professional development in mentoring.

The book addresses recent calls for endorsing an academic status to mentors' professional learning by suggesting an academic course of training.

Chapter 2
Learning to Mentor as Praxis: Situating the Conversation

2.1 Looking Back

What led to the conceptualization suggested in this book? Addressing this question necessitates a brief 'detour' to my own reflective research and experiential journey leading to the title of this book.

In 1997, when I began investigating the process of learning to mentor as experienced by two novice mentors, I proposed connecting learning to mentor with learning a second language of teaching. I argued, then, that the passage from being a teacher of children to becoming a mentor of teachers is a highly conscious and gradual process of reorganizing and reconstructing beliefs and understandings that the novice mentor holds as a teacher in order to make sense of the new context of mentoring (McIntyre & Hagger, 1996; Orland, 1997). Such a proposition defied commonly held conceptions of the passage from teaching to mentoring as starting from 'zero level,' urging us, instead, to define mentoring as connected to mentors' expertise as school teachers, rather than through other domains such as therapy or organizational psychology (McIntyre & Hagger, 1993).

In my initial work, the main construct that emerged from novice mentors' account of their learning was their ability to *tune in to the mentee*, also referred to as *cuing in*, *zooming in*, or *finding the right window*. Mentors' recurrent use of these phrases to describe the ways in which they were learning *to communicate* with their mentees led me eventually to conceptualize learning to mentor as a process of learning to communicate in a new language in the context of professional learning, or, metaphorically, *learning to mentor as learning a second language of teaching* (Orland-Barak, 2001).

Seven years later, informed by important findings from studies conducted in other contexts and by my own investigation, I had recreated the initial metaphor of learning to mentor as 'acquiring a second language of teaching' to *learning to participate in competing discourses of practice* (Orland-Barak, 2005b). The new metaphor implied a view of the practice as socially constructed and understood within the particular discourse community within which it is created and sustained (with its unique language, ideological, historical, cultural, and social heritage) (Gee, 1996, 1999).

L. Orland-Barak, *Learning to Mentor-as-Praxis*, Professional Learning and
Development in Schools and Higher Education 4, DOI 10.1007/978-1-4419-0582-6_2,
© Springer Science+Business Media, LLC 2010

The metaphor of participation was rooted in the strong sense of vulnerability that mentors attributed to their work in the findings of my own investigations. These pointed to dilemmas of accountability, carrying conflicting values and ideologies, often positioning mentors as 'juggling' competing and conflicting discourses (Orland-Barak, 2002).

Present studies, thus, shed light on issues of morality, expertise, context, conditions, and power relations that play out in learning to mentor. In a recent article entitled Lost in Translation: Mentors Learning to Participate in Competing Discourses of Practice (Orland-Barak, 2005a, p. 364), I wrote the following epilogue:

> The reflective research journey has sharpened my awareness of the importance of accounting for the systemic, political, and ideological context within which a practice is acquired...just as research on teaching and on learning to teach has gradually shifted...to [focus on] how the educational and sociocultural context(s) shape teacher–pupil interactions...research on mentoring and learning to mentor needs to extend its focus from the acquisition of skills, to how the contexts within which mentors work shape the character of their work, the skills that they develop, and the nature of the passage from teaching to mentoring. Viewed in this broader perspective, and constituting an important aspect of teacher education, mentoring must also be understood as "an intellectual, cultural and contextual activity" (Cochran-Smith, 2004, p. 298).

2.2 Continuing the Conversation

Drawing on my evolving understandings of learning to mentor as an intellectual, cultural, and contextual activity, this book continues the above conversation to suggest a framework for conceptualizing learning to mentor-as-praxis that attends to these extended meanings. At the outset, it seems important to position 'learning to mentor' in relation to extant competing approaches to mentoring and professional learning, with a focus on the praxical (or nonpraxical) character of each approach.

2.3 Approaches to Mentoring: Competing Perspectives on a Practice

As mentioned in the introductory chapter, the term Mentor is rooted in Homer's Odyssey and it is used to denote the capacity to guide, instruct, protect, and challenge the novice protégé as envisioned in the role of Mentor toward Telemachus (Anderson & Shannon, 1988). To date, mentors' roles have been expanded to include modeling, instructing, cothinking, inquiring, evaluating, supervising, facilitating, and learning companionship (Zanting, Verloop, Vermunt, & Van Driel, 1998).

The orientation toward functioning in any of the above extended roles depends, to a large extent, on the espoused approach to mentoring, whether of a more apprenticeship nature or of a personalistic and collaborative nature. Specifically, mentoring seems to be shaped by competing therapeutic, apprenticeship, and reflective collaborative approaches to the practice, aligned along a continuum that ranges from 'outside-in'/top-down views of mentoring as product to 'inside-out'/bottom-up views of mentoring as process (Orland-Barak & Klein, 2005).

In this section, I discuss competing approaches to mentoring and their connection to five prevailing views of adult learning (Carr & Kemmis, 1986): common sense, applied science, philosophical, practical, and critical. I suggest that a particular approach to mentoring aligns with a corresponding view of adult learning and professional knowledge, guiding mentors into idiosyncratic modes of reasoning and behavior. Understanding learning to mentor as an intellectual, cultural, and contextual activity in praxis speaks to reflective and collaborative approaches to mentoring. These are rooted in sociocultural theories of learning, embedding practical and critical views of professional knowledge development. The latter is explored in detail in the last section of the chapter.

2.4 Apprenticeship-Instructional Approaches: Common Sense and Applied Views

Mentoring practices that follow an apprenticeship/instructional/top down orientation are of a predominantly prescriptive nature, based on modeling and on repeated behaviors. According to this approach mentors determine the starting point for the mentoring conversation, deciding what is listened for and for what purposes. Prioritizing and attending first and foremost to the mentor's interpretation of the mentoring situation, the mentor functions as a model and as a charismatic figure to the mentees, guiding them toward the acquisition of defined patterns of behavior, as determined and regulated by external agendas and authorities (Giroux, 1996; Halley, 1967). In this deliberative approach (Valli, 1990) to mentoring, the mentor stresses a practice which is characterized by instructing someone in the right behavior or ideas of what morally 'ought to be done,' as represented by external codes and educational agendas of the 'authoritative discourses' (Bakhtin, 1981) that they are accountable to.

Apprenticeship/instructional approaches speak to Carr and Kemmis (1986) 'commonsense' and 'applied science' view of professional competence. Aligning with a 'common sense' orientation to professional knowledge as grounded in practical common sense experience rather than in theory, the task of the mentor, then, becomes to facilitate the successful teachers' traditional patterns of conduct (Carr & Kemmis, 1986). Furthermore, according to the common sense view, professional development is exhibited through the skilful use of an existing pool of pedagogical knowledge. Hence, learning to mentor programs that abide by this view would stress the acquisition of a repertoire of pedagogical skills in mentoring.

Apprenticeship/instructional approaches also speak to an 'applied science' view of professional expertise. This view stresses the importance of acquiring technical skills for applying scientific theories and principles to educational situations (Ibid.).

Professional competence is, then, evaluated by the professional's effectiveness in achieving certain prescribed goals rather than by their capacity to formulate aims. The role of the mentor, then, becomes to transmit scientifically verified knowledge toward the effective implementation of preestablished educational goals. Learning to mentor programs that abide by this view would, then, stress training mentors to acquire technical skills for effectively assisting teachers in their practices.

2.5 Personal Growth/Inside-Out Approaches: Philosophical Views

Approaches that identify with a more psychological, philosophical stance follow a personal growth/inside-out/bottom-up orientation to mentoring, whereby the mentor acts closer to the role of 'therapist' and the mentee to that of a 'patient.' This personal growth and humanistic approach to mentoring stresses the value of the mentoring relationship for the development and growth of the mentee as a person. In this vein, the 'mentor-therapist' either 'talks to' the mentee (Fleming & Benedek, 1983; Yerushalmi & Karon, 1999), or the mentor and mentee 'talk to each other' in an effort to reach common understandings of the mentee's experiences (Goolishian, 1990; Rice, 1980). In his/her 'reading of the mentoring text' (Orland & Klein, 2005), the mentor accesses communication by prioritizing and legitimizing the text of the mentee, attending to the personal interests, values, and meanings that the mentee attributes to her experiences. This person-centred approach to accessing and sustaining communication implies covertly attending to the cultural, educational, and organizational codes that shape the mentees' particular context of teaching (such as prior personal and/or professional histories and experiences as students).

An inside-out/bottom-up perspective forwards a relational approach to mentoring (Valli, 1990), one which acknowledges a moral agenda that prioritizes and legitimizes empathetic understanding over rationality and abstract principles. This personalistic orientation is rooted in receptivity, relatedness, and responsiveness to the 'internally persuasive discourses' (Bakhtin, 1981) of the person as an individual. As such, the rational codes of behavior and 'authoritative discourses' of external forces and institutionalized systems are mitigated, allowing for attending to latent and silenced marginalized discourses (Giroux,1996; Gee, 1999).

Inside-out/bottom-up perspectives connote with more philosophical approaches to knowledge acquisition, which stress the need for practitioners to adopt a reflective stance toward the assumptions and ideals on which their philosophy of education resides (Carr & Kemmis, 1986). Professional competence is viewed as making judgments in accordance with fully articulated principles, values, and ideas. In this vein, the purpose of mentoring becomes to equip teachers with the necessary conceptual tools to formulate a coherent understanding of the nature and purposes of their roles as educators – with a focus on developing and articulating a personal educational theory and stance (Kelchtermans &Vandenberghe, 1994; Feiman-Nemser, 2001). Learning to mentor programs that endorse this perspective would, then, stress contents that raise mentors' consciousness of their own educational philosophies in mentoring as well as competencies for assisting teachers to articulate their goals as educators. It would also promote the development of communication strategies for engaging in interpersonal aspects of professional relationships, to allow for reflective exploration of dimensions of the experience which touch upon core reflective levels of their mission and 'being' as educators (Korthagen & Vasalos, 2005).

2.6 Reflective and Collaborative Approaches: Practical and Critical Views

As mentioned at the outset of this section, learning to mentor-as-praxis identifies with this orientation. Influenced by the 'reflective turn' (Schon, 1987), and attending to the value of dialogue and collaboration, reflective and collaborative approaches to mentoring stress the reciprocal relationship between the mentor and the mentee(s) who engage in learning conversations that stress the importance of all parties and participants being acknowledged, sustained, and voiced. Such a conversation is regarded as a communal, democratic dialogue whereby the cultural and educational codes and interests of all parties are legitimized and acknowledged.

Reflective and collaborative approaches are rooted in sociocultural theories of professional learning, suggesting that knowledge development is socially constructed, rooted in activity, and embodied in social and cultural practices (Bereiter, 2002; Wenger, 1998).

The notion of 'learning in praxis' stressing the complexities inherent at the meeting between ideologies and actions in a particular institutional, cultural, and historical context (Wenger, 1998) is, thus, central to this approach. As such, it supports the view that participants' coconstruction of professional knowledge is initiated and sustained through ongoing, progressive discourse among colleagues who interpret and (re)value work-related situations (Edwards, Gilroy & Hartley, 2002). This transformative orientation to professional knowledge (Tillema, 2005) is concerned with how participants identify problems and contradictions and resolve them, while attending to the tensions that appear in the system. Contradictions are manifested as problems, ruptures, clashes, and breakdowns in cooperation (Bardram, 1998) which, when overcome, can lead to development, transformation, and innovation of practices (Kuutti, 1994; Thorne, 2004).

Reflective and collaborative approaches rooted in sociocultural theories of professional learning connote with Carr and Kemmis' practical and critical views of knowledge competence. These views define professional competence as the development of a reflective and deliberative stance toward practice, which results in morally defensible decisions about practice rather than in the ability to apply scientifically acknowledged rules (Carr & Kemmis, 1986). The role of the mentor is, then, not that of an external agent providing solutions to educational problems, but that of a participant and facilitator whose task is to assist teachers to arrive at sound practical judgments. From this critical perspective, practitioners' educational problems are regarded as social matters requiring collective or common action if they are to be satisfactorily resolved (Ibid.).

Generic Attributes \ Approaches to Mentoring	Apprenticeship	Personal Growth	Collaborative-Reflective
Reading a mentoring situation	Identifying patterns of behavior.	Identifying the mentees' strengths and weaknesses.	Identifying points of convergence and divergence bt. the mentor and the mentees' codes of behavior, interests and agendas.
Appraising pedagogical practices	Assessing performance based on modeling, repeated behaviors, and external criteria.	Based on the mentees' understanding/interpretation of the experience. Based on the mentee's articulation of beliefs as they relate to actions.	Looking at communities of practice, how the various players in a system connect and collaborate to arrive at joint re-evaluated activity.
Observing pedagogical practices	Observing behaviors of the mentee as modelled by the mentor.	Observing signs of personal growth as defined by the mentee.	Identifying contradictions and breakdowns while attending to emergent tensions and gaps.
Recording appropriate modes of support	Documenting standard-based evidence of professional learning.	Identifying particular needs, lacks, and wants in order to find appropriate modes of support for a particular context	Identifying relevant systems of support for a particular community of practice.
Assuming diverse supportive roles	Enhancing apprenticeship of observation processes. Mentor /of mentors as a caring role model figure.	Assuming the role of nurturer and carer to empower the mentee in his/her individual search.	Assuming the role of co-thinker, critical friend and enhancing group support.
Managing accountabilities	Representing the system and the external agendas set by policy makers.	Surfacing competing and often contradictory messages in the mentee's voices.	Co-constructing understandings in shared talk to surface differences and articulate conflicts of interests.
Establishing and sustaining professional relationships	Maintaining asymmetry of roles between expert and novice. Mentor/ of mentors as charismatic figure.	Encouraging awareness of personal attributes to enhance professional growth.	Establishing relationships based on communal dialogue and reciprocity-acknowledging a variety of views and opinions.
Tuning In	Identifying gaps between expected and realized behaviors.	Identifying gaps between espoused personal beliefs and realized behavior of the mentee.	Identifying convergent and divergent views, ideologies and actions in shared activity.
Articulating teaching, learning, and subject matter	Communicating and conveying principles, rules, and regulations as defined by the system.	Exposing the mentee's professional text.	Engaging in joint elaboration of teaching and professional learning.
Mediating persons, context and content	Instructing for the right behavior or ideas of what ought to be done.	Reaching an in-depth understanding of the mentee's experiences, values, and ideologies.	Engaging in the co-construction of shared understandings through social activity and talk.

Fig. 2.1 Approaches to mentoring and generic attributes of the practice

Learning to mentor in this critical extended sense, thus, attends to how ideologies, rituals, values, belief systems, and behaviors play out in mentoring interactions of different social, cultural, ethnic, and religious backgrounds. In this sense, reflective critical and practical views resonate with a conception of praxis, as a reflexive encounter stranded in tensions and dilemmas at the intersection between personal theories and pedagogical action.

Figure 2.1 illustrates the connection between the different approaches to mentoring and generic attributes of the practice.

Chapter 3
Learning to Mentor-as-Praxis: Toward a Conceptual Framework

3.1 Praxis and Social Theories of Learning

The impact of constructivist and social constructivist thinking on learning, education, and teacher education in the late eighties (Engeström, 2001; Korthagen & Vasalos, 2005; Loughran, 2003), along with a 'come back' to concepts such as learning from experience (Dewey, 1933), has led to a shift from the 'theory–practice divide' to a view of theory–practice as constituted dialectically *in praxis*, referred to as 'reflective practice' (Schön, 1987). Praxis is also used to appraise professional learning in practice. It stresses the development of informed and disciplined understandings of personal rituals of practice tuned to specific concrete cases and complex or ambiguous situations (Korthagen & Kessels, 1999), as practitioners engage in participation and in improvisation 'in situ.' In the process, they call on intuitive and simultaneous thinking, connecting between environment, persons (with their beliefs ideologies), and actions. Connecting us back to the writings of educational philosopher John Dewey (1933), teacher education as 'praxis' calls for educating 'reflective practitioners' to make meaningful connections between theory and practice. In the reflective process, practitioners frame and reframe problems, constantly evaluating the gaps and contradictions that emerge between personal theories and beliefs, and practice or actions in the classroom. Reflection, then, becomes a dialectical process of looking inward at one's thoughts and outward at how these play out and often contradict each other in the actual situation (Carr & Kemmis, 1986). As such, it moves away from earlier rationalistic, dichotomous orientations to 'levels' of reflection (Schön, 1987) stressing, instead, the situated and embedded character of activity in action, through simultaneous connections between the planned and the immediate (Fendler, 2003; Yinger, 1990). In the context of critical pedagogy, praxis involves the process of action-reflection–action that is central to the development of a consciousness of power and how it operates (Lewis & Ketter, 2004; Wenger, 1998; Fairclough, 1992). It is the complex combination of theory and practice resulting in informed action. It is a form of practice necessary to all professional activity.

L. Orland-Barak, *Learning to Mentor-as-Praxis*, Professional Learning and
Development in Schools and Higher Education 4, DOI 10.1007/978-1-4419-0582-6_3,
© Springer Science+Business Media, LLC 2010

3.2 Situating Praxis in the Philosophical Discourse

Praxis is rooted in the word Praxeis, a Greek term whose literal meaning is action (Gadotti, 1996). Praxis has, by and large, implied the integration of theory and practice. As such, it juxtaposes 'pure,' objective, and abstract reason which is disconnected from practical concerns. In praxis, the ideas which guide action as well as the action itself are subject to change. As informed action, it remakes and reviews action constantly (Carr & Kemmis, 1986), expressing intentional, reflective meaningful activity situated within the dynamic, historical, and cultural contexts that shape and set limits on that activity (Freire, 1970, p. 36).

In recent feminist and critical discourse, and drawing on the political-philosophical discourse of Karl Marx and Paolo Freire, praxis connotes with activism and consciousness about one's work: ...*Praxis* [is] *reflection and action upon the world in order to transform it ... The praxis that defines human existence is marked by its historicity, this dialectical interplay between the way in which history and culture make people even while people are making that history and culture ... the practice of freedom, as critical reflexive praxis, must grasp the outward direction, meaning and consequences of action, and also its inward meaning as the realization and articulation of a self ...* (Glass, 2001, p. 16).

As such, it calls for the integration of practice and theory, for combining reflection and action, and for working *with* the people and working to cause change (Seng, 1998). Praxis connotes with the pedagogical idea of dialogue not merely as the encounter of two subjects who look for meanings, but also as an encounter which is predominantly social and takes place in 'praxis'– in participation, action, and reflection; in cultural responsiveness; and in social transformation (Gaddoti, 1996). Praxis, as an extension of dialogical thinking, embeds two major notions that deserve attention as a basis for thinking about learning to mentor as praxis: dialectics and phronesis.

3.3 Praxis as Dialectics and Phronesis

The concept of dialectics is integral to the notion of praxis. Going back to ancient Greece, the word 'dialectic' evoked a specific manner of argumentation. In general, dialectics can be described as the opposition of a thesis against its antithesis, with a new synthesis being arrived at when the thesis and antithesis are reconciled. Dialectical thinking, thus, involves searching out *contradictions*. Contradiction distinguishes from paradox (Gaddoti, 1996) in that whereas paradox suggests that two compatible ideas will remain inertly opposed to one another, contradiction implies that a new resolution can be achieved.

For example, let's consider the story of Fatin, whom we will return to at several points throughout the book. Fatin's 'thesis' that as an Arab mentor she can serve as a bridge for communication between Arabs and Jews by implementing the Sesame Street program in her school is opposed with an 'antithesis' that the implementation of her agenda is perceived as betrayal and lack of solidarity toward her own people. Fatin, eventually, does not 'resolve' this contradiction but merely opts for putting her ideology aside so as not to endanger her image as being committed to the Palestinian Arab cause in the eyes of the teachers. This contradiction could be resolved had she, for example, responded to the teachers' resistance by sharing overtly her own sense of frustration, to gradually arrive at a resolution that would attend to her espoused educational ideology, on the one hand, and to her teachers' sensitivities, on the other hand.

Dialectical thinking, thus, involves breaking through the 'taken for granted zone' and dominant beliefs and actions, and questioning them back and forth with a sense of agency to transform practice (Habermas, 1973; Solits, 1984). In the process, contradictions may be discovered, which by virtue of reflection lead to new constructive action. To arrive at finer understandings the parties must, then, learn to be responsive to each other and to engage in informed meaning making as the conversation develops. To engage in this form of participation and improvisation in order to meet the interests of the people served, the leader (in our case the mentor) must be attentive to nondominant forms of strength and resistance and gain confidence in the people's ability to think, to want, and to know (Gadotti, 1996). Trust, reciprocity, and responsiveness are, then, critical components of the relationship that leaders/mentors must have with the people with whom they work.

Going back to Fatin's case, we might contend that although she exhibited sensitivity and was responsive to her mentees' resistances, her mode of participation did not, eventually, lead to new constructive action. In the language of dialects, dominant 'taken for granted' beliefs and forms of practice were not opened up, reevaluated, and questioned collaboratively with the mentee, to uncover contradictions which by virtue of reflection would lead to new constructive action. What might Fatin have to learn in order to manage inherent contradictions in her work as a mentor? The chapters in the book address this question.

Praxis is always guided by a moral disposition to act truly and justly (Kristjánsson, 2005; Carr, 1999). The moral in phronesis is grounded in human mission as it occurs in activity (Aristotle, 1985). This kind of knowledge is referred to by Aristotle as 'phronesis' or the prudent understanding of what should be done in practical situations (Gadotti, 1996). Phronesis, thus, sees education not as technical (or using Aristotle's notion of 'techne') but as essentially practical and strategic. In contrast to modern and postmodern notions of technical rationality (Van Manen, 1991), phronesis connotes with practical wisdom or with 'the right reasoning about what is to be done' (Aquinas in Gaddotti, 1996, p. 73). In praxis, phronesis involves knowing how to apply general principles in particular situations, embedding the ability to act so that the principle will take concrete form (MacIntyre, 1981). As such, it speaks to the situated, creative, critical, and reflexive nature of praxis as the enhancement of practical wisdom through perceptual experiences of concrete particulars (Kessels & Korthagen, 1996).

A dialectical perspective to learning to mentor-as-praxis also attends to the place of intertextuality in the shaping of texts' meanings by other texts. Emergent in the sixties from radical theories of writing and based on Derrida's deconstruction of reality, the practice of intertextuality underscores the relational and transformative character of identity, meaning, subject, and text. Hence, in intertextuality, meaning is not transferred directly from writer to reader (or speaker to speaker), but is mediated, instead, by 'codes' imparted to the writer, reader, and speakers by other texts (Kristeva, 1986). Mentoring as an intertextual activity would, then, call for attending to how mentoring texts are constantly being transformed and mediated by the social and professional texts that dynamically emerge in and through mentoring interactions. Texts, in this broader sense, constitute the multiple discourses (both verbal and nonverbal) that professionals as social actors participate in (Gee 1996), carrying multiple and often conflicting identities and voices (Lather, 1992; Orland-Barak & Klein, 2005).

3.4 Domains of Praxis in Mentoring: Beyond the Acquisition of Skills

Positioned within critical and reflective-transformative views of professional learning *beyond the acquisition of skills,* learning to mentor-as-praxis entails learning to plan and improvise, observing the consequences and sources of participation systematically. It also entails appreciating the contexts within which others work and responding to the situational constraints of a particular strategic action. The role of the mentor is, then, to promote and respond to teachers' continuous deliberations and critical discussion of how political and social structures relate to and influence educational aims and practices. It also entails improvising conditions of free open dialogues to promote practitioners' self-understandings.

The practical and critical views of professional learning undergirding reflective and collaborative approaches call for extending the contents of a curriculum for learning to mentor from the acquisition of skills in practice toward the acquisition of professional competence and performance within *domains of praxis.*

3.5 Foundations for Domains of Learning to Mentor as Praxis

Taken together, dialectics and phronesis offer important principles for understanding praxis (Gadotti, 1996). These principles align with social theories of professional knowledge, competence, and performance, serving as interpretative lenses for making sense of the conflicting values and ideologies that emerged from mentors' stories, as they juggled in competing discourses of practice (Orland-Barak, 2002, 2005). Taken together, these principles provide the following foundations for the domains of *learning to mentor-as-praxis*:

- Everything is related and nothing can be understood in isolation but rather as part of reciprocal action. Reality must, then, be *appreciated* as a concrete totality and learning be understood as actions and activities integrated in a complexity of institutional, cultural, and historical practices. This implies looking at contexts for learning about innovative practices as developing in larger contexts within their historical, social, cultural, and institutional conditions, with specific resources and constraints, some of which are explicitly and some implicitly articulated.

We are also looking at work in practice, at interconnectedness of how one factor affects the other, and at how creative and new ways of thinking are dependent on prior understanding of experiences. Taken to the realm of mentoring, this principle connotes with learning to 'read a mentoring situation' both as a whole, that is, *appreciating* what this is 'a case of' in mentoring, its uniqueness as shaped by particular discourses, power relations and dominant educational agendas, and *appreciating* the extent to which these two reciprocate and contradict each other 'in action.'

- Every opinion inherently possesses a contradiction, uncovering multiple and contrasting voices (Bakhtin, 1981) which are, in turn, required for transformation and change (Gadotti, 1996). This implies identifying the problems in activity and resolving them while attending to the tensions, potential contradictions, and while focusing on cooperative breakdowns as a way to make sense of the dynamics of co-operative work. Mentors should, then, learn to become aware of the contradictions inherent in the competing discourses of practice within which they *participate*. This, as a way of developing a critical and disciplined stance toward the versatile nature of their roles and practices and for pursuing ways of managing contradictions as a source of growth and directed change.

- Everything is transformed and nothing is static. Understandings are dynamic and grounded in continuous reflection through ongoing deliberation. Professional learning is, therefore, a matter of ever changing deliberation and change, and is nonconformant with general traditions or narrowly specified prescriptions of practice. Exploration and a search for meaning occur in context, and knowledge development is constantly reshaped by the boundaries within which professionals work and participate. As such, learning to mentor would be attentive to how *improvisation* plays out in mentoring interactions and to how different voices and texts are attended to in mentoring conversations. It would also focus on developing responsiveness to the dynamic and social/political character of mentors' interactions and relationships with their teachers, colleagues, school principals, and project leaders. Learning to mentor would also attend to the roles that mentors play in *improvising* conditions to sustain free open dialogues on how changes in political and social structures might shape educational aims and practices.

- Professional learning entails *appreciating* how specific, concrete cases and complex or ambiguous situations are informed by personal and cultural rituals of practice. Learning to mentor, thus, calls for developing a role of the mentor as appreciator of how teachers' practical judgments and reflections are enhanced or limited by particular ideological and political mechanisms that operate in the educational system within which they function. It also entails engaging in the dialectical process of looking inward and outward at one's thoughts, recording how personal theories, beliefs, and actions play out and often contradict each other in actual mentoring situations.

- Professional learning is regarded as a communal, democratic dialogue in which the cultural and educational codes and interests of all parties involved in the learning process are legitimized and acknowledged. Professional learning embeds *appreciation* of the contexts within which others work and response to the situational and practical constraints of a particular strategic action. Learning to mentor, thus, implies encouraging *participation* in dialectical processes of constructing, reconstructing, and coconstructing theory through reflection for, in, and on practice. It also implies *improvising* through intuitive and simultaneous thinking by connecting between environment, persons, and actions, observing the consequences and sources of participation systematically. It also calls for *improvising* and responding to meaningful connections between theory and practice and to the framing and reframing of problems.

- The following three chapters expand on each of the three domains, providing *situated illustrations* of how ideological, political, and moral considerations shape modes of *Participation*, *Appreciation*, and *Improvisation*.

3.6 Representing Mentoring as a Discursive Practice

Drawing on social theorists Foucault (1997) and Fairclough (1992), a discourse can be defined as a way of *talking about* and *acting* upon the world which both constructs and is constructed by a set of social practices. Rooted in particular institutions, discourses embody their idiosyncratic culture, hence guiding actors to adopt particular constructions and positionings for appreciating, participating, and improvising social roles and behaviors. Thus, actions and the acts they accomplish make up discursive practices. In discursive terms, actions are intentional utterances, meant as something. Actions become speech-acts when they are taken up by the others to whom it has been addressed, that is, when they represent ways *to do* things for particular social contexts. A discursive practice is, then, *the repeated and orderly use of some sign system, where these uses are intentional, that is, directed to or at something* (Harre & Gillett, 1994, p. 32).

Adopting a discursive stance to learning to mentor-as-praxis called for the challenging task of finding the appropriate mode of representation that would faithfully convey the overriding message and orientation of the book.

Developing such an organizing structure has been, I must say, an exigent but extremely stimulating endeavor. Goodall (2000), in his persuasive and provocative book Writing the New Ethnography, elaborates on this challenge. Quoting rhetorical theorist and critic, Kenneth Burke (1989), he writes:

> After all, *I* am the one authoring this account, am I not? My credibility as a writer depends on how well I *develop a relationship* with my reader, which is largely determined by the *character* I reveal on the page ... My job as a writer is to vividly and dramatically arouse a readers' interest in my topic ... deploy language to shape the account into a coherent narrative unity that resonates with the life experiences of the intended reader [and] move the reader to a sense of completion, to a conclusion that satisfies or satiates the readers original quest for the experience of reading, or knowledge, or both (Burke, 1989)

Goodall's words have particularly resonated throughout my journey of representation of two major conceptual challenges:

1. Representing the way in which participants *position* themselves in the discourse in respect to the local conventions of rights and duties, judgments, acts, and so on.
2. Representing the way in which they *construe* experience through the language used as they position themselves in relation to the social acts that they perform.

In doing so, I had to be particularly attentive to how the various uses of language and language acts represented in the texts reflected particular points of view both about the world and the use of mind in respect to this world (Bruner, 1990). In this sense, Bruner's ideas about language spoke to the discursive character of the three domains of praxis:

> ... language necessarily imposes a perspective in which things are viewed and a stance towards what we view [in our case Appreciation] ... The medium is the message. The message itself may create the reality that the message embodies [in our case improvisation] and predispose those who hear it to think about it in a particular mode [in our case participation] ... the most generative aspect of language is not grammar but its possible pragmatic range of use [in our case, in order to appreciate, participate, and improvise one needs to perform certain acts]. In this view, a culture is as much a forum for negotiating and renegotiating meaning and for explicating action [improvisation] as it is a set of rules and specifications for action [participation] ... it is the forum aspect of a culture that gives its participants a role in constantly making and remaking the culture [appreciation and participation], their active roles as participants who play canonical roles according to the rule when the appropriate cues occur [appreciation of the cues]. (Bruner, 1990, pp. 80, 82)

To meet the challenge of representing vividly and coherently the *discursive character of the three domains of praxis* in mentoring, I have found it useful to organize Chapters 4, 5, and 6 according to the following structure:

(1) First, I describe the praxical underpinning of each domain, which grounds the notions that provide a discursive and dialogic basis to a particular form of mentoring practice.
(2) Then, I characterize the dialogic basis of each domain as it plays out in relevant practices of mentoring. The dialogic basis of the domain is constituted by how participants *position* themselves in particular discourses of practices and how they *construct* meanings on which to act upon in these practices. The *encounter* between generic practices of mentoring and forms of positioning and construction distinguishes and shapes the praxical character of a specific mentoring practice.
(3) The praxical connections between forms of practice and dialogue in the specific domain are then consolidated into an integrative framework, highlighting the *acts* that are constituted in the various praxical connections.
(4) Each chapter then *zooms in* to the specific acts constituted in each domain, illustrating particular forms and meanings that these acts take in the context of authentic stories, cases, critical incidents, and excerpts from learning conversations in a variety of mentoring contexts.
(5) The presented texts are critically explored and interpreted, to illustrate their discursive, dialogical constitution, with a focus on how mentors *position*

themselves in the discourse and *construct* particular communicative acts (i.e., support, challenge, probe, clarify) in a particular domain.

(6) In order to encourage connections between the illustrative cases and the reader's context of practice, I provide a series of relevant reflective questions to frame personal interpretations of a particular text. These are phrased as *thinking in practice bubbles* prior to the introduction of the text.

3.7   Toward an Extended Conceptual Framework

Figure 2.1 offers a two-dimensional platform for conceptualizing the essential attributes in mentoring as they relate to the major evolving orientations to professional learning to mentor. This book *extends* on the critical/praxical orientation, suggesting a third dimension to the two-dimensional platform – one which embeds the three domains of learning to mentor-as-praxis: appreciation, participation, and improvisation. This can be illustrated as follows (Fig. 3.1):

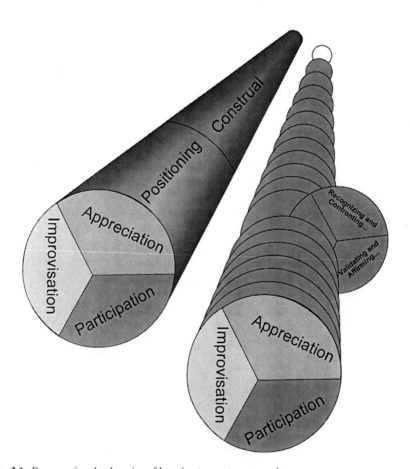

Fig. 3.1   Representing the domains of learning to mentor-as-praxis

Chapter 4
Domain of Appreciation

Ap·pre·ci·a·tion
əˌpriʃiˈeɪʃən [*uh*-pree-shee-**ey**-sh*uh*n]

–noun

1. gratitude; thankful recognition: *They showed their appreciation by giving him a gold watch.*
2. the act of estimating the qualities of things and giving them their proper value.
3. clear perception or recognition, esp. of aesthetic quality: *a course in art appreciation.*
4. an increase or rise in the value of property, goods, etc.
5. critical notice; evaluation; opinion, as of a situation, person, etc.
6. a critique or written evaluation, esp. when favorable

The generic meaning of *appreciation*, as the dictionary defines, associates with recognition, estimation, perception, evaluation, and opinion. While appreciating we estimate, critique, appraise, acknowledge, and esteem a particular situation, person, or object in a given context, at a particular time and place, and for a particular audience and purpose: We take a stance, adopt a perspective, and make an informed judgment.

4.1 The Discursive Character of Appreciation in Mentoring

As a discursive activity of a praxical character, appreciation engages us in multiple *forms of dialogue* with a particular *form of practice*. In the process, we *construe* new and more informed meanings of that which is observed, recognized, or appraised, as we adopt various *positionings* in relation to the particular subject, object, and/or practice.

Taken to the realm of Mentoring, *appreciation as a discursive activity* engages the mentor in *dialogue* with his/her mentoring practice, as he/she reads a situation, appraises and observes pedagogical practices, and records appropriate modes of support. In each of these 'dialogues of practice,' mentors engage in the process of *positioning* themselves in relation to the particular historical, social, cultural,

L. Orland-Barak, *Learning to Mentor-as-Praxis*, Professional Learning and
Development in Schools and Higher Education 4, DOI 10.1007/978-1-4419-0582-6_4,
© Springer Science+Business Media, LLC 2010

and institutional character of the mentoring context, while *construing* idiosyncratic understandings about how practices develop and can be enhanced in specific conditions, resources, and constraints.

4.1.1 Appreciating as Positioning in Dialogue

How do mentors learn to appreciate their context of practice? What rules do they extract as they become attentive to the stories of practice that emerge in that context?

4.1.1.1 Recognizing

Appreciating as *positioning* means making something out of the situation as one participates in it and according to one's perceptions of it. It also means recognizing and becoming attentive to the stories of the context, to how these stories are told, and to Discourses embedded in those stories (Gee, 1999) – through the language of practice that represents them. In the process, the mentor contemplates and takes a perspective as he/she makes judgments and characterizations of the teaching and learning context, and recognizes and confronts inherent gaps between his/her codes and norms and those within which the mentee operates.

4.1.1.2 Evaluating and Empathizing

Appreciation as positioning eventually develops into an evaluative judgment which can be either (Harre & Gillett, 1994) moral (good or bad, moral or immoral), aesthetic (emotional, satisfying, or the opposite (Eisner & Powell, 2002)), or prudential (warning, fear). Thus, an important outcome of learning to appreciate as positioning are the gradual appraisals of a particular pedagogical practice, by identifying the evaluative moral, aesthetic, and prudential judgments attributed to particular acts in a particular setting. In the process of reframing understandings (Korthagen, 1995; Loughran, 2003), one might develop what in Eisner and Powell (2002) is referred to as empathic reasoning and knowledge, which is an understanding of and identification with another's emotions, experiences, and motivations, or the attribution of one's feelings to an object (Eisner & Powell, 2002).

4.1.2 Appreciating as Construing in Dialogue

What are the narrative conventions or the ways in which stories and texts are told and represented in those contexts?

4.1.2.1 Signifying and Taking Perspective

Whereas positioning focuses on recognition, evaluation, and reframing of a situation, construing suggests signifying, that is, taking perspective and recognizing that there is a situation on the one hand, but also a quite different representation and understanding of oneself and of others in that situation. Signifying moves us, then, to interpreting where and how the [mentee] locates his or her current behavior in...the structure of rules and practices of the context within which she moves (Winch, 1958 in Harre & Gillett, 1994, p. 20). As Haree and Gillett (1994) suggest, it is the active role of meaning in structuring the interaction between a person and a context so as to define the subjectivity of that person in the situation and their positioning in relation to certain discourses implicit in that subjectivity... (pp. 23–24). In the process of construing or signifying a situation, people negotiate events in such a way as to reconcile various constraints: The need to adapt to situations that are often independent of one's will; the attempt to make a given occasion coherent or hang together, which would require making adjustments; and balancing integration of different discourses into unique complex subjectivities (Harre & Gillett, 1994).

Thus, *appreciating as construing* occurs at the intersection of influences or meeting points of many significations in a variety of discourses. This connotes with Kelly's (1955) the notion of constructive alternativism, which underscores our constant reinterpretations and representations of our environment: We build systems of personal constructs upon which we place interpretations of events. Thus, through an abstraction process we construct meaning of events for ourselves (Kelly, 1955, p. 50).

4.1.2.2 Typifying and Building Repertoires of Practice

Appreciation as construing also embeds a process of typifying, which entails, according to phenomenologist Alfred Schutz (1970), the construction of conscious guidelines or 'dramatic rehearsals' for future actions. Such rehearsals enable us to imagine or fantasize the planned action as already finished, enabling in turn the anticipation or 'typifications' of future events and the building of repertoires of practice. These idealizations, Schutz argues, enable people to express their confidence in the basic structure of the life world, perceiving it as remaining unchanged and reliable for future conduct. Construing as typifying in mentoring, however, also entails becoming conscious that absolute certainty is impossible: that during the execution of a project the actor's system of relevance inevitably undergoes changes resulting in a different perception and understanding of the situation, because as Schutz (1970) contends, 'Foresight differs from hindsight' (pp. 26–27). In the process, mentors make educational construals and anticipate recurring and unique patterns of action in new scenarios of practice.

4.1.2.3 Contemplating

Appreciation also calls for contemplation. As Yinger (1990) defines it, to contemplate something is to look at and think about it attentively and intently (p. 87). Contemplation implies observation and thinking in a place occupying a particular relationship to a larger community and cultural order. Contemplation is a way of being in the work even when the work is not being performed. It engages the individual in constant construal and representation of practice, merging intellect with feeling.

> Contemplation, in contrast to focused deliberation, allows the mind to roam widely over the terrain of focused practice ... it suggests that tradition, authority and circumstance should be the starting point for consideration...Contemplation is a generalist's stance-considering holistically in terms of order, balance, harmony, and symmetry and resisting the lure of autonomy and control ... (Yinger, 1990, p. 88)

Contemplation as a state of balance and harmony with feelings and thoughts 'in place' engages us in different positionings and construals of a particular situation. It also calls for the capacity to perceive which, in discursive terms, ... is an active process which includes the search for the most important elements of information, their comparison with each other, the creation of a hypotheses concerning the meaning of the information as a whole and the verification of this hypothesis by comparing it with the original features of the object perceived ... it is about pattern recognition (Luria, 1973, p. 168). As an aesthetic experience, contemplation occurs during reflection or meta-analysis while finding patterns, juxtaposing information, or using a tried or physical strategy to aid figuring out a problem (Eisner & Powell, 2002, p. 156).

Hence, contemplation and perception in mentoring would call for acquiring techniques and skills for construing information from the holistic environment, as informed by the stances and representations that we constantly make out of our interactions with practice.

4.2 Appreciating a Mentoring Text: Putting It All Together

The above notions underlying appreciation as positioning and construing provide a *discursive platform* for appreciating a mentoring text. While perceiving, typifying, judging, and anticipating, the mentor engages in reading, appraising, observing, and recording *the uniqueness* of a particular context. He/she also develops an orientation toward assisting the mentee to conceptualize experiences that are similar but not identical.

This entails both building repertoires of unique cases as well as judicious replications of experiences across contexts, encouraged through questions such as 'What is this a case of?' (Shulman, 1986), both on the level of 'what does it represent in my mentoring context' as well as on 'how this case might differ from other similar cases encountered'. It also entails articulating dispositions to act through questions such as 'What am I learning about my developing concept of mentoring?, What teaching/learning conditions typify my particular mentoring context and the teaching situation and how might these alter in new contexts?, How might different interactions influence decision making?'

Appreciation as multiple encounters between forms of practice (reading, appraising, observing, and recording) and forms of positioning and construing (such as

Table 4.1 Praxical connections between forms of practice and dialogue in the Domain of Appreciation

MENTORING AS A DISCURSIVE PRACTICE		
DIALOGIC BASIS OF APPRECIATION		
Practices of Mentoring	**POSITIONING**	**CONSTRUCTION**
Reading a mentoring situation	*Recognizing and confronting gaps between the mentor and the mentee's codes and norms of behavior* *Reframing perspectives on ingrained assumptions and ideologies*	*Typifying the mentoring context and signifying emergent cooperative breakdowns* *Taking perspective: Making educated conjectures and connecting the parts to the whole*
Appraising pedagogical practices	*Recognizing role boundaries* *Evaluating ducational interventions as rooted in moral stances* *Reframing perspectives on resistances as rooted in contradictory values* *Reframing rigid views about effective pedagogical practices*	*Signifying contradictory and competing accountabilities*
Observing pedagogical practices		*Contemplating to build repertoires of practice*
Recording appropriate modes of support	*Anticipating contradictions*	*Making educational construals for future use*

typifying, anticipating, placing judgment, perceiving, and signifying) speak to Gadamer's (1975) concept of understanding as a back and forth, to and fro endless play of significations. It also speaks to a view of dialogue as 'represent[ing] a continuous, developmental communicative interchange through which we stand to gain a fuller apprehension of the world ourselves and one another' (Bakhtin, 1981, p. 69).

Taken together, as mentors *read a situation*, they *recognize* and *confront* gaps between codes and norms of behavior; *contemplate* the physical, relational, and professional context of mentoring; *typify* emergent cooperative breakdowns; *signify* ingrained assumptions and ideologies and *take perspective* by *making educated conjectures* and connecting the parts to the whole.

As mentors *appraise* pedagogical practices, they *reframe* rigid views about effective pedagogical practices; *signify* contradictory and competing accountabilities; *recognize* role boundaries; *evaluate* educational interventions as rooted in moral stances and *reframe perspectives* on resistances as rooted in contradictory values.

As mentors *observe* pedagogical practices, they *contemplate to build repertoires of* behaviors and their underlying messages. And, as they *record* appropriate modes of support, they make *educational construals* and *anticipate* contradictions of interest that might be inherent in different forms of support. In the sections that follow, I explore the different encounters between forms of practice and forms of positioning and construing, as they unfold in authentic exemplars of mentoring practices in a variety of educational contexts.

Table 4.1 illustrates the dialogic basis of Appreciation.

4.3 Reading a Mentoring Situation

In an earlier study (Orland-Barak, 2001b) learning to read a mentoring situation was defined as the process of gradually uncovering and reconstructing meanings as the mentor encounters dynamic and complex mentoring interactions. Thus, the mentor as 'reader' constantly engages in revising his/her own judgment of the meanings inherent in the target 'mentoring text' in light of the

Practices of Mentoring	POSITIONING	CONSTRUCTION
Reading a mentoring situation	*Recognizing and confronting gaps between the mentor and the mentee's codes and norms of behavior*	*Typifying the mentoring context and signifying emergent cooperative breakdowns*
	Reframing perspectives on ingrained assumptions and ideologies	*Taking perspective: Making educated conjectures and connecting the parts to the whole*

dynamic, multiple, and unique nature of the dilemmas that her mentees face and manage. In the process, the mentor learns to become "... sensitive to the subtleties of the situation of the other [the mentee]... to know what the situation means to the person and not just what the situation is, as a way of understand[ing] what the person [the mentee] is doing..." (Harre & Gillett, 1994, p. 35).

Focusing on the discursive character of reading a mentoring situation as participation calls, then, for attending to how mentors recognize and confront gaps between codes and norms of behavior; contemplate the physical, relational, and professional context of mentoring; typify emergent cooperative breakdowns; signify ingrained assumptions and ideologies; and take perspective by making educated conjectures and connecting the parts to the whole.

4.3.1 A Developmental Journey

To begin unpacking the discursive character of reading a mentoring situation in appreciation, let us engage in the developmental journey that Randi, a novice teacher, undertook as she was learning to appreciate her mentoring context. Randi is a novice school mentor working with 14 novice and experienced English teachers from both elementary and high school in a comprehensive community school project in the north of Israel. Randi was appointed by the Ministry of Education as part of a larger reform to raise pupils' achievements and to foster reflective teaching and local educational leadership. Specifically, her role entailed observing and supporting individual teachers at schools, and organizing workshop sessions to advance communicative language teaching and heterogeneous teaching, which were new policies advocated by the English Inspectorate in Israel.

The town to which Randi was designated was largely populated by Russian new immigrants and most of the teachers in the school were residents of the same town. Most of these teachers were, then, former Russian immigrants who had arrived in the country as already experienced teachers of English in Russia. Coming from rigid political regimes, these teachers held strong ideas about effective frontal, noncommunicative methods of teaching which stressed streaming classes according to levels rather than working heterogeneously. These teachers also held deep-rooted beliefs about the importance of teaching grammatical rules and using translation methods that focus on accuracy. Of an epistemological nature, these context-related beliefs about knowledge and the structure of knowing are known to be difficult to eradicate, as the work of Schommer (2002), Hofer and Pintrich (2002), Mason (2005), and others suggest. Furthermore, teachers' ingrained beliefs contrasted starkly with the reform communicative, holistic agenda to language teaching which Randi espoused, both as a teacher of English and as a mentor of English teachers. Moreover, the teachers had had little experience and training in collaborative modes of teaching and in engaging in reflective modes of thinking about their practices in the company of their peers (Orland-Barak, 2001b).

4.3.2 Unpacking the Journey

Let us explore what and how Randi learned to read her mentoring context to eventually challenge her ingrained views and practice as a mentor (Note 1).

When the project started, Randi spoke at length about her strong convictions regarding teaching in heterogeneous classes:

> The main problem here is that teachers do not work in heterogeneous classes ... one of my main goals is to get teachers to work heterogeneously... I also want to convince them [the teachers] that even though it is more work for the teacher, it is more success-ful to work as a staff than isolatedly. I want to work on deepening staff thinking... I have experienced the great change that our school went through when we moved into teaching heterogeneously...the teachers in our school began to work more collaboratively and the children, especially the weaker ones, did not feel labeled anymore...

Drawing on her experience as a teacher working with heterogeneous classes and with the successful implementation of a similar project in her own school, Randi envisions replicating a similar agenda in her work as a mentor.

Indeed, as McIntyre, Hagger, and Wilkin (1993) suggest, mentoring does not start from zero level, hence her reasoning is strongly influenced by her exper-tise as a school teacher (Orland-Barak, 2001, p. 53). Her reading of the situation at this initial stage 'mirrors' the conditions and forms of collaboration that play out in her own 'culture of teaching' with little regard for the unique back-ground of the teachers in the intervention project. Notice her use of the word *convince*, denoting an unequivocal and prescriptive reading of 'what ought to be done.'

4.3.3 Something is Not Working Out...

As Randi began to meet with the teachers as a group, though, she soon realized that the physical and relational conditions of the community were inconsistent with the ideas that she had initially envisioned. This was made apparent to her as the teachers began to express resistance toward her and toward the intervention project in gen-eral. She also began to notice the lack of cooperation and tensions that characterized the culture of teaching in the schools, especially between the administration and the staff of teachers.

Exploring the relationship between contexts of mentoring and mentoring prac-tices, Jian Wang (2001) reminds us that it is important to consider not only the relevant experiences of mentors but also to identify if mentors' conceptu-alizations of their work are congruent or not with the expectations, structure, and norms and demands of the mentoring context. Indeed, the tensions that Randi was experiencing reflected the incompatibilities that were gradually emerg-ing. Already during the first group session, she began to realize that *something* [was] *not working* the way she had expected. This is elaborated in the following section.

4.4 Recognizing and Confronting Gaps Between the Mentor and the Mentee's Codes and Norms of Behavior

What embarrasses and puzzles me?
What kind of resistances does it create for me?
How do I react to my own resistances? How do I
transform them into learning opportunities?

Randi had prepared a session on learning styles as a bridge to thinking about catering for the different styles of learners in the heterogeneous classroom. The room was organized in half a circle to enable teachers to see and relate to each other more easily. The workshop was supposed to start at 2 o'clock but nobody showed up until 2:30. At 2:30 only five teachers showed up. The other four, from the other high school, did not show up at all. The coordinators from both schools were not there either. Randi decided to start the session despite the small number of participants. As the discussion was beginning to develop, Adina, the coordinator of one school, suddenly entered the room. She excused herself for not being able to come earlier because she had *other important things to do at school.* Then she immediately demanded from Randi to tell her what they had been doing. Randi stopped the discussion and handed out the questionnaire to Adina. But Adina responded abruptly *What's this? How am I supposed to fill it in? Do you really want me to fill it in now?* Randi was quiet for a few seconds. She gave me a puzzling look as if not knowing how to react and then she said to Adina *You know something? O.K. don't do it now. You can do it at home and we'll talk about it after the session.* A few minutes later, Adina opened her notebook and began to copy down other things which were not related to the topic of the session. She did not participate during the rest of the session. Adina did not wait to talk with Randi at the end of the session. Again, she excused herself for not being able to stay because she had to be back home on time.

Randi felt puzzled and embarrassed by Adina's attitude. It had been a powerful experience for Randi, namely, because she had been confronted for the first time 'face to face' with teachers' resistances to take part in the project. Moreover, she was beginning to *recognize* profound gaps between what she expected from teachers as appropriate codes and norms of professional behavior and what was actually happening in the workshops. At this point, in her reading of the situation, she was not sure whether it had to do with the set up of the school or with the teachers' reluctance to work with her as their mentor. In positioning her discourse in relation to Adina's, she was gradually *confronting* the resistances that she was developing toward the way in which Adina was functioning as a coordinator, which stood in stark contrast with her own ideas and expectations: ... *Something is not working and I am not sure whether it's the set up or it's me ... what kind of example was Adina setting as a coordinator to others by not doing anything?*

In the session that followed, the same number of teachers participated. Adina did not show up but the other coordinator did. Randi said that she felt that it was again a frustrating and unsuccessful session because none of the teachers came back with feedback on the activities that she had asked them to implement from the previous sessions in their classes. In learning to read her situation she was, thus, positioning herself in relation to the norms and codes of behavior of her mentoring context. This entailed recognizing and confronting contrasting views regarding observable forms of professional behavior.

4.5 Typifying the Mentoring Context and Signifying Emergent Cooperative Breakdowns

What makes my mentoring context unique and different from what I know from other experiences? What am I surprised to discover? How does it challenge my personal convictions? How is my role different from what I thought it was?

Randi was beginning to *construe* new understandings. She was realizing that what had worked well for her school did not necessarily speak to the teachers in the new mentoring context. In her designated role as agent of change from 'above,' she was beginning to recognize that her own ideas about the role of the administration and the coordinator in implementing change clashed with the codes, norms, and rituals of the mentoring context. She could not figure out, though, why the teachers were showing so much resistance to participating in the meetings. In her critical narrative of teacher community in the midst of school reform, Cheryl Craig (2009) discusses one of the sources to such resistance as rooted in conflicting notions of professionalism: Professionalism, according to the PLC [professional learning community] conceptualization intentionally introduced to the school context, has a great deal to do with teachers walking the administrative party line and being accountable to that line: working as curriculum implementers partaking of reflection that served that purpose of the reform (not teachers' personal and shared learning as curriculum makers); not questioning the nature of the reform that stripped them of voice and agency ... not taking into careful consideration the slippery boundary between public and private relationships ... (p. 17).

Unaware at this point of possible emergent tensions as those suggested by Craig, Randi *typifies* the cooperative breakdowns that she was encountering as a case of teachers not having an instrumental motive for getting together. She also *typifies* the school as one which does not embrace heterogeneous teaching:

... I mean they go for each other's birthdays ... socially they get along well. But I don't see them as community in teaching, part of it is because of the set up of the school ... When you work with tracks according to levels you can't plan together ... you have different materials different things ... they are not going to sit together because it's the nitty gritty of the daily work what occupies most teachers and it's not something they can share.

Randi adds on to her reading of the situation by further *signifying* it as a question of multiple accountabilities in the system:

... because I have too many bosses I have no connection here or there I have to go to the meetings with Julie and then I can't attend the meetings with Leah. They don't know the timing in advance and when they do know its three days beforehand and that's too late I can't change my plans...

Randi *construes* her understanding of the situation by *typifying* and *signifying* emergent cooperative breakdowns between her various positionings (Harre & Gillett, 1994) in relation to the competing discourses she is accountable to – between her personal pedagogical and educational ideology, her mandated (and expected) reform agenda, and the school's rituals of practice:

I feel that my job was different from what I thought it would be. It's definitely different from what July [the inspector] thought it would be .... I think that the expectations were not realistic, within the given the circumstances .... we haven't been able to create this community although we want to treat them as if they are a community of teachers in professional contact with each other...

4.6 Reframing Perspectives on Ingrained Assumptions and Ideologies

How do my ideas about meaningful learning reflect my personal background? How might these clash with teachers' ideas who come from different backgrounds?
How do I put aside my own views to make place for recognizing the potential of learning opportunities which I have not valued until now?

thinking in practice

The middle of school year marked an important shift in Randi's *construal* of her mentoring practice, as she took part in a one-week workshop session with a group of mentors from all over the country. Randi spoke of the course as an opportunity for her to clarify her role. She said that it had raised her awareness of the importance of letting the mentee determine the direction of the conversation to enable the mentor to ... *hook up to where the person is coming from ... and to really understand what his situation is ...* She had also begun to *reframe* perspectives regarding her own underlying codes and ideologies:

I have had this basic question in my mind since I started as a mentor: When does the mentor have the right to implement her world view on the person and when is it her responsibility to help her find her own way?

The course, which was of a reflective, personal growth character, highlighted for Randi the fact that many mentors were resistant to the reflective character of the course, and that whereas her own educational and cultural background as an American had encouraged questioning assumptions, other participants hadn't. Such awareness helped her, eventually, to transfer these understandings to the difficulties that she was experiencing in trying to get teachers to connect to the conversational and self- reflective nature of her sessions:

> This one mentor from Rumania told me that she was never taught how to question, that she couldn't question anything they were learning.
>
> . . I learned from what happened that I could reflect better than other people in the group because as an American I was expected to reflect and to question all the time . . .those who lived in the USA in the 60s 70s we were more skilled in reflecting. Now I understand why many people in my group [of mentees] kept on saying: let's stop talking about things in the air and look for more concrete ways. . .

In trying to signify the cooperative breakdowns in light of her own experience of being mentored, Randi was *reframing* her perspectives, attributing the emergent breakdowns to teachers' cultural, educational, and social background. Put differently, her construal of the situation entailed a new appreciation of how participants' dispositions are ingrained in culture:

> By being a learner with Yosi [the mentor of mentors in the course] I was in a different position.
>
> And this made me realize that not everything is for everybody and not everybody has to do everything . . .
>
> And once you've realized that there is an automatic shift into acknowledging that different people do different things . . . .
>
> . . . I felt in many cases I was butting my head against a brick wall. And I realized that one of the reasons was once again that I was imposing my own attitudes on situations that were different and on people who were different. And the ability to be able to see that there could be things that are better for that particular person but do not work for another . . . Because maybe these are wonderful teachers even though they don't use any of the methods that I think are the best ones.
>
> I have also realized that there is resistance to the idea of imposing a framework from the outside, not to me personally, and I can understand that better now . . .

Randi's reframing seems, now, much closer to Craig's ideas about why school reforms can often fail:

> Experts external to Yager [the school] who . . . advocate for particular narrative fragments being added to existing stories of school to produce certain results need to consider how their philosophical and theoretical additions practically fit . . . with what is already under way in particular campus contexts and with what is concurrently being introduced (Craig, 2009, pp. 16–17).

Indeed, Randi can now *construe* a more informed appreciation. As her reading becomes more sophisticated while typifying her mentoring context and signifying emergent cooperative breakdowns, she can now reframe understandings regarding teachers' resistances. In the process of reframing, she recognizes that the ideas that she is trying to promote, ingrained in her own idiosyncratic world views, are incompatible with the world views of the participants, especially because most of them come from regimes in which they were not open to feedback or to questioning their teaching.

> They are all new immigrants they either come from Russia or from Rumania ... and they are not ready to open themselves to others, in fact I think that they see reflective conversations as a waste of time. Everything they do in the classroom is very secretive and they become very uptight when we start questioning attitudes or things they have done ...

Randi's emergent insights speak to the strong influence that representation structures, social order structures, and regulatory functions of a particular regime can have on how a particular population might interpret reform changes (Lechner, 1997 in Stromquist & Monkman, 2000, p. 18). In our case, teachers coming from rigid political and social regimes had internalized relationships with administrators, teachers, parents, and students which were based on teacher cultures of either balkanization or fragmented individualism (Hargreaves, 1992, p. 238) rather than of collaboration or even contrived collegiality. Randi was gaining powerful insights in her journey of appreciation on these aspects of the context, leading her eventually to stop conducting general sessions for a while and focus, instead, on working with individual teachers and on establishing channels of communication with them individually.

4.7 Taking Perspective: Making Educated Conjectures and Connecting the Parts to the Whole

How do the gradual insights that I am gaining help me to understand the 'big picture?
How does the big picture guide me to decide what to do and how to do it?

thinking in practice

As Randi adopted various positions within different discourses during the year, she gradually began to identify the objective conditions of the context, and *construe* a more informed picture of how these conditions affected the teachers' dispositions and resistances to the views that she was trying to promote. Her developing perspective taking about how conditions of the workplace bear a strong influence on collegial relationships, on dispositions to change, and on the way on which teachers talk about teaching and learning is well documented in the literature of professional learning. As Warren Little (1993) points out, in schools with developed norms of collegiality and norms of experimentation, teachers talk frequently and specifically about practice, observe one another teach, collaborate in instructional planning and preparation, and are willing to advise and teach one another (Little & McLaughlin, 1993) – this was certainly not the case of Randi's school.

In her broader appreciation of the norms of collegiality and experimentation that characterize her workplace, Randi gradually construes a more coherent perspective of the constraining factors that affect her own performance as a mentor working with a community of teachers. She calls this level of appreciation *seeing the whole picture*: *Its' seeing the big picture, that is seeing the pieces as part of a process, being able to generalize and make conclusions from all the pieces The content of mentoring is the process of figuring out how the pieces stick together... and also being able to break the process down into small steps and back to the big picture again without getting stuck in the small steps.*

Toward the end of the year, Randi had construed a comprehensive picture of the conditions, motivations, and dispositions of herself, of the English teachers, and of the school system inherent in the mentoring context. She had also arrived at a consolidation of what it meant to work as a mentor with a group of teachers which was expected to be treated as a potential community of teachers but in fact it wasn't.

In her reading of appreciation, Randi can now *make educated conjectures and connect the parts to the whole*. In doing so, she is exhibiting a new *perspective* of the context: *Its' a combination of things. First, I don't think there is a tradition of studying in that school .... I don't think there is a tradition of working or improving yourself, and therefore they don't see the need ... so this has to do with the systemic effect: how the school works: in a school where people are not expected to work as a staff it's difficult ...* As she connects between parts, she construes a deeper understanding of the 'whole,' that is, the consequences of educational reforms imposed from 'top–down' especially on populations categorized as failing: *...here there is resentment from the beginning that the project was imposed on them that they were defined as a failing school ... already that's an attitude that develops...*

Randi's evolving perspectives speak to Craig's theory–practice–policy divide, "one where neither theory nor practice nor policy engages in fruitful conversation with one another (Craig, 2009, p. 19)". They also suggest her increasing understanding of how Tayloristic, canonical orientations to reform at the workplace can become restrictive and tricky, and generate resistance if they fail to recognize the situated demands of the context, overlooking at the importance of noncanonical improvisations that emerge while learning in practice (Bourdieu, 1977; Suchman, 1987; Orr, 1990).

4.8 Appraising Pedagogical Practices

In its basic definition as a component of assessment, appraisal of pedagogical practices pertains to the careful analytical judgment of practitioners' quality of performance according to set criteria and standards. As a formative practice of assessment, appraisal involves the continuous process of recording and monitoring

of the mentee's profess-
ional growth and con-
strual of relevant practice
experiences (McMillan,
2007; Tillema, 2009)
across an extended
period. In the process of
providing (in)formative
feedback to direct the
mentees' development
and help them gain
insight into performance
(Boshuizen, Bromme, &
Gruber, 2004; Brown &
Glasner, 1999; Feiman

	POSITIONING	CONSTRUCTION
Appraising pedagogical practices	*Reframing rigid views about effective pedagogical practices*	*Signifying contradictory and competing accountabilities*
	Recognizing role boundaries	
	Evaluating mentoring interventions as rooted in moral stances	

Nemser & Remillard, 1996), the mentor also engages in appreciation of the social, cultural, and political features of the context that he/she is appraising. It is in this extended sense that appraisal becomes a discursive practice – engaging the mentor not only in formative assessment of the mentee but in continuous appreciation of his/her own practice. In the process, he/she reframes views about effective pedagogical practices, recognizes role boundaries, evaluates mentoring interventions as rooted in moral stances, and signifies contradictory and competing accountabilities while appraising a particular pedagogical practice. Appraisal as a discursive practice also speaks to the idea of shared appraisal engaging multiple participants, a notion which is widely adopted in work-related settings in many professional fields (i.e., nursing, hospitality management; Baum, 2002 in Tillema, 2009). Appreciation through multiple appraisal sources recognizes that no single source in the appraisal of performance has ultimate legitimacy or warranty (Byham, 1996; Cochran Smith & Fries, 2002). Moreover, to arrive at a balanced and multidimensional weighting of the many-faceted nature of professional expertise, a combined overview of several dimensions in appraisal is needed (Tillema, 2009).

4.9 Reframing Rigid Views about Effective Pedagogical Practices

What am I prepared to change regarding my views about good teaching and about effective modes of staff collaboration? What core values do I want to preserve in the process of reframing?

thinking in practice

Randi's new reading of the situation challenged her initial rigid beliefs about teaching in heterogeneous classes and about forms of staff collaboration. Through Adina's case she could appraise her pedagogical practice anew, by *reframing* her interpretation of the meanings she had initially attributed to teachers' resistance in mentoring:

> ... She had a lot of resentment for the whole program and I don't think specifically for me. For a long time I felt I couldn't quite discern where it was coming from ... then I understood that she felt put off because she couldn't do a course she wanted to do at the university because my workshop had been imposed on her

Randi's journey of appreciation consumes with an appraisal of the conditions that need to be created to sustain collaboration within a community of teachers. As she positions herself in the new discourse of practice, she reframes her views about effective pedagogical practices, construing various forms of understandings integratively: social-interpersonal aspects (identity and pride) with social-professional aspects (professional contact). These conditions connote with what we know about sustaining successful communities of practice: a creative basis; a shared knowledge base or common ground; a reciprocal basis for extended perspectives to develop; an internal basis of commitment and accountability; and an external organizing basis (Wenger, McDermott, & Snyder, 2002).

> ...it's three things: 1. To do with the identity of the members: how they see themselves as part of a system. 2. To have an infrastructure, a channel of communication, professional contact among members 3. A pride in the community. These are the conditions ... and all these three elements were missing. . . .

Notice how her language of appreciation has changed too. Her initial accounts were predominantly descriptive and impressionistic, whereas at this later phase of her journey she exhibits a professional language (Freeman, 1993), with a focus on articulating her conceptualization of the experience.

4.10 Recognizing Role Boundaries

In what cases does my experience as a teacher assist me as a mentor and when does it block my interpretation of the situation?

thinking in practice

Mentors' appreciation of the gaps, contradictions, and breakdowns between their personal ideologies and the dominant ideologies of their mentoring contexts foregrounds the complex web of positionings that operate in mentoring, as mentors *appraise* the personal, interpersonal, and professional character of the practice (Roberts, 2000; Semeniuk & Worrall, 2000; Miller-Marsh, 2002b). Miller-Marsh's (2002b) account of how she positioned and repositioned competing identities and ideologies in the discourse of two contrasting mentor–mentee relationships is particularly illuminative of this point. In her conclusion she suggests:

As teacher educators we are in the business of promoting ideologies through the discourses that we choose to use as we work with prospective teachers ... to promote an awareness of how the discourses in a particular field of education have been, and continue to be, socially, culturally, historically and politically constructed ... (Miller Marsh, 2002b, p. 345)

In the process of articulating identities, mentors learn to recognize the boundaries of their role, often related to how 'the teacher and the mentor in them' play out in mentoring interactions (Orland-Barak, 2002).

Notice how, in the excerpts that follow, mentors appraise their practice by articulating convergences and divergences between teaching and mentoring:

D: *"...there are certain characteristics that you have to have ... maybe they can be learned ... you know ... you can be a teacher of teachers. That you can do. You can stand in front of a classroom of teachers in a session and you can lecture them on all subjects but you are not a mentor then, you are a teacher giving information ..."*

C: *"I see a continuation between being a good teacher and a good mentor. The same power that pushes us to being teachers pushes us to being mentors at a later stage...*

M: *I thought to myself, the same way I am a good counselor to children I can be a good mentor. For me these two roles complement each other."*

L: *"Can a good teacher be a good mentor?"*

The mentors' questioning of their roles as they look inward and outward into their assumptions and inner contradictions remind us of Daniele Blumenthal's (1999) notion of a mobile, multiple, and divided 'self' that emerges out of relating to different people, in different situations and across time (p. 381). The process is cocreated in collaboration with others, and is 'connected to our previous selves ... which may pop up the present at any time' (Blumenthal, 1999, p. 383). Likewise, the questioning of roles speaks to the dynamic character of teacher identity, shifting under the influence of internal factors such as emotion (Rodgers & Scott, 2008; Van Veen & Sleegers, 2006; Zembylas, 2003), and external individual factors such as job and life experiences in particular contexts (Flores & Day, 2006; Sachs, 2005).

Mentors also *recognized* which aspects of 'the teacher in them' help them to assist other teachers, as well as those aspects that are new to them. Consider, for example, Debbie's comment *I have the skills in terms of discussing activities ... I can teach them from the practical to how to apply theory ... I've been there, I've done it all, I've experienced it on an emotional level .... but I have less skills when talking about why something works.* Likewise, Randi contends that the *new teachers like to hear from experienced teachers what works. What's been tried, what according to experience should be done. So in a sense I'm the driver's seat and they can trust me and I didn't lead them astray. I didn't tell them something that isn't true. And they are always looking for rescue ...*

Recognizing role boundaries in mentoring also entails *positioning* oneself in relation to how professional responsibility plays out differently in teaching, counseling, and mentoring:

...So then I started thinking and comparing the role of someone who's in the position of a mentor ... as a coordinator I feel I have to lead the staff according to what I think is the best way to deal with things. On the other hand, as a mentor you sort of help a person learn to do better what she does rather than teaching him to do what she doesn't do ... and a coordinator doesn't have the time to do any serious mentoring ... it's a question of responsibility. In mentoring I don't have to live with these teachers they are the ones who have the responsibility in the long run. All I'm doing is scaffolding, giving them crutches giving them tools, giving them a direction as opposed to having ultimate responsibility for what goes on in a particular department.

Mentors' concerns over issues of professional expertise, as reflected in the quote above, are well supported in a recent study on mentoring in collaborative settings (Elnir, 2005). The study sheds light on mentors' strong tendency to promote professional talk, that is, talk about teaching subject matter (which they regard as 'known territory') over personal talk, that is, encouraging talk about dynamics of interactions, about feelings, concerns, moral dilemmas, and so on (which they regard as 'unknown territory').

Recognizing the multifaceted character of role boundaries often *positioned* many mentors as novices in a state of 'living professional contradictions' (Whitehead, 2000):

Take the comment by Debbie, who is a novice mentor, as an example:

I have all these emotions. What can I give them? What am I going to do with them? How am I going to present them so that they say: Wow! You really have something to give...I am a first year teacher again. It's all coming back to me I mean my lesson plans! I have to have a lesson plan for them on Sunday.... If they don't become excellent teachers after one year, did I fail as a mentor?... now, I have very short term goals: first get over the Sunday session, will the teachers want to come back?

Consider, now, Dalia's reflection, who is an experienced mentor:

.... I see mentoring as supporting the teacher in her on-going work and I see teaching as supporting the pupil. But with me ... it seems that I cannot distinguish between my behavior as mentor and my behavior as teacher. When I am doing mentoring, I allow teachers to manipulate me into helping the children with their computers. As I think about it, it maybe that it is more comfortable for me that way, to do teaching, because that's what I know best having worked with children for so many years. I keep asking myself... do I function more as a teacher than as a mentor when I do mentoring?

In her reflections, Dalia appreciates gaps, inherent tensions, and possible contradictions that emerge as she *appraises* the complexities of establishing role boundaries between her known, familiar, professional 'self-as-teacher' and her new 'self as mentor'. Her inner debates as novice-expert speak to Glaser's (1987) contention that as people gain expertise nonmonotonocities and plateaus occur, suggesting the complicated and 'messy' nature of the stages of developing expertise (Feiman-Nemser & Parker, 1993; Korthagen & Wubbles,1995; Day,1998). This implies that practitioners move backward and forward between phases during their working lives, due to different personal, contextual, and social factors such as taking on a new role, changing schools, or teaching a new group age or a new syllabus (Day, 1999). Indeed, mentors' reasoning and behavior may fluctuate between a novice and an expert stage depending on the situation, illuminating on the multifaceted forms and meanings that expertise might take in the context of moving from one role to another within the same domain, such as the passage from teaching to mentoring (Orland-Barak & Yinon, 2005).

4.10.1 Evaluating Mentoring Interventions as Rooted in Moral Stances

What kind of moral dilemmas do I face in my work? What are the pedagogical, ideological, and cultural roots of these contradictory encounters? What forms do they take in my daily work with teachers, principals, project leaders etc? What do I choose to voice? What do I choose to consciously avoid and what are the consequences?

thinking in practice

Let us now consider a different dimension of Appraisal in Appreciation: evaluating mentoring interventions as shaped by moral stances at the meeting between different cultures and beliefs.

The following vignettes illustrate how mentors from three different ethnic/religious groups (Jewish, Moslem, and Christian), all working with teachers in Arab-speaking schools in the Arab sector, *evaluate* the contradictions and inner conflicts that they experience in mentoring interactions. These take the form of moral dilemmas, as mentors struggle to *position* themselves in relation to tensions of ideological and cultural character, tensions related to contrasting beliefs, norms of behavior, and pedagogical orientations. The vignettes illuminate on mentors' appraisal of the situation as they evaluate their personal subjective educational theory in light of the cultural beliefs and norms of practice of their mentoring context. These subjective personal theories, which are the personal interpretative frameworks that professionals construe in the course of their career, are shaped by the collective discourses that surround them and by the changing contexts that shape their identities within 'a changing professional knowledge landscape' (Connelly & Clandinin, 1999, p. 120). While evaluating, then, the mentor also appraises the various identities that he/she is displaying, such as being a carer or creative cothinker (Søreide, 2006), a critical friend, or a supervisor. While engaging in such discursive activity, he/she also reifies, endorses, and makes significant the different identities that play out in communicational practice (Sfard & Prusak, 2005, p. 16).

Let us begin with Sanna's case. Sanna is an Arab-speaking Christian mentor of elementary school teachers in Moslem Arab-speaking schools. In conversation with Sanna on the dilemmas that she faces in her work as a mentor she comments:

On the one hand, teachers are resistant to mentoring. This comes across as showing unwill-
ingness to fulfill a particular task, or through statements such as 'I don't need this it doesn't
suit my class' or 'we know this already' ...very often I feel that I am wasting my time in a
particular school.

Although Sanna feels that *things do not move as quickly as expected*, she is
willing to continue because the mentees treat her with respect:

...They treat me with respect. So, on the one hand, I am expected to cover certain material
and arrive at certain products but, on the other hand, I cannot say that I don't want to come
to them because it's not that they are being impolite or not nice to me. They don't like doing
new things and working too hard but on the other hand they respect me ... I say to myself
that this is the school that the inspector chose for me to work with and it is not my place to
say to the inspector that I don't think they are doing much. I don't want to be disrespectful.
So I have decided to accept the situation as it is, because it is in the end the inspector who
decides whether I continue or not, and I don't want to be rude or impolite to someone who
is of a higher authority...

Sanna's evaluation of her intervention as a mentor is strongly rooted in her
appraisal of the values she believes in and cherishes – politeness and respect towards
authorities. These, she is not prepared to negotiate, even if this would mean less
effective outcomes. This is evident in her decision to stay in the school, not because
she thinks she will be able to implement radical changes, but because teachers
respect her and because it is rude, impolite, and not of her place to refute the
inspector's decision about her work in a certain school.

Similarly, identifying herself as a mentor who believes in processes of learning over time, Samara, a Moslem Arab-speaking mentor, evaluates conflicts of
accountability between her process orientation to mentoring and her inspectors' product-oriented agendas that expect achievements within a short period
of time:

In my work I focus on processes of change in teaching methods, but to achieve any kind
of change we all know it takes time. This means it is not enough to spend one year with
the school staff, it takes at least three years to see any kind of higher order change in the
way in which teachers work with their pupils. But every year my inspector appoints me to
a different school. I constantly face the dilemma of whether I should give up on my idea of
change as a long term process or adopt a more realistic objective of short term products as
might be expected from a one year intervention, which is what my inspector expects ... I am
torn between my belief of change as a long term process and my supervisors' expectations
to produce outcomes in a short period of time....

Although Samara's espoused discourse as a mentor is strongly marked by her
personal educational beliefs about learning as a process, she eventually decides
to comply to her inspector's expectations because, like Sanna, she cannot be
disrespectful to authorities:

Eventually I have decided to avoid confrontation with my supervisors because he is the
authority after all...I respect his decision and try to work as much as I can on processes in
the hope that I will be hired to continue in that same school the year after...

For these mentors, coming from tight religious backgrounds, their ingrained
beliefs and values related to respect for authorities, politeness, honor, and preserving

hierarchy of roles, are core to their appraisal of their practice. These cultural values, as the above cases surface, are strongly influential to the way in which they position themselves in relation to their course of action and mode of intervention. Hence, mentors' evaluations of their dilemmas around issues of accountability and around their roles as 'mandated' agents are strongly embedded in their cultural values. The illustrative examples of mentors' elaborations of their dilemma reveal how their idiosyncratic 'readings' into their dilemmas are endorsed by social, cultural, and political values.

4.11 Signifying Contradictory and Competing Accountabilities

What kind of 'red borderlines' I am not prepared to *thinking in* *cross as agent of change? In what ideologies, beliefs* *practice* *and dispositions to act are these borderlines rooted?* *Who are the various players in the system that I am expected to be accountable to?*

Strategies for coping with resistance is an extensively dealt practical area in mentoring, especially when mentoring interventions are imposed 'from above' and policy makers create modalities of support through contrived collegiality structures in top–down fashions (Hargreaves, 1992).

As mentors appraise how their pedagogical practices might clash with participants' perspectives, they also signify the sources and nature of participants' resistances. In the following case, Rita signifies her dilemma as a case of a 'liberal, democratic' mentor working in a school where teachers are highly accountable to an authoritative, traditional school principal. In her account, Rita appraises teachers' resistances by construing the situation as a dilemma of contradictory values (liberal versus authoritative) and as a case of loyalty and accountability to the various players in the system. It is interesting to notice that her construal of the situation is mainly shaped by the cultural–political differences that she attributes between the mentor's liberal code of ethics and her mentees' authoritative code of expected behavior:

> In the school I work at, the principal is very authoritative and everything he asks, the teachers do without any questions even if they don't always agree to what he wants. As a mentor I am considered as a democratic and liberal person since it is very important to me that they work with motivation and collaboratively... But the teachers were very resistant to me and did not want to cooperate much with what I had planned...I have always said to the teachers that I am not an inspector, and not a principal. I stressed that I would never pass on information about what we do together to the school principal and that I am there for

them to assist. Many times I considered talking to the principal about it but then I reminded myself of what I had promised the teachers and besides knowing the principal I thought it would harm the teachers. But the teachers only took advantage of my liberal mode and did not do much. I still wonder whether I should stick to my beliefs or involve the principal to make teachers work and arrive at some outcomes...

Mentors' significations of the underlying codes, contradictions, and interests that are at stake in their mentoring contexts are often endorsed by strong social, cultural, and political values. These values guide them in managing tensions that emerge around issues of accountability to certain mandated roles, to their work with school principals, and of commitment to the teachers they work with. They also guide their appraisal of their visions as agents of change and of the kind of 'red borderlines' that they are not prepared to cross when finally deciding on a course of action to manage resistances (Orland-Barak, 2003c).

4.12 Observing Pedagogical Practices

Appreciation engages the mentor in informed observation of pedagogical practices. As a discursive activity, it is inherently constructive and builds on informed contemplation in order to build knowledge around repertoires of observed practices.

Practices of Mentoring	POSITIONING	CONSTRUCTION
Observing pedagogical practices		Contemplating to build repertoires of practice

Observation as contemplation integrates both 'seeing' and 'knowing,' that is, as mentors-as-observers bring their repertoire of past experiences, images, examples, understandings, and actions, they are able to 'see' and make sense of new situations (Kvernbekk, 2000). Thus, new observed situations, although directed by former ones, are not automatically subsumed under meanings, but examined in terms of similarities and differences to the familiar situation, requiring recognition and judgment of similarities and differences (Kvernbekk, 2000). Observation as contemplation is also a conceptual, theory-laden undertaking which involves perceiving in and awareness of a particular situation, leading to appropriate courses of action (Kvernbekk, 2000, p. 359) and to the development of perceptual practical wisdom (Kessels & Korthagen, 1996). The product of observation is, then, a record of what has been seen 'to be the case,' influenced by the theories that we accept and are able to observe (Hanson, 1958; Kvernbekk, 2000; Suppe, 1977), but also by those which influence our choice of what not to observe (Orland-Barak & Leshem, 2009).

4.12.1 Contemplating to Build Repertoires of Practice

How do I observe teaching? How does it reflect my views about forms of support? How does it assist the mentee?

Meaningful observation would entail, using Yinger's (1990) terms, contemplating, that is, looking at and thinking about something attentively and intently. In mentoring, contemplation would also involve looking and thinking about practice 'in action', 'on action,' and 'for action.' Consider how contemplation plays out in Leah's experience of observation. Leah is a teacher counselor working as a mentor of new teachers. She entitles her story 'Big Mistake'. As you read her story of an unsuccessful observation visit to a teacher, consider how, through contemplation in and on the experience of observation, she can construe understandings that can guide future reasoning and action in similar experiences:

> As a teacher counselor, I was asked to visit a class of a new immigrant teacher to assist her in her first year of teaching in the country. As we sat down at the beginning of the lesson, the children started bombarding her with questions: 'Who is she?' 'Why is she here'? The teacher turned to me and suggested that I answer. I introduced myself and without thinking, I said I was a teacher-counselor for the English staff and that I was there to help the teachers in their class. BIG MISTAKE!!!! I totally miscalculated the teacher's reaction. Despite the fact that the children accepted the explanation (or so it appeared to me), the teacher looked mortified, although she said nothing to me at the time. She felt that her role as authority in the classroom had been undermined and that she had been humiliated in front of the class. I immediately lost her trust and her willingness to cooperate and allow me into her lessons. She didn't really state it; she just always had a reason why it was inconvenient. Only much, much later did the true reason come out. I was advised by a colleague to confer with the teacher in advance about how (or if) s/he wanted me to introduce myself.

Although recent study points to the benefits of observation for making assumptions, for taking a stance, for articulating new insights, for triggering connections in teaching and learning, and for confronting educational beliefs (Orland-Barak & Leshem, 2009), it is not always perceived as such. In fact, reiterating Lortie's (1975) discussion of teacher individualism, Hargreaves (1982) maintains that "... teachers guard their autonomy 'jealously'. They do not like being observed, still less evaluated, because they suffer competence anxiety and are fearful of criticism that may accompany evaluation.... Autonomy ... is the polite word sued to mask teachers' evaluative apprehension and to serve as the rationale for excluding observers" (Hargreaves, 1982 p. 206). Furthermore, the interpersonal layer of power relations and authority created when the mentor comes to 'observe' or 'supervise' (in the language of super-vision) embeds not only power relations but also the personal interpretations that both mentor and mentee bring to the act of observing – as rooted in cultural rituals of practice and authoritative discourses they have experienced.

Leah's case is, indeed, illustrative of the gap between the mentor's ideas and interpretation of her role as 'cothinker', colleague, and critical friend (Feiman-Nemser & Parker, 1993) and the teacher's interpretation of her visit as 'supervisor' and expert. The apparent clash between these two opposing discourses (partly rooted in the participants' respective backgrounds), not voiced during the interaction before the lesson, created a cross-cultural misunderstanding about the purpose of observation for the mentor (to assist rather than test) and for the mentee.

As the mentor contemplates on her 'big mistake' while observing the mentee, she is able to *construe* a more informed appreciation of the novices' resistance, as a case of cross-cultural misunderstanding and not as a question of being personally resistant to her mentoring:

> This situation is not about feedback. It is, however, about an issue that must precede feedback – that of having sufficient background information about, shared schematic knowledge with, and /or cultural awareness of the teacher with whom one is working as a mentor. Had I realized how insecure this teacher was about my visit to her class, or had I been aware that because of her background I represented a threat to her and loss of face in the eyes of the pupils, I certainly would have handled the situation differently. My conclusion, therefore, is that first of all, one should get to know the teacher and her background as thoroughly as possible before observing her. Secondly, even when a mentor knows a teacher well, she must constantly be aware of the possible impact of her words.

The mentor couldn't have phrased it better. Her words resonate with the power of language and its influence on the kind of mentoring relationship that might develop as a result. As Zeichner and Tabachnick (1985) suggest, perspectives (ideas and actions) are reflected both through professional behavior as well as through the language used when talking about such behavior. Hence, what is said, how it is said, and what is done, that is, language and behavior, are complementarily constituted to affect interpretation (Orland-Barak and Hassin, 2009).

Leah's case illuminates on the contemplative nature of appreciation, engaging the mentor in constant construal in and about practice, while challenging and reexamining emergent assumptions of the 'observed'.

4.13 Recording Appropriate Modes of Support

By contrast to objective documentation of evidence which is devoid of value judgment or of an ideological, social, or educational stance, recording engages the mentor in intersubjective systematic gathering of experiences that would

Practices of Mentoring	POSITIONING	CONSTRUCTION
Recording appropriate modes of support	*Anticipating contradictions*	*Making educational construals for future use*

allow for informed anticipation and construing of an appropriate mode of support for a particular audience, in a particular time and place. Recording, then, is the value-laden documentation of the recurrent interactions, performances, and mentoring experiences, whereby 'experience' and its articulation are not regarded as a static and absolute entity but rather the product of an educational, social, and political undertaking and process.

While recording, the mentor identifies and establishes an alliance with the experience, staying optimally in touch with the nature of the mentee's experiences, and constantly identifying cues about confusion, anxiety (Fox, 2001), potential contradictions, and tensions of power relations. In the process of anticipating contradictions and making construals for future action, the mentor reflects back his/her emotional and intellectual state and tracks the processes of change (Ibid.).

4.13.1 Anticipating Contradictions and Making Educational Construals

What guides my decision to assist a mentee? Have I ever suggested that a teacher is not fit to continue teaching?

While recording an observed mentoring practice, the mentor collects information and positions himself/herself in relation to the observed teaching scenario in order to make an 'educational construal' – an abbreviated rendering of events and construction of alternative meanings for future use (Schutz, 1970). An important aspect of the process entails anticipating contradictions of interest that might emerge when the mentor opts for a particular form, as the following case shows. Irena, the narrator, is a mentor of novice teachers. Appointed by her inspector, her work consists of organizing workshop sessions and observing new teachers in their work. Irena shares her story with a group of mentors. Her story revolves around Dalia, a novice English teacher:

> In one of our sessions Dalia shared with us her discomfort and anger about being visited by the school inspector immediately at the beginning of the year. What's this supposed to mean? she said to us angrily. I haven't even gotten to get to know my class properly and the inspector appears???. I suggested to come to one of her lessons and made it a point to stress that I was not coming to test her but to help her. Dalia finally agreed and we set a meeting.
>
> When I got to her class I asked Dalia what she was planning to do. She said that since they were about to have a test in reading comprehension in a few days, she had planned to give them a handout with exercises so that they could practice. I must say that already at the beginning it seemed rather odd to me that knowing I would be coming to see her she had decided to spend most of the lesson having them work to complete a handout. Dalia also said that this is a especially problematic 7th grade class and very heterogeneous which made it very difficult for her to work.

I entered the class. I saw a class with a relatively small number of pupils – twenty the most. The lesson went on like this: Dalia handed out the worksheets and announced that they were going to practice for the test. She began reading aloud the first question in the handout. Two or three pupils answered, the rest did other things. Then she moved on to the next question in the same manner. She then told them to continue on their own. Several pupils finished early and started looking for other things to do. She then said in a loud voice to those who had finished: "What's the matter with you? Why can't you work together with everybody??' and then turned to me saying:" You see? They are impossible!! The lesson went on and everybody was relieved (including me) when the bell rang. I looked at the handout of the reading passage with the questions. The text was an interesting one and she could have done so many things with it. I wrote to myself what she could have done to talk to her about it.

We went to the teachers' room. The moment she came in I realized that Dalia had other problems besides bad teaching: She sat apart from all the other English teachers (who usually sit together) and she did not establish any kind of communication or eye contact with anybody. Worse of all, the school principal approached Dalia and reprimanded her in front of everybody for being late to class. One of the English teachers approached me then and said that it was about time that she be scolded about her lateness and that she always takes material from everybody but never does anything or shares anything and that they are all 'fed up' with her.

In her account of the incident, the mentor records the situation she is observing by rendering a kind of factual recollection of the events that took place during the lesson. She, then, makes an 'educational construal', based on a more comprehensive appreciation of the novice's incompetence as a teacher and as a professional colleague. Considering the teacher's novice stage, any of us in Irena's place would probably wonder whether to invest time and effort to assist and support Dalia or whether this is a case of being unfit to work as a teacher. True, Dalia had gotten a teaching certificate from a teacher training institution. But personality wise should she be encouraged to stay or is it in her (and the school's) best interest to suggest her to look for other professional routes? Irena's concern in regard to these questions, as she records the entire situation, positions her in relation to an additional discourse – that which considers the needs of the system alongside a felt duty to serve as gate keeper by establishing norms of entry into and exit from the profession (Ben-Peretz, 2009; Tillema & Smith, 2000). As she construes her appreciation of the situation she anticipates emergent contradictions between her responsibility as a teacher, as a mentor of novices, and as a colleague:

In Israel there is a shortage of English teachers and that's a well known fact. It is, then, my duty to help any new teacher to become successfully inducted into the system. True, all new teachers are faced with infinite problems and struggles of professional survival, but how does one help someone who shows no awareness whatsoever of her basic responsibilities as a teacher as a colleague who is part of a school system with rules and duties?

Irena's dilemma resonates with previous dilemmas in earlier sections pertaining to the moral duty of the mentor and his/her sense of commitment and accountability to the various players in the system. What is particularly interesting about this case, however, is how in the process of recording the situation, the mentor's construal is guided by her sense of duty toward the profession in recruiting English teachers to the system. Her appreciation of the complex interplay between the right kind of pedagogy, professional conduct, interpersonal relationships, and personal attributes is also influenced by an almost survival and pragmatic need to preserve the interests of the profession. Irena's sense of moral duty as a teacher and as a mentor speaks to David Hansen's (1994) vocational character of teaching (and mentoring) which, as social practices, bear a feeling of agency and commitment to the work that embodies the belief that he or she has something to contribute to it and go hand-in-hand with questions, doubts, and uncertainties, some generated by the nature of the work, and some by the sheer fact that the person treats the work as more than a routine task. (Hansen, 1994) p. __.

In this chapter I have discussed the conceptual roots of Appreciation as a Domain of Praxis in Mentoring. I have also illustrated these roots as grounded in authentic cases, examples, excerpts, and empirical sources from preservice and in-service mentoring settings.

The following *dimensions of praxical connections* between forms of practice and dialogue constitute the Domain of Appreciation. Taken together, they yield a discursive portrayal of the domain of appreciation in mentoring, as illustrated in Table 4.1.

- Reading a mentoring situation

  Recognizing and confronting gaps between the mentor and the mentee's codes and norms of behavior
  Reframing perspectives on ingrained assumptions and ideologies
  Typifying the mentoring context and signifying emergent cooperative breakdowns
  Taking perspective: Making educated conjectures and connecting the parts to the whole

- Appraising pedagogical practices

  Recognizing role boundaries
  Evaluating educational interventions as rooted in moral stances
  Reframing perspectives on resistances as rooted in contradictory values
  Reframing rigid views about effective pedagogical practices
  Signifying contradictory and competing accountabilities

- Observing pedagogical practices

  Contemplating to build repertoires of practice

- Recording appropriate modes of support

  Anticipating contradictions of interest in forms of support
  Making educational construals for future use

Note 1: I should note that the stories in Chapters 5, 6, and 7 follow a set sequence that begins with illustrative examples of forms of positioning, followed by examples of forms of construing for each of the domains. Randi's story, however, does not follow that same sequence in order to preserve the continuity of her story.

Chapter 5
Domain of Participation

par·tic·i·pa·tion (pär-t $\breve{\text{I}}$s^{l}ə-pā$^{\prime}$sh^{ə}n).

The act of taking part or sharing in something

Noun 1. **participation** – the act of sharing in the activities of a group; 'the teacher tried to increase his students' engagement in class activities'
involvement, involution, engagement
group action – action taken by a group of people
commitment – an engagement by contract involving financial obligation; 'his business commitments took him to London'
intervention, intercession – the act of intervening (as to mediate a dispute, etc.); "it occurs without human intervention"
group participation – participation by all members of a group
nonengagement, noninvolvement, nonparticipation – withdrawing from the activities of a group

2. **participation** – the condition of sharing in common with others (as fellows or partners etc.)
involvement

The dictionary defines *PARTICIPATION* as engagement, commitment, intervention, and sharing. Participation is also perceived as a condition, a status, an act. We participate in activity, as members of a group, at a particular time and place, and within a particular audience and purpose: We become involved, committed, take active part, hold, and are held responsible.

5.1 The Discursive Character of Participation in Mentoring

In participation, we *construe* new and more informed meanings about *persons* and contexts and about roles, relationships, and accountabilities, as we *position ourselves* in relation to a subject, object, or practice. In contrast to appreciation which focuses on observation, appraisal, recognition and record, *participation as a discursive activity* engages the mentor in *dialogue* with his/her mentoring practice as he/she mediates persons, context, and content; assumes diverse supportive roles; manages accountabilities; and establishes and sustains professional relationships.

L. Orland-Barak, *Learning to Mentor-as-Praxis*, Professional Learning and
Development in Schools and Higher Education 4, DOI 10.1007/978-1-4419-0582-6_5,
© Springer Science+Business Media, LLC 2010

5.1.1 Participation as Positioning in Dialogue

Participating as positioning focuses on the ability of the mentor to adopt various positions within different discourses, fashioning for himself/herself, intentionally or unintentionally, a unique complex of subjectivities with some longitudinal integrity (Harre & Gillett, 1994). Participation as positioning is dynamic and embedded in historical, political, cultural, social, and interpersonal contexts. In the process, the mentor defines himself/herself as having a place or places in various systems of location, a sense of responsibility as an agent located in a network of mutual obligations, and commitments to a manifold of other people (Harre & Gillett, 1994; Mullen & Lick, 1999; Hansen, 1994).

5.1.1.1 Commitment and Responsibility

Participation as positioning highlights the sets of rights, duties, and obligations of the mentor and mentee as speakers, particularly in respect to the social force (illocutionary) of what one may say (Harre & Gillett, 1994, p. 35). Put differently, knowing where and how the individual locates his behavior in relation to the context. Participation as positioning, thus, underscores commitment, responsibility, and selfhood, as discursively produced.

5.1.1.2 Agency

Agency is intentional action, and entails commitment to the course of action. Thus, if I withdraw my commitment then it is not my action (Hansen, 1994).

Positioning as agency in participation highlights mentors' initiation of action, significant in giving meaning to what he/she does or who he/she is. Above the mentor's own dispositions to react, he/she structures activity in the light of prescriptive norms or discursive validations which tell him/her how he/she ought to respond if he/she wishes to be understood in this or that way.

5.1.1.3 *Validating and affirming*

In participation, one engages in a process of validation, that is, giving a person a reason to opt for one orientation or way of thinking of a situation rather than another, and determining what counts as a reason for acting this way or that way (Harre & Gillett, 1994). As one enters into different discursive contexts, one comes into contact with different ways of conceptualizing and reacting to the same conditions. One must, then, position oneself in relation to these possibly conflicting ways of construing events. In the process, alternatives are exposed and presented, and subjective tensions that emerge from the contact between these discourses are affirmed. Affirming as positioning, thus, entails locating oneself in the value systems, ideologies, and power relations that characterize a particular discourse and establishing its location in relation to other competing, opposing discourses. In Gee's words, it would imply characterizing the positions from which participants speak and behave, as reflective of the standpoints, values, and concepts that they authorize and endorse as well as of those they marginalize (Rogers, 2004).

5.1.2 Participation as Construing in Dialogue

Through participation in discourse, the mentor develops skills for mediating and managing competing roles and for *construing* a professional self and identity in the sense of being located in space and having a position in the moral order of the group with which one is conversing (Hansen, 1994; Beauchamp & Thomas, 2006).

In the process, the mentor constructs a situated identity as agent of change within the various opposing viewpoints, social relations, ideologies, and standpoints that define the competing Discourses of his/her practice (Gee, 1999). In Foucault's words, it would involve scrutinizing the symbolic interactions and the conventions and relationships that either constrain or connect between particular interactions (Foucault, 1990).

5.1.2.1 Appropriating

It follows that participating as construing is a discursively learned skill of regulating one's behavior so that it conforms to the self-governed significations one endorses or that are endorsed in a given context (Harre & Gillett, 1994, p. 119). Put differently, it is learning how the discursive contexts inculcate the use of certain symbols that tend to structure the responses of individuals. As construal, it would entail the appropriation and mastery of physical and psychological tools as part of participation in collective and individual activities (Vygotsky, 1978) during which individuals engage in strategic activity, appropriating collective problem solving procedures and cultural tools as part of mediated activity (Wertsch, 1991).

Learning to participate as construal refers, then, to the appropriation of culturally valued mediational means or members' resources as part of participation in active, distributed meaning making. The key to understanding learning is, thus, analyzing how the appropriation of mediational means occurs or not across time and in interaction.

5.1.2.2 Interdiscursivity

Participation as construal is interdiscursive, that is, it assumes the presence or trace of one discourse within another. Interdiscursivity occurs when one participant appropriates and reconstructs discourses associated with other participants. The process involves a generative reconstruction of a discourse rather than a recapitulation or imitation. As such, it is a process associated with learning and is initiated and sustained through ongoing, progressive discourse. Through interdiscursivity participants actively construe *professional situational understandings* in and from contexts through continuing, progressive discourse, interpreting, and (re)valuing work-related situations. Construing as situational understandings is a type of progressive understanding of situations that occurs in collaborative discourse about action in real contexts.

5.2 Participating in Dialogue: Putting It All Together

Participation in mentoring engages the mentor in *mediating, supporting, managing, establishing,* and *sustaining* relationships in dialogue. Through positioning and construing he/she acts upon the conventions, the rights, duties, and obligations of the mentor and mentee as speakers. In the process, he/she constantly confirms and validates how forms of interaction and participation that unfold throughout the discourse are constrained and shaped by the formal and informal rules of interaction of a particular context. At the interdiscursive encounter between forms of practice and forms of positioning and construing, the mentor appropriates mediational tools. These are informed by his/her sense of responsibility and commitment as agent, participating in manifold networks of professional and relational texts.

In this extended sense, 'texts' are the verbal and nonverbal symbolic interactions that can bring about changes in our knowledge, beliefs, attitudes, values, and experience, and are mediated by meaning making. Thus, we learn from our involvement with and in texts.

Participation in dialogue speaks to the situated interactions of mentors as social agents, whose agency is enabled and constrained by social structures and social practices. It underscores the way in which participants' resources are privileged, appropriated, rejected, and deployed in mentoring activity. As such, it recognizes forms of cooperation, negotiation, and shared activity, as well as struggles and contradictions which characterize interpersonal activity (Fairclough, 1989; Linell, 1998).

Taken together, as mentors mediate persons, context, and content they validate and affirm interactions, they carry out agency, and they appropriate mediational tools to reconcile between different educational texts.

As mentors assume supportive roles, they recognize culturally diverse texts, they intervene guided by a sense of commitment and responsibility, and they are activists informed by an ethics of care, recognizing privileged and rejected discourses in activity.

As mentors manage accountabilities, they negotiate contradictions in interaction and deal with conflicts of loyalty and commitment while carrying out agency.

As mentors establish and sustain relationships, they attend to culturally valued texts in potentially intimidating interactions, they appropriate texts from teaching and mentoring interdiscursively, they engage in validating and affirming reciprocal communal learning, and they hold themselves responsible for modeling formative leadership agency.

Table 5.1 represents the dialogic basis of participation.

Table 5.1 Praxical connections between forms of practice and dialogue in the Domain of Participation

MENTORING AS A DISCURSIVE PRACTICE		
DIALOGIC BASIS OF PARTICIPATION		
Practices of Mentoring	**POSITIONING**	**CONSTRUCTION**
Mediating persons, context and content	*Validating and affirming interactions Carrying out agency*	*Appropriating mediational tools to reconcile between different texts*
Assuming diverse supportive roles	*Recognizing culturally diverse texts and privileged and rejected discourses*	*Intervening guided by a sense of commitment and responsibility* *Activism informed by an ethics of care*
Managing accountabilities	*Negotiating contradictions in interaction*	*Dealing with conflicts of loyalty and commitment while carrying out agency.*
Establishing and sustaining professional relationships	*Attending to culturally valued texts in potentially intimidating interactions* *Engaging in validating and affirming reciprocal communal learning*	*Appropriating texts from teaching, mentoring and leadership interdiscursively*

5.3 Mediating Persons, Context, and Content

Mediation in professional learning draws strongly on Vygotsky's idea of cultural mediation of actions as the triad of subject, object, and mediating artefact (Vygotsky, 1978, p. 40). The notion has been lately extended to the concept of mediated activity as comprising of complex dialogic interrelations between the individual subject and his/her community (Engeström, 1994).

Practices of Mentoring	POSITIONING	CONSTRUCTION
Mediating persons, context and content	Validating and affirming interactions	Appropriating mediational tools to reconcile between different texts
	Carrying out agency	

Mediation is grounded in and supported by existing social conditions. Hence, mediators have a range of available linguistic forms and discursive strategies or resources on which they draw and which they use to build up a repertoire that reflects and reinforces the institutional and contextual/situational requirements of the mediation process. Mentors as mediators are both pragmatically and ideologically driven. In the process, they validate and affirm interactions, carry out agency and appropriate mediational tools, to reconcile between competing and often contradictory discourses of practice (Fineman, 1988; Adler, Lovaas, & Milner, 1988).

5.3.1 Validating and Affirming Interactions

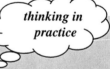

How does my ethics of care play out in mentoring new teachers? What guides my decision to intervene and often prescribe certain behaviors?
What are the consequences for the relationships I establish with the mentees?

As stressed in earlier sections, mentoring is a moral practice and, as such, it constantly engages the mentor in participatory modes that call for ethical and pedagogical action and reasoning, influenced by their strong sense of moral obligation toward the well being of the mentee. Resorting to their moral stances as experienced teachers toward administrative, educational, and professional matters, mentors validate and affirm interactions as carers and as moral agents to their mentees. In doing so, they mediate interactions drawing on their values, such as integrity, care, and caring, responsibility and commitment, as experienced teachers, while validating and affirming what novices often ought to do in situations where their well being might be at stake (Orland-Barak, 2003b).

Participation in mentoring entails, then, constant mediation between persons and content in value-laden contexts of practice. As mentors position themselves discursively in a mentor–mentee relationship, they have to mediate contradictory and often opposing interpretations, reactions, and modes of action to a specific critical incident in teaching. In the process, values and codes of behavior are validated and affirmed, guiding a particular orientation and determining the choice for a certain mode of action in an ethically conflictive situation.

The following vignette illustrates how, through validating and affirming interactions, the mentor positions herself in the discourse to mediate and eventually act upon her professional ethics of care (adapted from Orland-Barak, 2003b).

Consider the story of Maya, a veteran teacher and mentor working in conservative, religious Jewish schools with novice teachers:

> In my work with novice teachers I am often confronted with situations in which I am not sure what the best way to act is. Such is the case with Darra, a novice teacher I have been supporting throughout the year. She told me that a few days after the school year ended, one of the pupils in her class had come to her home with his mother with a big garland of flowers, a satin scarf and a thank you note. She told me how proud she was about the gesture, especially because she had had a real tough year with that pupil's class and getting a token of appreciation had made her feel very good and optimistic about next year.

In her effort to mediate between her appreciation of the situation and her mentee's interpretation, Maya affirms to herself the dilemma of participation she is faced with:

> Darra's comment that she felt so proud and complimented by the gesture kept resonating in my ears. But I also knew I had to make it clear that she was putting herself in a risky position. Working in a small conservative community where everybody knows everybody and ethical codes of behavior are so important for certain groups within the community might get her into real trouble.

Should Maya act upon her duty to prevent the mentee from breaking ethical rules in teaching (accepting presents from pupils) and from getting into a situation that might probably harm her in the long run? Instructing the mentee to return the presents because it is unethical, however, might also put the novice in a very fragile situation in front of the child and the parent, especially because giving presents (and not returning them) was, in this family's cultural tradition, considered to be a gesture of respect.

Maya also engages in critical validation of her own mediation and actual course of action:

> Eventually I told her that she should speak to the pupil's mother and let her know about the problem – she would probably better understand the situation than the pupil...I knew that was the right thing to do, I had to protect her from something she wasn't even aware of. But I knew that I was putting the novice in a very stressful situation – I felt as if I was punishing her for something that she had eventually been appraised for! What right did I have as a mentor to ruin the novice's feeling of achievement after having gone through such a hard year?

Maya's mediation by telling the novice to return the presents was affirmed by her sense of moral obligation as a mentor to protect the novice from the system, and by her internally validated code of ethics as a teacher. Such a choice of action backgrounded, however, the novice's strong need to feel recognized and appraised. In prescribing a clear-cut answer, Maya had attended to her personal ethical code as a teacher of what constitutes right and wrong behavior. Mediating at the crossroads between morality and instrumental reasoning (Goodlad, Sodler, & Sirotnik, 1990), she positions herself as a 'carer' to validate and affirm her mode of participation in order to protect those cared for (Noddings, 1988; Mayeroff, 1971). Maya locates herself as mediating between contradictory discourses: her own codes as a teacher, her knowledge of ethics in teaching, and the novice and pupils' codes of ethical behavior.

In the process, she exposes and affirms the alternatives presented by the different constructions, locating herself in order to cope with emergent subjective and intersubjective tensions.

5.3.2 Carrying Out Agency

> *To what extent do I have the right to pursue educational views I feel very strongly about as a mentor and agent of change?*
> *Am I prepared to go against the majority for something I really believe in?*
>
> *thinking in practice*

The process of validating and affirming through mediation is directed and initiated by a strong commitment to agency. Such a commitment gives meaning to and carries intention for the mentor's mode of participation and his/her positioning in the discourse. In the process, he/she structures activity by considering the norms and validations which tell him/her how he/she ought to respond, while considering the constraints and expectations of the context.

From the perspective of professional identity, carrying out agency becomes the active pursuit of professional development and learning as directed by the practitioner's goals (Day, Kington, Stobart, & Sammons, 2006; Holland, Lachicotte, Skinner, & Cain, 1998; Parkison, 2008).

The following example illustrates how the mentor-as-agent mediates between intentions, expectations, and commitments to act. As he positions his views in relation to the school teachers' discourse, he debates with himself as whether to remain faithful to his commitments and ideological agendas or to reconcile his views with competing orientations and ideologies that are voiced by the majority of the teachers at school:

As a school mentor I am head of the committee for writing a new school code both for Elementary and High school. This means collaborating and working with groups of teachers, coordinators and principals who often hold rigid and strikingly different world-views, educational values and ideas about what ought to be done. This makes it very difficult to consolidate rules and arrive at a consensus about what to include. For example, not long ago we had the following debate: One teacher claimed that students should be exposed to different political views and that school should encourage political awareness in order to educate future conscious citizens. Many teachers expressed their fervent disagreement saying that it is our role as teachers to 'teach' and not do politics. I tried to mediate to create a critical dialogue around the different views. My views on the issue are that as educators it is our role to promote political awareness. And this is something I would really like to translate into our new curriculum and school code. I see it as my personal mandate as agent of change – but I am in a minority-most teachers strongly disapprove. (Shapira & Orland-Barak, in press).

In his treatise of teaching as a vocational practice, David Hansen calls our attention to how a person with a sense of vocation brings to bear a feeling of agency and commitment to the work that embodies the belief that he/she has something to contribute to it. The process is shredded with questions, doubts, and uncertainties, some generated by the nature of the work or by the fact that the person treats the work as more than a routine task (Hansen, 1998). As agent of change with a sense of vocation, the mentor in the above case, indeed, debates with important questions, doubts, and uncertainties brought about while trying to mediate between the ideologies underlying his construal of agency and the expectations and commitments to act as represented by the school.

A similar dilemma of agency as ideological, intentional action shredded with political struggles and dilemmas related to choice of content is voiced by a Jewish mentor working with Arab History teachers. The dilemma revolves around mediating subject matter, persons, and context in the teaching of History:

I keep coming back to this dilemma when I work with history teachers especially in the Arab sector.... To what extent should I go into political implications of certain sections in the curriculum? For example, Arab teachers often feel that the whole chapter on Israel's Declaration of Independence is problematic for their students...

I think that it is important to voice these issues both amongst the teachers and with the pupils, and I see that as part of my own ideology and sense of legacy as a mentor... but it is not something that I can do on my own ... I'm part of an entire system that expects certain behaviors on the part of the teachers on the one hand, and on the part of the inspector who has a certain agenda on the other hand ...

In his conflict, the mentor struggles with delicate issues of agency as related to identity and to the kind of content knowledge that 'ought to be taught' and included in a curriculum. Mediating content, persons, and context while carrying out agency in a context that is politically fragmented is particularly fervent when it comes to the teaching of History (Goldberg, Porat, & Schwartz, 2006; Kizel, 2008). Indeed, in his narrative the mentor hints at the inherent problematic character of his identity as agent – a Jewish mentor of History teaching working in an Arab-speaking school. As he shares his concerns, the mentor displays a strong sense of involvement, stressing the problematicity inherent in construing an identity as agent of change while managing emergent tensions (Day et al., 2006; Parkison, 2008; Sfard & Prusak, 2005).

5.3.3 *Appropriating Mediation Tools to Reconcile Between Different Texts*

thinking in practice

What makes me decide to move student teachers to a different placement during practice teaching?
What kind of strategies help me to resolve misunderstandings and settle amongst the different players involved?
When do I fail to mediate?

Mentors in participation construe appropriated strategic activity, as they signify problems and procedures in a given context. The school–university triangle (student teacher–school mentor–university mentor), which is core to the process of learning to teach in initial teacher education, calls for constant appropriation of such strategies through various mediation tools, in order to maintain a participatory dialogue amongst the various forms of mediation with all parties involved.

Mediation tools are, according to Vygotsky (1978), the physical or symbolic mechanisms or channels through which humans negotiate processes of interaction with the world. Symbolic tools empower humans to organize and monitor mental processes such as voluntary attention, logical problem solving, planning and evaluation, voluntary memory, and intentional learning. Such symbolic tools can include mnemonic devices, diagrams and graphs, and, most importantly, language. Physical and symbolic tools are collaboratively constructed by the members of a culture over time, the former being outwardly directed toward objects, while the latter inwardly directed toward subjects (Lantolf, 1994).

In teacher education, mediation tools entail the use of verbal and nonverbal forms of participation, geared at assisting the mentees in the complex task of making sense of the experience of learning to teach. Such mediation tools include different types of mediational questions (i.e., clarification, elaboration, probing, prediction, metacognition, intentionality questions); the use of nonverbal triggers to elicit the gist of a teaching–learning experience and to encourage associative thinking (i.e, line drawing, the use of pictures and objects); portfolio, journal writing, and guided observation tasks; learning conversations; and so on. These mediational tools are seen as valuable means for encouraging and advancing the student teacher's learning in and from experience, for monitoring learning processes, for articulating insights and understandings, connecting between experiences, making relevant links between theory and practice, thinking through cases, and so on (Feiman-Nemser, 2001; Grossman, Smagorinsky, & Valencia, 1999; Orland-Barak & Yinon, 2005).

Yet, the use of mediation tools is often a delicate, tricky, and not always fully accomplished endeavor. In many cases, their appropriation for a particular context is shredded in ethical and pedagogical dilemmas, in conflicts of responsibilities and accountabilities, and in competing views regarding the envisioned profile of the 'ideal' cooperating teacher who should function as a school mentor to support and advance student teachers' learning.

The following journal entry, written by Dita, a college pedagogical mentor, surfaces some of the above tensions and ethical issues of participation that emerge while mediating between the student teachers' text, the cooperating teacher's text, and her own text.

> I had two very good student teachers placed in an Elementary school since the beginning of the year. Towards the middle of the year, they came to me and asked to be transferred to another school because in their words, they 'weren't learning anything new from the teacher at that point'. I tried everything to keep them in the school, especially because I knew that the cooperating teacher had a good reputation both as a teacher and as a mentor. I also encouraged concrete connections between what they were observing and experiencing at school and what we were learning in our sessions at the college, which I thought were helpful, so I couldn't quite discern why they 'really' wanted to leave. They were also in the middle of writing a project related to that school. It was their last year of study and it wasn't easy (to say the least) to move them to another school. Eventually, I convinced them to stay but then, two months later, they returned to me insinuating quite outspokenly that it would have been 'so good to have written the project in another school...'. At that point I felt really bad, as if my decision to make them stay (for all the reasons I had thought to be the right reasons) had not been the most appropriate one. I felt that I should have done more to help them have a more meaningful learning experience. These were very good students and I wanted them to finish the program with a positive sense of accomplishment and disposition to teach.

In her espoused text as carer, supporter, and educator, Dita sees herself responsible for maximizing student teachers' learning opportunities and for supplying a context of learning to teach with ample possibilities for developing a positive disposition to teach and for encouraging concrete connections between what they were observing and experiencing at school and what they were learning in their sessions at the college. Guided by this text, her students' complaints disturb her deeply, and prompt her to appropriate mediation strategies to reconcile between the student teachers' texts and her envisioned text as teacher educator: moving the students to another school and explaining her motives to the cooperating teacher in open talk, while being careful not to offend her or underestimate her expertise:

> So, at that point I said to them: OK, I am moving you to another school. I knew that meant finding another school and another teacher, being careful not to offend the cooperating teacher who is a good teacher after all.

> That week, I went to the school and had a long conversation with the cooperating teacher – I decided to tell her directly what was going on, reassuring her about our positive experiences of collaboration in previous years. She was taken by surprise and felt even insulted, as if her expertise was being questioned. But I had made my decision. Eventually, I moved the students to another school. I worked hard to find a teacher that would be both willing to accept the students and has a good reputation as a mentor. I had a preliminary meeting with that teacher to coordinate expectations on both sides. For me, this meant starting a whole new project with the students but I am completely fine with my decision: Our first duty is towards the students – to provide them the best kind of training possible – so if there is a bad experience or connection between the cooperating teacher and the student, no matter when, we should do everything in our power to protect the student teacher. I don't care if everybody in the school tries to convince me otherwise.

Reflecting upon participation, Dita articulates her considerations for moving the student teachers to another school. These are mainly directed by her professional duty to protect and support the student teacher, her main concern in the mentoring triad. To this end, she is determined to mediate in the best interest of the student teachers, even if this might put her in a difficult and unpleasant situation. In trying to reconcile between the various texts in the triad, Dita appropriates a number of mediation tools, yet not fully successfully. For example, her determination to move the students to another school is guided by a strong subjective (almost impulsive) fear that she might be spoiling the experience of teaching for them and that might have implications for their future motivations. Driven by this worry, she overlooks at possible strategies of mediation at her disposal, such as initiating a conversation with all parties involved (the students, the cooperating teacher, and college teacher educator) to jointly share the different standpoints, feelings, and possible courses of action. Students could be encouraged, for example, to write a self-reflective project that would articulate the 'twisting path' of their learning experiences or how the barriers that they encountered can be translated into opportunities for learning. The encountered problem could, then, be signified in more creative ways, prior to deciding on appropriating certain actions and procedures. The result is that although Dita is quite complacent about her mediation at the end of the story, she has not, in fact, fully engaged in a comprehensive reading of the situation. Thus, in her effort to reconcile first and foremost between her initial sense of 'having let the students down' and the students' sense of frustration, it seems that she fails to construe a more complex and broader understanding of the triadic dynamics of participation.

5.4 Assuming Diverse Supportive Roles

Assuming supportive roles speaks to the core of mentoring as a helping relationship (DeCoster & Brown, 1982; Hunt & Michael, 1983; Kram, 1985), striving to attend to culturally diverse discourses of practice and to scrutinize possible tensions 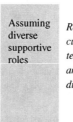 *Assuming diverse supportive roles* — *Recognizing culturally diverse texts and privileged and rejected discourses* — *Intervening guided by a sense of commitment and responsibility* — *Activism informed by an ethics of care*

that emerge between privileged and rejected discourses throughout a professional relationship. As an intensive interpersonal relationship, adopting diverse supportive roles enhances the development of therapeutic competence, underscoring 'who one is' in addition to what one does. It also entails intervening guided by a sense of commitment and responsibility for engaging in mutual reflection on the dynamics of the mentoring encounter and interaction. As an activist informed by an ethics of care, the mentor creates a space for deep expression, responsiveness, self-disclosure, and identification with the other. This involves developing a disposition of empathy, a positive regard, respect, interest and understanding, tact, commitment and obligation, acceptance and expectation, empathy, and agency alongside genuineness and congruence.

Through an ethics of care, mentors can transform their own vulnerability into awareness and creativity, providing a mirror for reflecting emotional, intellectual, and interpersonal processes of knowledge construction (Bullough, 2005). By sharing perceptions and subjective reactions, a space can be created for the mentees to develop an internal means to maintain esteem and tolerate ambiguities, uncertainties, and failures (Proctor, 1982; Bradburya & Koballa, 2008; Hawkey, 1997; Gratch, 1998).

Assuming diverse supportive roles speaks to social support theory, broadly defined as 'information leading the subject to believe he is cared for and loved, esteemed, and a member of a network of mutual obligations' (Cobb, 1976, p. 300). House (1981) proposes four dimensions of social support:

Emotional support (esteem, affect, trust, concern, listening); appraisal support (affirmation, feedback, social comparison); informational support (advice, suggestion, directives, information); and instrumental support (aid-in-kind, money, labor, time, modifying environment). Within this broad range of categories, 'assuming diverse supportive roles' in mentoring embeds both emotional and social-interpersonal aspects of the mentor–mentee relationship, alongside informational, instrumental, and practical aspects of assistance – as determined by the mentor's reading of a particular situation (House, 1981, pp. 524–525).

5.4.1 Recognizing Culturally Diverse Texts and Privileged Discourses

How do I support student teachers who come from a different cultural and ethnic background?
What kind of problems do I encounter?
What do I need to be aware of?

thinking in practice

When student teachers are placed in a practice teaching setting which is different from their own culture, they often find themselves as strangers in a new unfamiliar context (Mazor, 2003). As such, they experience hardships beyond the familiar difficulties that any student teacher would experience in their classroom, namely difficulties in relationships 'outside the classroom doors' with the school staff and with their mentors. Seeing themselves as strangers to the new school culture, they often attribute their hardships to their different social and cultural background. For mentors working with culturally diverse populations of student teachers, it calls for assuming supportive participatory roles that build on their appreciation of the uniqueness of their context.

The student teachers in the vignettes that follow (Einat and Amal) typify their hardships in practice teaching in the Jewish school as informed by their life world, rooted in their experiences both as former pupils in Druze schools and as Druze women in the Jewish college. Their typifications play out as their personal interpretive framework, informing their significations of the situation and the consequent actions and forms of participation that they choose to undertake in the new context of practice teaching.

The centrality of the expressive aspect in student teachers relationships with the staff, and especially with the cooperating teacher, underscores their expressed need to be accepted by the school staff as equal and at the same time acknowledged as different. As the literature suggests, the success of the stranger's attempts to be accepted and to belong in the new group is reflected through the way the members of the group relate to him. Put differently, it is rooted in the 'expressive structure' of the relationship (Kimberly, 1984) (i.e., the way in which participants signify and interpret a particular interaction as guided by their feeling of belonging and of being accepted (or not) by the norms of behavior and participation followed by the members of the group). Thus, one's need for acceptance into the group is validated through participants' behavior, indicated through norms of equality, support, and protection within the group and toward members of other groups. With these understandings in mind, mentors are called upon to assume supportive roles that are attentive to how the student teachers' underlying texts of acceptance and belonging play out in participation. This also implies recognizing the extent to which participatory modes of support privilege certain discourses over others.

In the excerpts that follow, I illustrate how the 'expressive' plays out in student teachers' definition of their relationship with the mentor. The vignettes, written from the student teachers' perspectives, focus on a very specific population – Druze student teachers placed in Jewish schools. Nevertheless, their content depicts a much broader issue when examined through the lens of mentoring as a discursive, dialogic praxis: the need to assume forms of participation grounded in supportive roles that sustain expressive aspects of the experience of learning to teach.

In the first vignette, Einat defines her situation as being rejected and used by their mentor/cooperating teacher, and keeps recurring to the phrase, *It's all because I am a Druze*. In her narrative, she discloses her feeling of being distanced by the cooperating teacher and ignored by the school staff. Her account is illustrative of how, in the eyes of the student teachers, the mentor fails to recognize privileged and rejected discourses implicit in expressive norms of behavior. This intensifies their feelings of estrangement and detachment, eventually blocking their learning:

It isn't fair!

This incident happened to me one day when the cooperating teacher was absent from school, and we [the student teachers] had to substitute for her throughout the entire school day. During recess we were told by the principal assistant "Girls you have to be on duty outside". I was upset especially because I knew Terry [cooperating teacher] is not supposed to be on duty that day. I thought it was not fair, and that they were using us. When Terry came back I told her about the incident, and her only reaction was 'well I don't know what to tell you'. I felt something was really wrong in her response and it hurt me that I did not receive what I deserved. I am fulfilling my job, substituting for her so why can't she help me? There are other students here from the college. But they only come to us, the Druze student teachers. With us she knows we would not say 'no'. Maybe it's because they see us as Druze girls and they do not expect us to say no.

Einat's definition of her situation as 'being used by the system' and not being protected by her mentor suggests something about her expectations to be treated as equal and to be represented and granted protection. Einat's concerns, thus, focus on norms of equality and protection toward her. Put differently, they focus on the expressive aspect of the relationship with her mentor (Kimberly, 1984), which she typifies as being related to the fact that she is a Druze. In her expected supportive role, her mentor had failed to acknowledge the culturally diverse text that Einat brings to the experience of practice teaching.

Issues related to substituting teachers, being on duty during the break, and contact with the mentor and other staff members are known to be an integral part of any student teachers' reality in schools during practice teaching (McNally, Cope, Inglis, & Stronach, 1994). But for these Druze students, incidents like the one they described by Einat convey connotations of being rejected and distanced not as student teachers but as Druze in a Jewish school. Devoid of expressive forms of participation in the mentor–mentee relationship, these student teachers could not 'make space' for focusing on their teaching in the classroom. Einat recounts: *I am telling you, I am very bothered by the fact that if I don't feel warmth and acceptance neither on the part of the teachers in the teachers' room nor on the part of my cooperating teacher...I can't even begin to start thinking about what I can learn here....*

The mentor's positioning in relation to the student teachers, devoid of a culturally sensitive mode of participation, causes the student teachers to avoid contact with her: *We are afraid to talk to her and to consult with her. I guess afraid is the right word for how we feel here ... I think it is better not to talk to her at all and do what I think should be done....*. The students' choice of detachment and distancing from their cooperating teacher in order to protect themselves from being hurt is also supported in early studies of mentoring, underscoring the image of the cooperating teacher/mentor as responsible for the student teacher's well being in the school (Feiman-Nemser, 1994).

Consider now the second vignette told by Amal. In contrast to the first vignette, this is a story of successful culturally responsive participation in mentoring: Amal shares her experience of being supported and protected by her mentor as expected. Still, like in the first vignette, her interpretation of her mentor's behavior as supportive is grounded in the same expressive norms of behavior which led Einat to feel disappointed and hurt in the first story. These pertain to how her mentor managed to connect to her identity as a Druze. In typifying her mentor's participation as protective and supportive toward her as a Druze, she can now 'make room' for focusing on her actual teaching:

In my first day of school I was called to substitute. My mentor didn't like this so she immediately told the principal's assistant "It's their first day here, they don't even know the school, they don't have to substitute today. They should only substitute in English lessons [both students are learning to become teachers of English], not in Hebrew". And when I did substitute for my English teacher she came immediately after the lesson and wanted to know if I was O.K. if I had had any difficulties. She wanted to know how I felt about it. It gives me a very good feeling that our teacher protects us. I think she cares and she is sensitive to us, and she understands our difficulties as Druze.

Amal tells us about her mentor's norms of behavior, geared to protect her as a 'stranger' from possible injustices of the system, and to stand for her in front of the school authorities. Notice Amal's recurrent use of first person 'I' and 'me': She interprets her mentor's supportive mode of participation as first and foremost concerned with her personal well being (rather than with performance or with the pupils' learning). By recognizing and foregrounding the student teacher's privileged texts as a Druze, the mentor succeeds in assuming expressive norms of participation, which allow the mentee to feel accepted while preserving his/her unique identity (Kimberly, 1984), in this case being a Druze in a Jewish school. This grants the student teacher support, safety, and stability (Blau, 1964; Tajfel, 1978; Bershfield, 1994).

Amal makes sure to stress this point. *She said to me: I wouldn't let anyone treat you any other way. You are new for them, as student teachers and also from a different culture and they need to get to know you. This really calmed me down as if she divided the responsibility of getting to know each other...not leaving it all to me because I am new, I am Druze .*

Both Einat and Amal interpret supportive mentor–mentee relationships as grounded in expressive norms of participation. This constitutes, for them, an essential condition for being receptive to the potential learning opportunities that they are exposed to in the new unfamiliar context of practice teaching. As Amal describes it:

It may be that beforehand I didn't have time to think about teaching because I was so preoccupied with other things like feeling different from the rest of the school, I mean they related to us differently. The important thing now is that our mentor treats us as equal, and stands side by side with us when we need her. Now we can focus on teaching once again . . . .

Notice that in her account, Amal's language moves from the use of first person singular 'I' to first person plural (us, we, our), reflective of a shift in how she signifies and interprets the mentor's supportive role. Supportive roles grounded in forms of participation that attend to expressive aspects of the mentee's experience call for recognizing diverse culturally embedded interpretations, and for validating them in forms of participation that are sensitive to the prioritized texts that mentees bring to the relationship.

5.4.2 Intervening Guided by a Sense of Commitment and Responsibility

How do I act in situations where the well being of the mentee might impinge on the well being of the pupils? To what extent do I act guided by genuine concerns for protecting the mentee from the system?

Different mentoring contexts call for different forms of participation, each of which construes a particular type of supportive role. Across the broad spectrum of participatory roles, issues related to the nature and scope of intervention strategies have been a recurrent concern in the literature of mentoring (Achistein & Athanases, 2006; Tomlinson, 1995). For example, it is often claimed that the mere notion of 'intervention strategies' conveys an implicit 'top-down' form of support. In the context of school mentoring, whereby the mentor is also a teacher in the same school, intervention acquires a more complex connotation, since it is entrenched in competing collegialities, dual responsibilities, and accountabilities to the pupils, the community, and the mentees on the one hand, and to the school principal and the inspectorate on the other hand. In the following story, a school mentor shares her dilemmas of participation as she supports a novice teacher in her school. The story foregrounds the moral considerations underlying forms of intervention in subject matter mentoring, a dimension that has not been dealt with in previous sections. As we will see, the mentor's construal of her intervention strategy was guided by a strong sense of commitment and responsibility for the various parties involved (pupils, parents, and the novice). In prioritizing a discourse around the novice's basic lack of subject matter knowledge, the mentor finds herself confronting important issues regarding the nature of her supportive role and the consequences of her form of intervention for the novice's well being:

In the school I work I hold three roles: I am a geography teacher, a coordinator of the 8th grade level and a mentor for all the new teachers in the school. A new geography teacher joined our teaching staff this year and I was asked to assist her and support her. I have a lot of experience with the hardships that new teachers experience, but this time it was different. I noticed that she kept making severe pedagogical mistakes in her class. It was both a question of teaching wrong geographical facts and not being able to control the class. This was brought to my attention by teachers and parents. I used various strategies to get her to share the source of the problems that she was facing and to guide her professionally throughout the year. She was very receptive and took my comments seriously. Indeed, classroom management gradually improved but her subject matter knowledge was weak and she kept making serious errors in what she taught. It wasn't anymore a question of relationships but a big problem as far as teaching geography is concerned – more so, since she was teaching High School. I felt a strong sense of responsibility for her but also for the pupils she was

teaching. On the one hand, I felt I could not 'teach' her subject matter knowledge anew –
she needs to retake certain courses at the university or other professional frameworks to
gain more expertise in her subject matter knowledge. On the other hand, she has been very
cooperative and has improved on the interpersonal side. But the teachers and the parents
do not respect her anymore and she has gained a very bad reputation of being incompetent.
This was a not going to be a win-win case! The pupils were not getting what they should
as far as learning geography is concerned and the teacher was trying her best but the result
was not good enough. . .

In the end I gave up, I told her that although she had a teaching certificate she should take a
number of core courses in geography and then start anew – in another school – start fresh.
I suggested to her that I would help her as much as I could in the future. I acted from a
concern for the pupils' well-being – first and foremost. Then I felt that the best way to
protect the teacher was to suggest to her quitting the job in the school before she is fired by
the principal. She could, then, have a fresh start somewhere else. But I cannot stop thinking
that I could have helped her more, I just didn't want it to be at the expense of the pupils.
Nira [the novice teacher] was very offended. She left the school but never got back to me
since then. . .I feel I let her down.

In her narrative, the mentor shares the tensions and dualities that she experiences as she participates to 'protect and support' the mentee and her sense of
obligation toward the standards of her profession and toward the pupils. In her
construal of her intervention strategy, she surfaces the intrinsically moral and ethical character of subject matter knowledge for teaching (Ball & Wilson, 1996),
foregrounding dilemmas of participation at the intersection between discourses of
care and discourses of knowledge expertise. Eventually, the mentor opts to intervene in the role of 'professional gate keeper'. Yet her decision is mainly guided
by her discourse of care for the pupils. Subject matter mentoring is usually discussed separately from issues of caring in mentoring. Whereas support, care, and
self image align with humanistic, personal growth paradigms of teacher development, issues related to promoting subject matter knowledge and scaffolding learning
speak to more cognitivist/constructivist views of mentored learning. In their recent
book Mentors in the Making (Achinstein & Athanases, 2006) and in earlier publications (Athanases & Achinstein, 2003) provide a comprehensive account of the
crucial aspects of knowledge needed for effective mentoring to guide focus on
individual learners. Such knowledge base, represented through different dimensions of knowledge, suggests a comprehensive conceptual umbrella for thinking
about different aspects of knowledge in mentoring (including subject matter and
caring): '. . .knowledge of both students and teacher learners; of classroom community and contexts, as well as professional contexts that inform teacher decisions;
of teaching as it relates to students, as well as teaching, tutoring, and mentoring
as they relate to adult learners as new teachers' (Athanases & Achinstein, 2003,
p. 1491).

The above case illuminates on the dialectical character of the knowledge base
for mentoring, extending current views of subject matter mentoring as mostly dealing with issues of content knowledge, to include the entrenched forms of caring
that surface at the meeting between supportive roles, subject matter mentoring,
responsibilities, and accountabilities in participation.

5.4.3 Activism Informed by an Ethics of Care

Do I ever decide to act against regulations guided by a sense of ideology and moral duty?

thinking in practice

From a feminist and critical discourse perspective, mentors are critical pedagogues and activists, exhibiting consciousness in their contexts of participation (Freire, 1970; Smith, 1991). Guided by an ethics of care and a moral obligation for the well-being of the mentee, mentors-as-activists often assume direct intervention roles that defy taken for granted norms and rules. In the following story, the mentor acts against some of the regulations and stated views of the mentoring project she is accountable to, participating in ways that might impact on her career. As she narrates her story of participation and support, Betty takes pride in her actions, considering her intervention as one of the most critical and memorable ones in her entire career as mentor. Betty is an in-service mentor of novice teachers. She is part of a holistic intervention project, sponsored by the University and the Ministry of Education to help novices' induction in their first year of teaching. She entitles her story 'Rescuing Sarah' (Adapted from Orland-Barak, 2003b):

> Sarah, a novice teacher, joined the group [of mentees] at the beginning of the year although she still didn't have a teaching placement at the time. During the first two meetings she sat frustrated listening to her peers' stories and envying them for having a placement as teachers at school. Even hard stories about discipline did not prevent her from wanting badly to teach and from seeing these as challenges rather than as difficulties. She would note down every single tip, always ask questions and try to connect what she had learned at the university with her peers' stories of practice...she was actually longing to have a class of her own. Since my approach to mentoring had always been rather protective, I decided to call someone I know to help find a job for Sarah. And, eventually Sarah found a full time job as a first year teacher to teach a class after three different teachers had left that class for all sorts of reasons. Her 'entrance conditions' were therefore more like those of a 'substitute teacher' and every novice knows that such a beginning is hard. This shows the obstinacy of the system when it comes to novice teachers. Her entrance conditions therefore predicted failure: A new teacher looking desperately for a job, falls into a hard class with discipline problems, teaching the last hours of the day, and following the failure of the previous teachers: and here this new teacher comes and the kids are ready to 'devour her'.

> Her lack of confidence was reflected from day one. Sarah shared with us her problems [during the mentoring sessions]. We constantly tried to help her in the group discussion by analyzing the problems collaboratively and proposing various solutions from the floor ... But when the pupils sabotaged the wheels of her car and most of the teachers did not even ask her how she had felt about it, I thought that her suffering had to come to an end. It was better to look for another placement than to come to a school which was like a battlefield and where she got absolutely no support from the staff.

Betty's decision to move Sarah to another school is strongly guided by her sense of care and a moral obligation. Acting from a concern for the well-being of the mentee, Betty acts as an activist, assuming a direct interventionist role:

In our project [the mentoring project described in previous sections] we are not supposed to interfere in the schools. We are not even supposed to visit the teachers or interfere at schools but only focus on what the novice brings to our meetings from her perspective, that's her truth and our concern, and this is where we start from. So what was my duty as her mentor? I said to myself: the atmosphere of the school will eventually push her out and she is already having second thoughts about teaching. . . . On the one hand, I realized that the system in which she functions is impossible. On the other hand, this is not part of my mandate, I might get into trouble professionally if I intervene in something that is not part of my mandate: I am not supposed to go to schools and talk to the principals. Still, despite my hesitations and the risk I was taking, I thought that at this stage I had to intervene.

I phoned the school and asked for help. The reaction was extreme. Sarah was called by the principal and scolded for 'spreading the word' outside the school. She was also told that at the end of the year her behavior would be taken into consideration (loyalty to the school and inability to handle discipline). Her future destiny was being decided upon in the most unfair manner.

On my part I tried to assist her every time she phoned but I couldn't sleep at night thinking that my intervention had actually caused her damage.

One day, an object was thrown into her class from the window. . . The police came in, and the person in charge of discipline interfered. Needless to say that her family began to put pressure that she not go to school because she was physically in danger.

At this point I decided to intervene again and suggest that **she not go back to school** [bold stressed as in original text]. I sent her to the teachers' union and they helped her. I also made sure to phone her previous teachers at the university to get a letter of recommendation. Needless to say that that same year she got two other job offers. And despite the hardships of substituting she finished the year with optimism.

My complaints are to the system: It can be that a person is not competent to teach. Many people decide eventually that the job is not for them and quit. But the system has to absorb new teachers differently. All the factors at school, the principal, the coordinators, the teachers, the counselors etc/have to give the new teacher the feeling of support. . . I did the right thing to intervene.

Betty's construal of her mode of participation through direct encounter with the authorities is informed by a strong sense of activism grounded in an ethics of true care for the well-being of the novice (Webb & Blond, 1995; Noddings, 1988). She shares with us the possible implications of her positioning and consequent participation as activist in the discourse, considering the dangers of assuming a role which goes beyond her designated mandate as mentor. In Nodding's terms, her decision to intervene is 'an inescapable risk of caring' (Nodding in Webb & Blond, 1995, p. 620), with a political undertone of advancing the rights of the least advantaged (in this case the novice), and resisting any institutional agendas that might impede that advance (Valli, 1990). Her actions, however, reflect a role which is more in tune with that of a carer rather than critical pedagogue (Giroux, 1996). In trying to protect Sarah, Betty does not explicitly confront her or encourage her to gain awareness of how conflicting agendas and interests might shape her situation. Put differently, her actions as mentor do not consider cultural, social, and political features of the context that might affect the way in which practices are validated and legitimized (Berger & Luckmann, 1966; Hansen, 1998).

Betty's case is clearly a case of how the mentor, faced with competing agendas (those which represent the interests of the project as opposed to her own moral judgment of the situation), actually opts for a supportive role and mode of participation that rescues the mentee from quitting the system.

The cases in this section illustrate how mentors assume supportive roles by construing modes of participation that are informed by a strong ethics of care and a sense of mission toward the profession. These two sources of activism, care and mission, are strong in Korthagen's six stage model of reflection in realistic teacher education (Korthagen & Vasalos, 2005). The most central core levels of the model call for a serious consideration of identity and mission as they relate to professional behavior, connecting the personal with the professional.

5.5 Managing Accountabilities

Contexts of participation in innovative practices develop in larger contexts within their historical, social, cultural, and institutional conditions, with specific resources and constraints, some of which are explicitly and some implicitly articulated (Wenger, 1998, p. 79). In this discursive sense, then, participation as managing

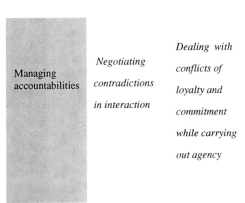

Managing accountabilities

Negotiating contradictions in interaction

Dealing with conflicts of loyalty and commitment while carrying out agency

accountabilities considers the larger context of the educational system within which mentoring is practiced, and with it the way in which systems of accountability are created, sustained, and legitimized. As agents of change in those systems which control policy, mentors have to manage emergent contradictions of interests, and deal with conflicts of loyalty and commitment while carrying out agency roles. As a relational practice of support and mediation, mentors are often required to participate in agendas imposed by policy makers, creating occasions of 'contrived collegiality' (Hargreaves & Dawe, 1990; Grimmett & Grehan, 1992) administratively imposed from above.

5.5.1 Negotiating Contradictions in Interaction

thinking in practice

When do I feel that I am being accountable to too many people in my work?
How does that affect my actions and decisions?

When mentors manage accountabilities they are informed, on the one hand, by their own cultural and social codes of behavior and, on the other hand, by the cultural tradition, conventions, and symbolic interactions of the workplace. Different populations of mentors would then position themselves distinctively as they negotiate contradictions that emerge from managing issues of accountability. The following excerpts, selected from a conversation group of novice and experienced mentors from diverse cultural backgrounds, illustrate these differences. (Adapted from Orland-Barak, 2002).

We begin with Jamal, an experienced male mentor in the Arab sector, who tells the group the following story:

> ... The principal asked me to go into Tamara's class [a teacher in the school] to see whether I can help her with the discipline... and I think that we managed to come up with some good strategies that would help her with the class... but after the incident [one child cursed the teacher and the teacher left the classroom] I felt I had to report back to the inspector... I felt he should be informed...

The mentors from the Jewish sector in the group reacted fervently to Jamal's story. For example, Yehudit, an experienced mentor of literacy contended:... *how could you report to the inspector without consulting with the teacher first!!!??... the teacher has the right to know and you should share the problems and conflicts that this might cause...* Supporting Jamal, Habed, another mentor from the Arab sector replied: ... *but she* [the teacher] *knows and everybody knows that the inspector sent him to intervene... so why go round in circles pretending that he* [the inspector] *doesn't exist...???*

Tali, a novice mentor added: ... *it's not nice to say it but frankly... Habed has a point... and I have expressed this on other occasions here... after all, the inspector is the one who hires and fires!*

The short interaction around Jamal's mode of participation underscores the distinctive ways in which mentors from different cultural contexts and levels of experience manage issues of accountability in mentoring, each bringing different motives and ideological discourses to their appreciation of negotiation processes.

Notice, for example, Tali's comment. As a novice, and in tune with her survival stage (Fuller & Bown, 1975; Conway & Clark, 2003), she is mainly concerned with being recognized by the system. Positioning herself as 'survivor' in relation to the 'dominant discourse' that hires and fires (in her case the inspector), Tali does not perceive any contradictions inherent in Jamal's mode of participation and consequent managing of accountability issues in his work. In contrast to Tali's instrumentality, Jamal's motives for being accountable first and foremost to the inspector have a strong cultural grounding. In the Arab sector, the role of the mentor is defined as being closer to the role of an inspector, hence his felt need to inform the inspector. Habed coming from the same culture can, thus, understand Jamal's management of accountability, by suggesting that it is 'common knowledge' that the mentor works hand in hand with the inspector. By contrast, Yehudit, who is an experienced mentor working in a more liberal school context with an explicit open educational agenda in the Jewish sector, cannot accept Jamal's choice of action. Unlike the rest, she exposes her strong belief in negotiating the contradictions that might emerge in such a situation. Working in the Jewish sector, but contrary to Yehudit's explicit unquestionable position on the matter, Irit, an experienced mentor of computer assisted learning, brings a more elaborate, dilemmatic, and vulnerable perspective to her management of accountabilities. Notice how, by accepting her principal's request, she is caught in a conflict of accountability to the teacher, to the principal, and to her own educational beliefs:

> ... my role is to assist individual teachers or groups of teachers according to the needs of the school... in one of the schools to which I was assigned I was asked by the principal to train the biology teacher in the school because the principal and the pedagogical advisor had decided that sciences would be the first area to integrate computers... In my first encounter with the teacher I was confronted with a frustrated teacher who did not want to engage in any new projects... first, I explained to her that she had been chosen by the principal because she was seen as someone who can lead change.... I remained with the dilemma: should I work with the teacher despite her negative attitude and try to convince her and motivate her or should I confront the principal on her wrong choice and go for what I believe is a better way: to search for other people in the team who are motivated to try without having to force them into change...? (Orland-Barak, 2002)

In her story, Irit shares the ambiguities and conflicts of participation that she experiences in the various discourses that she encounters in her practice. In her struggle to attend to the different voices that she feels accountable to, Irit 'makes place' for her own voice only toward the end of the story, giving it a minor focus in the whole discourse. Speaking the voices of others, surfaced uncertainties as to whether by being accountable to those voices, she was eventually silencing her own voice, which 'spoke' differently about how to manage the contradictions that she was experiencing.

I should note that Irit's management of the case is not meant to serve as illustrative of what 'ought to be done' but rather illuminative (as with the rest of the examples in this book) of the tensions, ambiguities, and contradictions that mentors have to manage in their work.

5.5.2 Dealing with Conflicts of Loyalty and Commitment in Agency Roles

To what extent am I sensitive to power relations between the various participants at the workplace? In what instances do I feel that my credibility as a mentor is being questioned?

thinking in practice

The previous section focused on how different populations of mentors *position* themselves in relation to the various kinds of contradictions and accountabilities that they are required to negotiate. This section focuses on how mentors, as agents of change, construe their participation in a variety of competing 'discourses of accountability'. Such construals call for managing issues of commitment and responsibilities toward the various players and participants (in mandated reforms, often referred to as 'clients or recipients' of mentoring). As a result, mentors' construal of the situation positions them as jugglers in relation to conflictive rights, duties, and obligations – sometimes more and sometimes less successfully. The following case illustrates the latter – a mentor's failure to manage accountabilities as she encounters conflicts of loyalty in her agency roles (Adapted from Orland-Barak & Yinon, 2005):

Hanna, an in-service mentor assigned by the Ministry of Education, was asked by her inspector to conduct a needs analysis questionnaire with the teachers of the schools she works with, in order to identify the type of intervention that was needed for a particular school. After having met with the teachers in all of the schools, she compiled the findings of the need analysis for each class and delivered them to the school principal in each of the schools. In one of the schools, the principal approached her telling her that she was not pleased with the 'results' of the questionnaire for one of her teachers. Without consulting anybody, she called the teacher to her office and scolded her for having done such a 'poor needs analysis' in her class. The teacher was deeply offended and accused the mentor bitterly for having revealed the results of the questionnaire to the principal without consulting her first. The week after the incident, when the mentor came back to school, she was completely ignored by the staff. Then she realized what had happened. She was so embarrassed by the situation and she didn't know what to do or how to respond. Eventually, she decided to talk to the principal and share her sense of distress from the situation. Together, they decided to have a meeting with the teachers in an effort to calm things down. Contrary to expectations, the meeting created even more resistance and anger toward her. The mentor tried several times to get the teachers together. She even planned a meeting in the evening without the principal in order to explain herself and restore the trust that had been lost. But only three teachers showed up. The teachers were not prepared to forgive.

Reflecting on her failure to work with the teachers and the principal, Hanna concludes:

> I had learned my lesson. In the eyes of the mentees, I had crossed the boundaries from being a mentor to the teachers to becoming the principal's right hand person.

> I quit working in that school but I learned about the price I paid for not having been sensitive enough to the dynamics between the principal and the teachers

Although Hanna had not explicitly positioned herself as accountable to the principal's discourse, she had been seen by the teachers as acting on behalf of the principal. Hanna was caught in a situation which was fundamentally conflictual: On the one hand, her mandate called for involving the whole school population, including the school principal. This implied being accountable both to the teachers and to the school principal. In reality, this didn't happen: By agreeing to conduct the survey and by delivering its results to the principal, she had been disloyal and acted unethically toward them. Had she, on the other hand, decided not to deliver the results to the principal, she would have been unaccountable to her mandate, that is, to involve all parties in the whole process including the school principal who (as is well documented in the literature), has a crucial and central place in the success or failure of any educational intervention at school (Craig, 2009; Hargreaves, 2001; Fullan, 1991). Insensitive to the competing accountabilities and interpersonal intricacies between the principal and the teachers, she did not foresee the implications of having handed over the results of the questionnaire to the principal. Hanna's story is illustrative of how she failed to construe an appropriate mode of participation that would appreciate the complex web of power relations and the conflictive rights, duties, and obligations called for in her designated role as agent of change. For example, she could have negotiated expectations and possible barriers and resistances both with the teachers and with the principal prior to distributing the questionnaire.

5.6 Establishing and Sustaining Professional Relationships

As a relational practice, mentoring calls for establishing and sustaining 'relationship constellations' (Kram, 1985) between an expert and a less expert/novice professional. As a relational praxis, however, mentoring relationships entails attending to the cultural and communal basis of a relationship, while appropriating diverse educational, pedagogical, and leadership texts to the particular discourse of practice within which the mentor participates.

| Establishing and sustaining professional relationships | *Attending to culturally valued texts in potentially intimidating interactions* | *Appropriating texts from teaching and mentoring and leadership interdiscursively* |
| | *Engaging in validating and affirming reciprocal communal learning* | |

5.6.1 Attending to Culturally Valued Texts in Potentially Intimidating Interactions

> *How are my decisions loyal to the values I cherish most? Am I prepared to pay the price in order to remain faithful to those values? If so, when?*
>
> **thinking in practice**

The way in which mentors establish and sustain mentor–mentee relationships is often guided by the fact that mentors' work is not recognized for tenure. This positions them as constantly being under the threat that their work might be terminated at any time (Orland-Barak, 2003a). In such a situation, mentors find themselves navigating between their mentees and their supervisors' expectations. The multiple roles imposed on mentors position them as lonely 'jugglers' who are constantly trying to please different players while always considering multiple possibilities (Orland-Barak, 2005). Such unstable status constitutes an important consideration in 'extremely emotionally loaded situations.' For example, Druze mentors often opt to position themselves neutrally, avoiding direct confrontation on dilemmas that touch upon political issues and which involve values related to national identity that might eventually impinge on them.

Rama, a Druze mentor, illustrates this position. In her story she shares the criticism that a Moslem teacher showed toward her because Druze people serve the Israeli army and in doing so they go against the Arab people. When she heard this she felt deeply insulted, but she didn't want to start any kind of argument on the issue. She also said she respected this teacher as a religious person but that she thought his belief was destructive. For a while she was not sure how to react but in the end she decided to avoid the issue. She also considered quitting the school but she felt committed to the teachers. For her, it was an issue of professional responsibility toward the teachers. Although she decided to remain working with the teachers in the school she notes, *I must say that every time I arrive at the school I feel bad.*

Rama remains insulted deep inside. Her management of the dilemma reflects the culturally valued text that informs her feeling of being caught 'in between' her commitment to the state of Israel and her Arab cultural heritage. Rama's decision to remain in the school is informed by her sense of integrity and duty to sustain a professional relationship with the mentees, despite the inner contradictions that she experiences. Her positioning in such potentially intimidating interaction could not be questioned – the values that she is committed to as a mentor constitute a core value for which she is prepared to pay the price of often feeling insulted and hurt over issues of national identity.

5.6.2 Engaging in Validating and Affirming Reciprocal Communal Learning

How do I support a community of learners?
What kind of relationships do I need to sustain and develop?

Participation in mentoring also calls for the establishment of reciprocal relationships in communal, collaborative learning contexts. These contexts, in whether versions of situated action (Suchman, 1987), situated learning (Lave & Wenger, 1991, Greeno, Collins, & Resnick, 1996), distributed cognition (Hutchins, 1995), mediated action (Werstch, 1991), and activity theory (Engeström, 1994; 2001), understand learning as actions and activities integrated in a complexity of institutional, cultural, and historical practices. The unit of analysis then is widened from viewing the individual as a 'solo learner' to including the learners' practice in relation to activities in the community.

Positioning oneself as mentor in these communities necessitates constant validation and affirming of the communal relationships that emerge in these contexts. This, in turn, calls for being aware of prevailing orientations, dispositions, and possibly conflicting ways of construing action that develop amongst participants in conversation. Such awareness necessitates strategies of validation and affirmation that are nonthreatening and that allow participants to 'speak their word' safely, openly, and with a sense of ownership to cope with tensions and challenges that emerge in the discourse.

We can learn a lot about successful participation in communal learning from recent work on star mentors (Orland-Barak & Hasin, 2009). For example, as a school mentor whose mandate is to move from school to school in order to provide ongoing support to teachers and to the school principal, Dorit builds on interpersonal relationships grounded in respect, trust, and reciprocity to validate and affirm reciprocal communal learning. She speaks of herself as a *mentor but also a friend who compliments a lot and want[s] to build trust relationships with each of the parties involved in mentoring: the principal and the teachers . . . so that no side is left unattended.* She calls this *authentic relationships, not martini relationships and dealing with real care.* Positioning herself in that way serves her well for the multiple relationships that she needs to sustain simultaneously when working holistically with the entire school staff. Her mentees, too, speak of her ability to affirm and validate relationships: *She does not come from above and never gives you the feeling that she knows and we don't . . . there is a feeling of partnership, a real collaboration between equals and not an expert with a novice . . . everything done with the right dose of sensitivity so as not to step on anybody's toes. . . .* Her ability to sustain multiple relationships based on safety, openness, and trust is also corroborated by the school principal: *Dorit is the closest person to me at school, she acts as a sound board to me and as a real partner . . . without damaging the relationship with the teachers.*

Orly, another star mentor stresses participation as developing openness and collaboration: *When there is a good relationship it is built on recognition and collaboration to accept and understand.* In the observations and conversations with her, she exhibits a very warm bond between her and the mentees. She is also open to sharing personal experiences and shows a lot of interest for the personal lives of the mentees. She contends, *There is a lot of laughter and jokes during the sessions, although sometimes it could be interpreted as crossing professional borders and becoming too open and intimate.* As one of her mentees contends: *The relationships are very open, the atmosphere very nice and during breaks we talk about family stuff and then come back again to talking about teaching and know how to move from one kind of talk to another . . .we can make that distinction with no problem. . .* The fact that Orly is training prospective mentors who need to learn how to articulate knowledge about teaching and how to build impersonal relationships probably directs her over attention toward sustaining this aspect of the relationship. Mirit, another star mentor, manages to create a community of learners characterized by interpersonal relationships that validate reciprocity. In her discourse, she mentions nonhierarchical relationships where *everybody can learn from everybody*. This is especially relevant for her context of in-service training with experienced teachers, who are expected to attend her workshops as part of their lifelong learning development. The compulsory nature of the professional courses that she leads probably shapes her decision to relate to the teachers she mentors as colleagues. She says, *I don't come from above I'm a colleague and this serves to mitigate resistances at the beginning to the fact that they are mandated to come* (Orland-Barak & Hasin, 2009 p. 6).

In contrast to 'star mentors' described above, mentors who participated in collaborative setting contexts in the study described in the earlier section (see Section 4.10, Recognizing Role Boundaries) eventually refrained from validating and affirming communal learning through relational and personal talk, aspects which they felt unprepared for. For these mentors, assuming what they interpreted as therapeutic roles was considered to be 'unknown territory' positioning them, instead, in a predominantly professional and pedagogical discourse.

5.6.3 Appropriating Texts from Teaching, Mentoring, and Leadership Interdiscursively

> *thinking in practice*
>
> *How does the teacher in me guide the way I communicate as a mentor?*
> *How is it reflected in the way I talk, support, challenge, advice and evaluate the mentee?*
> *What knowledge as a teacher helps me in mentoring? Which aspects 'get on my way'? How do I recruit other teachers from the school to become agents of change?*

Participation in mentoring is discursively construed. As such, it implies constant appropriation of behavior to conform both to the significations of a given context and to the various ideological and pedagogical texts that the mentor brings to participation from his/her own history. While construing, the mentor engages in mediated strategic activity, appropriating personal and collective problem solving procedures and cultural tools from the context.

The appropriation of culturally valued mediational means assumes the presence or trace of one discourse within another, as the mentor reconstructs associated discourses. As mentioned earlier, through interdiscursivity he/she construes professional situational understandings in and from contexts through continuing, progressive discourse, interpreting, and (re)valuing work-related situations.

What is the nature of these associated discourses? How are discourses of teaching and leadership present and traced in mentor's discourses?

How are texts from teaching, mentoring, and leadership appropriated in participation to guide mentors' construals of their participation?

The excerpt that follows of a novice mentor of English surfaces the way in which her discourse of teaching presents itself in her discourse of mentoring. These connections, between teaching and mentoring, highlight what research on mentoring makes clear: mentors' roles and practices are shaped by the ways in which other roles such as teacher, principal, and inspector are defined in the system (Elliot & Calderhead, 1993, Maynard & Furlong, 1993):

> ... this is my first year of mentoring a group of teachers. . . . the inspector told me to work with all the novice teachers in the Junior High school in order to help them to implement the new curriculum in their teaching. . . I myself still feel very insecure using the document in my own class. . . the teachers are counting on me to make it work. . . I don't want to disappoint neither the teachers nor the inspector, but I am not there yet. . . this was especially brought to my awareness when one of the teachers asked me a question about the principles of the curriculum. . . and I couldn't come up with the right answer. . . I'm worried that I have lost her trust in me. . .

Meira expresses her difficulty in transferring her expertise as a teacher to her mentoring context. This, in her perception, can lead to losing her mentees' trust in her. Such a concern highlights establishing and sustaining qualitative mentor–mentee relationships as the successful transfer from discourse to another. In Meira's case, feeling that she did not understand the curriculum as a teacher destabilized her functioning as a mentor. In her assertion, *the teachers are counting on me to make it work. . . I don't want to disappoint neither the teachers nor the inspector. . .*, she shares her strong motive for sustaining the multiple relationships that she feels accountable to in her work as mentor (teachers, the inspector, and the principal).

Mentors texts-as-leaders are embedded interdiscursively in mentors' construals of their participatory roles. Specifically, mentors often allude to their responsibilities as modeling formative leadership roles in their mentoring contexts. Thus, while construing mediated strategic activity, mentors appropriate roles that challenge and support the mentees to become autonomous lifelong learners – a view that speaks to formative leadership texts. Such leadership texts often appropriated for the mentoring context, stress challenging the protégés by setting high expectations and commitment to personal goals, and encourage them to think creatively and ask questions and approach problems in new and unexpected ways (Popper, Mayseless & Castelnovo, 2000).

Mentors texts as transactional leaders also intersperse in their work while attending to managerial, coordinating roles in the educational system (Silva, Gimbert, & Nolan, 2000), as well as roles related to curriculum and staff development and agents of change in their school cultures (Darling-Hammond, 1988; Silva, Gimbert, & Nolan, 2000; Lieberman & Miller, 1999; 2004). The interdiscursive character of mentors' roles as leaders seems to be stronger in contexts where the mentor functions as the agent of mandated agendas from above and is expected to perform and influence in a particular way.

In this chapter, I have discussed the conceptual roots of Participation as a Domain of Praxis in Mentoring. I have also illustrated these roots as grounded in data from preservice and in-service mentoring settings. The following *dimensions of praxical connections* between forms of practice and dialogue constitute the Domain of Participation. Taken together, they yield a discursive portrayal of the domain of participation in mentoring, as illustrated in Table 5.1

- Mediating persons, context and content

  Validating and affirming interactions
  Carrying out agency
  Appropriating mediational tools to reconcile between different texts

- Assuming diverse supportive roles

  Recognizing culturally diverse texts and privileged and rejected discourses
  Intervening guided by a sense of commitment and responsibility
  Activism informed by an ethics of care

- Managing accountabilities

  Negotiating contradictions in interaction
  Dealing with conflicts of loyalty and commitment while carrying out agency

- Establishing and sustaining professional relationships

  Attending to culturally valued texts in potentially intimidating interactions
  Appropriating texts from teaching, mentoring and leadership
    interdiscursively
  Engaging in validating and affirming reciprocal communal learning

Chapter 6
Domain of Improvisation

im·prov·i·sa·tion   (ĭm-prŏv'ĭ-zā'shən, ĭm'prə-vī-)

1. The act or art of improvising.
2. Something improvised, especially a musical passage or a dramatic skit

Noun
1. **improvisation** – a creation spoken or written or composed extemporaneously (without prior preparation)

   creation – an artifact that has been brought into existence by someone

2. **improvisation** – an unplanned expedient

   temporary expedient

   expedient – a means to an end; not necessarily a principled or ethical one

3. **improvisation** – a performance given extempore without planning or preparation

   extemporisation, extemporization

   performance– the act of presenting a play or a piece of music or other entertainment;

The dictionary defines *improvisation* as a temporary, spontaneous, unplanned act of performance. Improvising, in this restricted sense, connotes with immediate action and inventiveness, while 'making something up as you go along' and occurring as you 'do' and not as you 'think' or 'feel.' The common idea about the concept connotes with negative/low moral standards (i.e., unprepared, impulsive, snap, etc.) derived from western, rationalistic tradition of thinking: "The improvisatory act focuses on the gathering of energies, the freeing of possibilities of articulation, an alertness of giving and receiving, the establishment of connection. It, too, has to do with developing wholeness through developing the sense of self" (Frost & Yarrow, 1989, p. 145).

L. Orland-Barak, *Learning to Mentor-as-Praxis*, Professional Learning and
Development in Schools and Higher Education 4, DOI 10.1007/978-1-4419-0582-6_6,
© Springer Science+Business Media, LLC 2010

Yinger (1990) defines improvisation as "skilled performance that is especially sensitive to the moment and place ... it is highly patterned, intelligently composed and quite complex to learn (p. 85). Although especially suited to situations that discourage deliberative processes of planning, analysis, and reflection, it is a compositional process using as building blocks a set of situationally (contextually) grounded patterns for thought and action" (Ibid).

Yinger goes further to suggest a number of essential components to improvisation: patterns for thought and action that are holistic configurations of 'embodied thought' called upon the composed and enacted (lived) within the special constraints of the context; a retrospective working method which uses patterns from the past to other future action and draws on knowledge from the immediate context in its historical development; patterns and pathways that are incorporated in a way that is continually responsive to changing exigencies and purposes; constellations of knowledge, beliefs, and goals structured by action. Directed toward action, improvisation is synthetic and compositional and directed primarily toward the establishment and maintenance of relationship between actor and material, actor and instrument (tool), actor and other participants (p. 86).

In the realm of clinical supervision, improvisation would connote with reflection in action as theorizing in the context of practice (Garman, 1986),that is, understanding and depicting meaningful human action for the purpose of guiding practice. The process is represented through five steps: involvement in a scenario, a record of the scenario, making sense of the records, making an 'educational-construal,'an abbreviated, manageable rendering of events and meanings for future use, and a confirmation to determine whether the construal has meaning to other practitioners. Beyond theorizing, improvisation calls for "the merging of pre-rational dialectic knowledge which plays out as an aesthetic experience" (Steiman, 1971). As praxis, improvisation leans on personal theories of practice, generating new forms of merging between past experience, the present context, and future action. In contrast to earlier conceptions of reflection as stages for, in, and on action (Schön, 1987), improvisation entails nonlinearity and simultaneity, and is devoid of any sequential structure or order (Yinger, 1987).

6.1 The Discursive Character of Improvisation in Mentoring

The above elaborations underscore the dialogic character of improvisation at the encounter between embodied thoughts as *forms of dialogue* that merge positioning and construing with immediate action in situationally grounded *forms of practice*.

Taken to the realm of mentoring, improvisation as a discursive activity engages the mentor in dialogue with his/her mentoring practice, as he/she tunes in, articulates teaching, learning and subject matter, connects experience, beliefs and knowledge in action, and responds 'on the spot.' In each of these 'dialogues of enactment,' mentors construe by drawing on patterns from past action to compose and enact present action. These construals are grounded in 'here and now' positionings in relation to actors, tools, and participants. They are also echoed in the internally persuasive and authoritative dialogues that characterize participants' past and present discourses.

6.1.1 Improvising as Positioning in Dialogue

6.1.1.1 Discerning 'Here and Now' Meanings Through Skilful Action

> I call great character one who by his actions and attitudes satisfies the claim of situations out of deep readiness to respond with his whole life, and in such a way that the sum of his actions and attitudes expresses at the same time the unity of its being in its willingness to accept responsibility (Buber, 2002, p. 135)

Improvisation as positioning is the relationship of a person to the world through skilful action – these are both manual and discursive skills – used in symbolic inter-actions while explaining oneself to others (Harre & Gillett, 1994 p. 100). It entails discerning the 'here and now' meanings of a particular behavior or performance through the rules the individual is following at that particular point. Positioning as improvisation in mentoring involves interpretation and empathy rather than prediction and control, while the mentor encourages the mentee to discharge feelings in order to rationalize action. It entails examining discursive constructions as expressions of the mentee's underlying cognitive states, in the context of their occurrence.

6.1.1.2 Action as Guided by Interaction

Of a sociocultural nature, improvisation as positioning can be described as the orientation and purpose that guides action pathways as these react and respond to the dynamics of social interaction and conversation. In contrast to implementation, which is the activation of patterns within a framework prescribed by planning, improvisation as positioning can be described as alignment of patterns elicited by the demands of the moment (Yinger, 1990; Richardson, 1990). In tune with Schon's (1987) 'knowledge in action,' it is intuitively valid and, in contrast to decision-making models or reflective models of systematic inquiry (Dewey, 1933), it neither relies on a series of conscious steps in a decision-making process nor on staged processes of reflection (Yinger, 1990).

The knowledge is inherent, instead, in the action; it is based, in part, on the past experiences and 'wisdom of practice' of the practitioner interacting with the particular situation. Interacting with the situation as positioning 'in action' brings forth and expands upon a kind of tacit knowledge in an individual that is not consciously articulated at the time. It calls up on knowledge and procedures to demonstrate and direct action interactively, often described as 'pedagogical tact,' or the inner-reflective dialogue between representations of the 'I' and the 'Self,' while the former supervises the action of the latter at the time of action (Van Manen, 1991; 1995). In this vein, improvisation as action guided by interaction calls, on improvisational pedagogical skill of immediate thoughtful knowing (or pedagogical tact) of how to cope with situations of interactive learning.

6.1.1.3 Knowing in the Face of Uncertainty

Improvisation as positioning calls for drawing on one's wisdom of practice (Shulman, 1986; Goodfellow, 2003). Wisdom embeds, as Kitchener and Brenner (2003) propose, knowing in the face of uncertainty, an awareness of the unknown, and its implications for real-world problem solving and judgment: 'Wisdom is understood to promote superior understanding demonstrated in the ability to exercise good judgment about important but uncertain matters and deriving solutions to these problems' (p. 215). As such, it entails the presence of unavoidable difficult 'thorny' problems inherent in the lives of adults; a comprehensive grasp of knowledge characterized by breadth and depth; a recognition that knowledge is uncertain and it is not possible for truth to be absolutely knowable at any given time; and a willingness and ability to formulate sound, executable judgments in the face of uncertainty. Taken to the realm of education and professional learning, practitioners' wisdom of practice unfolds dynamically, through continuous pedagogical, practical, and curricular positionings in relation to the manifold experiences that they encounter (Shulman, 2004; Kitchener & Brenner, 2003).

6.1.2 Improvising as Construing in Dialogue

Whereas positioning in improvisation calls for attending to ways in which participants locate themselves in here and now relationships, construing transforms these positionings into interpretations and choices of action that allow for anticipating events and adapting to the here and now context (Harre & Gillett, 1994, p. 134; Kelly, 1955). As such, it embeds cognitive, social, and metacognitive constructivist processes of assisting the mentee in ways that are at the upper limit of his or her zone of proximal development (ZPD). It is, thus, the cognitive effort on the part of the mentor to identify recurring patterns that reflect those zones of development of the mentee that are in the process of maturing or which lie in the zone of proximal development. In the process, the mentor foregrounds connections between cultural codes, values, strategic, and pedagogic reasoning.

As practical wisdom, improvising as construing entails sound judgment in the use of personal/professional, theoretical, and practical knowledge, very often encompassing 'the invisible elements of practice' (Fish, 1998). Higgs & Titchen (2001) describe it as 'the possession of practice experience and knowledge together with the ability to use them critically, intuitively and practically... these qualities, skills and processes and their blending are built up through extensive introspection and critical reflection, and review of, practice (p. 275)'.

Improvisation as the deployment of practical wisdom calls for intuition and the ability to discern meaning through engagement with the context. Intuition, in turn, embeds the ability to see through things, read between the lines, and interpret messages gleaned through interactions with social and physical environments.

6.1.2.1 Composing Through Recurring Patterns

Improvising as construing connects recurring patterns within larger patterns (Yinger, 1987), links concepts to actions, and responds to connections between theory and practice 'in action,' both systematically and automatically. This requires the acquisition and development of skills that assist in identifying the conditions that play out to shape a particular situation. Performance is, then, accomplished on the spot by using knowledge and interaction patterns bounded by social participation structures, such as working together, demonstration, and working alone. The mentor's actions call up knowledge and procedures holistically associated with particular problem types. Action, in construing, calls for several recurring patterns of improvisation: Thinking aloud, explicating knowledge and debugging mistakes, getting to specifics, and decomposing/rebuilding problems. For any problem or conversation, these patterns are composed on the spot as part of the mentor's performance. While composing the interaction in activity, the mentor recognizes situational similarities and controversies, building on them to direct specific interactions and management of problems that arise on the spot (Yinger, 1990).

6.1.2.2 Responsible Responding

Improvisation as construing is also of a moral character. It is, as Buber would contend, responsible spontaneous response, which is of an inherently moral character. As such, it attends to voices and texts that are claimed and silenced, assuming non-confrontational intervention to mitigate conflicts and to connect emotionally and professionally to the mentee and his/her unique context. Responsible responding also calls for attending to and preserving the core values cherished by the mentor, while temporarily deconstructing the organized structures of the self in order to attend to those called for by the mentee and the context (Buber, 1947). As Buber suggests:

> In spite all the similarities, every living situation has, like a newborn child, a new face, that has never been before and will never come again. It demands of you a reaction which cannot be prepared beforehand. It demands nothing of what is past. It demands presence, responsibility; it demands you. (Buber, 1947, cited in Sidorkin, 1999, p. 51).

6.2 Improvising in Dialogue: Putting It All Together

Improvisation as dialogue entails multiple encounters between forms of practice (tuning in, articulating, connecting experience, beliefs, and knowledge in action) and forms of positioning and construing (discerning 'here and now' meanings through skilful action, action as guided by interaction, knowing in the face of uncertainty, composing through recurring patterns, and responsible responding). Taken together:

As mentors tune in to a situation, they connect emotionally and professionally to respond to contextual differences, identify recurring patterns, translate behavior into here and now patterns, and compose through recurring patterns.

Mentors articulate teaching, learning, and subject matter guided by the here and now interactions. They respond to connections between theory and practice in action, analyze practice systematically, and connect concepts to actions, encouraging the mentee to discharge feelings in order to rationalize action.

Mentors respond on the spot responsibly, connecting experience, beliefs, and knowledge. In doing so, they intervene to mitigate conflicts, connect emotionally and professionally to respond to contextual differences, foreground connections between cultural codes, values, strategic, and pedagogic reasoning and call up on knowledge and procedures to demonstrate and direct action.

Table 6.1 Praxical connections between forms of practice and dialogue in the domain of improvisation

MENTORING AS A DISCURSIVE PRACTICE		
DIALOGIC BASIS OF IMPROVISATION		
Practices of Mentoring	**POSITIONING**	**CONSTRUCTION**
Tuning In	*Connecting emotionally and professionally to respond to contextual differences*	*Translating behavior into here and now patterns and modes of assistance* *Composing through recurring patterns*
Articulating teaching, learning and subject matter	*Analyzing practice systematically*	*Responding to connections between theoretical concepts and practices 'in action'* *Encouraging the mentee to rationalize action*
Responding on the 'spot' by connecting experience, beliefs and knowledge	*Intervening to mitigate conflicts*	*Foregrounding connections between cultural codes, values, strategic and pedagogic reasoning* *Calling up on knowledge and procedures to demonstrate and direct action*

6.3 Tuning In

Improvisation in mentoring embraces the capacity to 'tune in' to the mentee during mentoring interactions. It implies identifying the mentee's perceptions of teaching and learning, and making use of that information as a starting point for a learning conversation. Mentors refereed to it as 'traveling unchar-

Practices of Mentoring	POSITIONING	CONSTRUCTION
Tuning In	Connecting emotionally and professionally to respond to contextual differences	Translating behavior into 'here and now' modes of assistance Composing through recurring patterns

tered waters or steering through the waters of unpredictability' or as 'the ability to look at the mentees' work retrospectively by establishing goals 'on the spot' according to how the conversation develops and where the mentee is at (Orland-Barak, 2001b). Interpersonally, tuning in can be best captured as leaving all our preconcieved notions, including our should's and must's in order to connect to the mentee. This requires a high degree of interpersonal sensitivity and social strategies that would enable the mentee to feel safe in the relationship and consequently to open up to the mentor. In this sense, tuning connotes tightly with humanistic, personal growth approaches to mentoring and mentored learning. As positioning, tuning in would suggest 'the empathic identification with the other, in our case the mentee, that helps the mentor to make sense of what the mentee is doing.....it [also means] being sensitive to the subtleties of the situation of the other...and to know what a situation means to a person and not just what the situation is, if we are to understand what the person is doing'... (Orland-Barak, 2001a).

The following quotes are selected from interviews with two novice mentors toward the end of their first year of mentoring new teachers. The excerpts exemplify the meanings that they learned to attribute to tuning in, as they were learning to improvise in mentoring interactions: (Orland-Barak, 2001b)

I am concerned now with tuning in, that is, knowing what to say that'll communicate the message that I understand you. Usually when we talk to someone we are talking from where we are at. The thing is finding the window that will enable me to understand what she really means and use that understanding as a starting point for the conversation...Tuning in for me means leaving all preconceived notions of how I interpret a particular situation, like a process of leaving me and entering the situation and the person I am communicating with. My inner 'me', that is, who I am as a person (like the fact that I like to help people or that I enjoy teaching) stays with me all the time when I am mentoring. What leaves me are all the 'shoulds' and 'musts' about my teaching. Instead, I try to connect to the teacher's should's and must's as a starting point...

The mentor's words above speak to Buber's demand of presence, responsibility, awareness of self, and acceptance as qualities of a 'great character' (see Section 6.1.1.1). They also associate with responsible responding which attends on the one hand to the mentor's core values and, at the same time, makes space for connecting to the mentee's values, beliefs, and feelings.

Similarly, but focusing on how the mentor temporarily puts aside her own beliefs and understandings in order to attend to those called for by the mentee and the context, another mentor shares her interpretation of tuning in:

> I've learned to listen to what the teacher is saying and to try to interpret as I listen what she means by that. . . .that all I have to do is help the people to realize what their own potential is and to use what's best for them. And in order to do that I have to be a better listener and I have to sort of be able to queue in to where they are coming from. . .I think this year I've learned that my job is not to solve problems, it's to help them solve their problems by themselves in the best way that is for them. . . (Orland-Barak, 2001).

For both mentors, tuning in entails positioning themselves differently in the discourse by detaching themselves both consciously and affectively from their own interpretations. By disentangling themselves from any predispositions or personal evaluations that they might be making of the situation, they can discern 'here and now' meanings as guided by how the mentee defines the situation and by how the interaction develops at a particular time and place.

6.3.1 Connecting Emotionally and Professionally to Respond to Contextual Differences

What do I do to connect to where the mentee is at?

thinking in practice

While tuning in, mentors position themselves emotionally and professionally in order to connect to the mentee. This calls for, first and foremost, establishing and sustaining positive interpersonal relationships that allow for associating between emotional, social, and professional aspects of learning (Evans, 2000). As quoted in previous sections in relation to other discursive aspects of the practice, we can learn a lot about tuning in from the study on star mentors: The different ways in which star mentors connected emotionally and professionally to their mentees were strongly reflected in how they spoke about tuning in by responding to the idiosyncratic conditions of the context. The various forms and meanings that these connections took ranged from emotional to instrumental and/or pedagogical aspects of teaching (Orland-Barak & Hasin, 2009).

For example, recognizing the importance of connecting emotionally to the mentee in her mandated role as agent of curriculum reform, Orly talks about tuning in emotionally to the mentee as a springboard for enhancing creative, innovative thinking about new curriculum: *It is important to connect to them and accept them even if they resist the process, processes of change are not simple and each is in a different place, they need the confidence in themselves first in order to think about new ways of teaching. . . ..* Her ideas find support in the mentoring conversations that were observed, which focused on encouraging the mentees to share critical events and personal incidents.

By contrast, Nurit alludes to tuning in to the mentees at personal, emotional, and professional levels. This is dictated by her context, since she works with novice teachers who need support at all levels. In the same vein, Nurit speaks about tuning in to the mentees in order to mitigate the resistances that they exhibit when a mentor is 'appointed from above':

As I connect to each teacher according to where she is at, I am delivering the message that every teacher has an individual style and that I am open to connecting to each of them according to their needs and to what is most appropriate for them. . . that also helps with managing their resistance to my mentoring, because don't forget that they were assigned by the principal to me, they didn't come to me on free will at the beginning. . . .. Thus, in this mandated context, she needs to be particularly sensitive to emergent resistances toward her presence as representative of the Ministry of Education and as supervisor of their performance during the first years of teaching.

Mirit connects to the mentees mainly professionally to *realize their potential to their maximum.* She talks about each mentee as possessing particular abilities and as her role to identify their strengths as a starting point for their development. As a regional math mentor who leads monthly group sessions, she does not have the possibility of establishing close ongoing contact with each teacher individually, a condition which backgrounds a focus on interpersonal relationships. By contrast, Dorit talks at length about connecting to her teachers emotionally in order to develop them professionally. She describes it as *knowing how to improve the mentee's practice but from where the mentee is at, in a democratic relationship. . .getting to the soul and feelings of the teacher.* As an internal school mentor, she has the time and the space to deepen into areas which are both of a personal and professional character. She mentions *encourag*[ing] *dialogue and allow*[ing] *for space to flow with the process. . .*

In all of the above cases, star mentors tuned in to their mentees by positioning themselves empathetically in the discourse, being sensitive to the subtleties of the situation, while appreciating the implications of a particular mode of participation or improvisation for a particular person and context.

6.3.2 Translating Behavior into 'Here and Now' Modes of Assistance

When do I decide to actively intervene in the mentee's work?
What guides my decision? What is the learning value (or not) for the mentee?
How often do I demonstrate and model behavior?
How might the experience help me in getting to know myself as a professional?

thinking in practice

Very often, tuning in to a particular situation calls upon the mentor's 'here and now' intervention during a lesson. Such a decision is informed by the mentor's construal of a particular behavior or performance as one which can assist the mentees to advance in ways that are at the upper limit of their zones of proximal development. By identifying recurring patterns of behavior that can be improved through direct assistance, the mentor uses knowledge and interaction patterns (such as demonstration) to exemplify, debug, and advance learning from experience.

In the following two vignettes, we are taken through a mentor's account of observing two different teachers, Dora and Betty, and through her construal of intervention modes that attune to their expressed difficulties. The vignettes illustrate the distinctive ways in which the mentor translated the mentee's behavior into a 'here and now' mode of assistance, as she tuned in to 'rescue them' and advance them in their respective teaching contexts:

> I was sitting in Dora's class at the back feeling that the lesson was not leading anywhere. I could even anticipate the discipline problems that were about to burst. I could understand now what Dora had told me about her discipline problems with that class because I saw it coming in the lesson…As I observed Dora, I could clearly see that she was not developing the lesson in a successful direction. This is when I began debating with myself what to do in order to help her. I didn't know what exactly to do at that point. On the one hand, I didn't want to interfere. On the other, I felt that Dora expected me to do something to help her.

Sarah, the mentor, continues to focus on a critical incident that had made her realize that she had to opt for a course of action on the spot:

> …so one of the children in the class stood up suddenly and said [in Hebrew] 'I feel that we are not learning enough. I don't understand why we do so much reading and speaking when we should be learning grammar! All the other classes are way beyond us!' I felt this was an escalation of the tension that was building up during the lesson and thought that poor Dora! She had to do something quickly otherwise she would loose the class completely. I was relieved to see that Dora did not hesitate and immediately answered by trying to explain to them that grammar is only one part of the language and, yes, they will learn it little by little…. but after that long speech, I felt even more strongly that she still wasn't getting to them and that she was loosing them even more. Dora looked at me as if signaling that she was asking for my support…. and then she was silent for a moment as if she waited for

me to say something. This is when I decided that I had to do something quickly in order to save the lesson and rescue Dora. I felt that she was kind of asking for me to interfere, to say something...

Sarah conjectured that if Dora hadn't managed to successfully overcome the pupils' resistances, the lesson could be ruined. She was also sensitive to tuning in to the hints coming from Dora, signifying that she wanted to be rescued by her, the expert teacher and mentor:

> ...from her look I could see that she was kind of slowly sinking and that she wanted me to say something... so I asked her for permission to get up and say something, which I have never done before... I got up and I spoke in Hebrew to make sure that there weren't any misunderstandings. I explained to them that grammar is only a framework and if you don't have anything to fill it with there is no point in learning it. I also said that I understand their feelings...and I think they felt a little bit better ...on the one hand I felt like I broke a boundary by interfering in the middle of the lesson. Like I crossed the border line that maybe I shouldn't have. On the other hand, I think that Dora was hinting to me strongly that she needed the reinforcement and support that I gave her. I also said to the children that they have a wonderful teacher and I think it gave her a little bit of support that she needed at that point in the eyes of the pupils... Dora said that it was good for her

Sarah tunes in to where Dora is at by expanding on the function of grammar, which is what Dora had started to discuss with the pupils. By staying close to Dora's text, she is legitimizing Dora's actions in front of the class. Employing clarification strategies, she construes her action drawing on the recurring patterns that she has recognized during the lesson. In discursive terms, she has attended and acted upon the voices that play out in the 'here and now' idiosyncratic context of interaction, carrying a particular pedagogical and educational orientation. She also appreciates the controversies that emerge between her own espoused orientation to mentoring and her informed choice of action. Her decision to intervene is, however, not devoid of moral dilemmas. As she resumes: ...*On the other hand, it's like...I feel it's a boundary that shouldn't be crossed very often...it was only a point of reference, as an explanation rather than a comment on anything that they were doing at the moment..*

The delicate borders that Sarah is cautious about crossing speak to mentors' ideas about the dangers of providing direct advice rather than letting the mentee find the direction (Zanting, Verloop, Vermunt, & Van Driel, 1998). It also connotes with Sarah's possible feeling that it would give the teacher the impression that she is not competent (Wildman, Magliaro, Niles, & Niles, 1992), or that she might be reluctant to incorporate her advice because it might not resonate with her own beliefs about teaching (Norman & Feiman-Nemser, 2005; Stanulis & Russell, 2000) or might feel overwhelmed by her demonstration and advice (Smagorinsky, Cook, Moore, Jackson, & Fry, 2004). Sarah's concern for providing support that focuses on 'teaching tips' and survival techniques speaks to concerns about novices being encouraged to replicate existing models of teaching rather than implementing more reform-based philosophies (Evertson & Smithey, 2000; Gratch, 1998;

Sundli, 2007; Wang, 2001), leading to continued implementation of current routines and the stifling of professional growth (Carter & Francis, 2001; Franke & Dahlgren, 1996).

Let us now consider the second story of Sarah's construal of her 'here and now' intervention mode while trying to rescue the mentee and at the same time advance her thinking on the issue:

> I have been working with Betty, a first year teacher, on how to organize oral activities in class because she doesn't know how to stimulate the children when doing oral work. We had planned together a series of speaking activities for her tenth grade and had decided that she would implement them while I would observe for feedback. The day before I was supposed to observe Betty, she phoned me home desperately announcing that she can't do it and asking me whether I could give the lesson instead of her. I was completely caught by surprise but I felt that as part of my duty I just couldn't say no. She wanted me to stand up and do it, she said that's what she needed to see at this point.

> After the phone call I became very uptight. Not only had I little time to come up with an interesting topic for the children to talk about, but I also knew that this particular class was very apathetic and difficult to activate. I was also aware that as a teacher I was coming from a different teaching context, one in which the pupils had a lot of exposure to English outside the classroom and therefore had no difficulty in speaking...I hoped that these activities would work for these children, because I sort of felt that I had taken them from a book and not really had time to think about how they would suit this particular class. I also hoped that the children would cooperate and that I would not be shy, embarrassed or uncomfortable.

At this point, the mentor was attending to her own voice and text *as a teacher* and examining the dualities and controversies that arise when juxtaposing it to the mentee's text. Talking from the teacher inside her (and not the mentor), all she could think about at this point was to successfully 'pass' this model lesson which had actually become a testing of her competence as a teacher. For her it had become a moment of truth. Here she was, exposing in the 'here and now action' the teacher behind the mentor. Furthermore, she had to prove to herself and others that her knowledge as a teacher would help her as a mentor.

Eventually, Sarah gave the 'model lesson' in Betty's class and it was a very successful one, as Sarah records it. She also shared later on with Betty the process that she herself had gone through when preparing for the lesson (both emotionally and planning wise). In resorting to this 'loop learning' strategy, the mentor was not merely suggesting alternative actions but also examining the appropriateness and propriety of her chosen actions, juxtaposing them with the mentees' values and theories (Greenwood, 2003). In doing so, she was legitimizing Betty's uncertainties, connecting pedagogical reasoning and action, and making space for legitimizing inner conflicts that are often backgrounded in mentoring relationships (Elnir, 2005). Sarah's positive disposition to respond to Betty's request 'here and now' also strengthened channels of communication and collegiality and prompted Betty to invite Sarah into other classes:

> Betty told me that it had opened her eyes to see that silence is not upsetting and that sometimes it takes a little longer for children to answer and that is OK...so Betty didn't react so much to the activity but rather to giving the children time to speak. I think this is what she learned most.

The experience was a powerful instance of improvisation for Sarah. In struggling through her own fears and resistances of having to function as a teacher in front of Betty, she could identify more closely with the mentee's fears and uncertainties while being observed by a supervisor. She had also become aware for the first time of how 'Sarah's text-as-teacher' interspersed with Sarah-the-mentor while planning the 'model lesson.'

In both cases of improvisation, Sarah drew on her wisdom of practice to position herself in the 'here and now' discourse, demonstrating her ability to exercise good judgment in the face of uncertainty. Tuning in successfully to each mentee also entailed recognizing recurring patterns of behavior in each of the novices' contexts, and construing strategies of responsible responding 'in action' to assist the mentees. Upon improvising, Sarah's actions called up knowledge and procedures of improvisation that tuned in to the particular problem type: Thinking aloud, explicating knowledge, clarifying pedagogical messages, debugging mistakes, getting to specifics, and examining controversies inherent in attending to the mentee's text. Sarah's construal in improvisation also carried a moral overtone. As Buber would probably contend, she engaged in responsible spontaneous response, which attended to the voices and texts that were being claimed 'on the spot,' connecting both emotionally and professionally in order to assist the novices.

6.4 Articulating Teaching, Learning, and Subject Matter

While improvising, mentors engage in the articulation of teaching, learning, and subject matter. In the process, they promote systematic analysis of practice and connections between concepts and actions, encouraging the mentees to

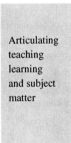

Analyzing practice systematically

Articulating teaching learning and subject matter

Responding to connections between theoretical concepts and practices 'in action'

Encouraging the mentee to rationalize action

access, conceptualize, and articulate their evolving practical and pedagogical content knowledge. The practical knowledge accessed from mentors carries their lived experiences that reflect the complexity of teaching, its contextual character, and the need for immediate action (Carter, 1990; Olson & Carter, 1989). In the process of articulating learning, teaching, and subject matter, the mentor engages in 'theorizing practice' (i.e., connecting and transforming local experiences into conceptual notions and theoretical propositions) and 'particularizing theory' (i.e., illustrating the unique forms and meanings that theoretical notions take in different experiential contexts) (Leinhardt, McCarthy Young, & Merriman, 1995). Articulating teaching, learning, and subject matter speaks to a robust view of 'educative mentoring' (Norman & Feiman-Nemser, 2005), one which responds to the mentees' present needs while helping them interpret what their students say and do and figure out how to promote their learning toward the development of principled teaching practice.

While articulating learning in improvisation, mentors also encourage the mentees to discharge feelings, hence, attending to their immediate needs and with the ultimate goal of encouraging informed rationalization of action.

6.4.1 Analyzing Practice Systematically

What kind of learning opportunities in my professional life have challenged me to re-examine ingrained convictions about good mentoring practices?
What underlies my choice of action in the mentoring context?
How do my actions reflect or clash with my views?
How do I connect my actions as a mentor with the mentee's actions and the outcomes in the field?

thinking in practice

Beyond sensitivity to the moment and place, improvisation, as defined at the outset of the chapter, calls for highly patterned and carefully composed processes of building contextually grounded patterns for thought and action. Furthermore, as Yinger (1990) contends, it assumes a retrospective working method which uses patterns from past action to guide and analyze future action. Analyzing practice in improvisation, thus, entails constant incorporation of new patterns through continuous construals and positionings, in order to respond to changing demands and purposes. Let us consider how Mirit, an elementary school teacher who has been involved in mentoring student teachers for five years, learns to articulate teaching and learning subject matter as she engages in systematic analysis of her practice and in making new connections between theory and practice (Adapted from Orland-Barak & Rachamim, 2009).

Mirit had been mentoring mainly through top-down apprenticeship approaches. Having undertaken a graduate course on reflective mentoring and action research (as part of her thesis track) she had become particularly curious to see how the new ideas that she had been exposed to could be implemented in her own mentoring of student teachers. In this section you will be taken through her journey of mentoring Chen, a student teacher, who studies in a leading teacher education college in the north of Israel. The undergraduate mentoring program at the college spans over a period of three years (out of four years of study) twice a week, throughout the entire academic year. Each year students are allotted to different schools in diverse educational settings, to encourage maximum exposure to a variety of teaching approaches. The approach to mentoring student teachers in these settings is relatively uniform and abides by preestablished criteria of observation and assessment of teaching, as established by the college mentors themselves. Chen, the mentee, is in her third year of studies.

Mirit's journey illustrates her systematic analysis of practice which informed her thinking and actions. In the process, she talks about how she learns to artic- ulate teaching and learning in new ways, and how reflection on action guides her improvisation in action.

6.4.1.1 Confronting My Instrumental Orientation as a Mentor

Having worked as a mentor of student teachers in my school for the past five years, I had never attributed much importance to the connections that could be made between theory and practice in my work as a mentor. I should also mention that, initially, my concern for the place of theory in my actions was strengthened by the fact that I was writing a dissertation. Adopting a research stance towards my practice increased my curiosity about the ways in which theory can be initiated into my work as a mentor. Reading the literature in mentoring problematized my views about theory and about how it plays out in practice. For example, reading about reflective practice challenged me to think about shifting students' thinking from a technical rationality orientation about 'what to do in the classroom,' which I was doing until now, towards an orientation geared to examining emergent gaps between assumptions and actions.

With these ideas in mind, and as part of my thesis work, I engaged in systematic action research cycles while mentoring Chen. Chen's lessons and our conversations that followed were video recorded and transcribed and were both used by Chen and myself to reflect on our respective practices (Chen watched her lesson and I watched the conversation on the lesson) and to guide the conversation that followed. Each of us watched our respective videos at home and came back to the next session with new insights from having reflected on our actions.

My analysis during the first Action Research cycle led me to realize that I was mainly concerned with the technicalities of the strategies that I was using. I was, indeed, displaying a rather technical approach to reflection. When examining the data of the first mentoring videoed conversations, I discovered that most of the conversation was led by me and by my questions. I could also identify long stretches of top-down 'pedagogical monologues' by me as compared to the short responses of the student. I also realized that during the discussion I had missed important opportunities to encourage connections between theoretical concepts, educational views, and assumptions about children's learning. This understanding led one of my questions for the second intervention cycle: 'How can I connect between theory and practice in my mentoring?'

I was determined to become especially attentive to burning issues in the mentee's teaching that she could relate to theory (such as classroom management). Watching the video prior to our next conversation gave me time to reflect on these issues and prepare for sharing them with Chen in the conversation that followed.

Mirit's journal entry offers a glimpse into her concrete step-to-step process of articulating emergent insights about her mentoring practice. Notice how she construes her improvisation process: First, she involves us in the appreciation of the scenario, making sense of the records that are part of it; then she makes an 'educational-construal' or rendering of events and meanings from her initial analysis to guide her future thinking and participation. Toward the end, she generates a new question to inform her future conversation with Chen, merging between reflection on the experience and her new emergent understandings of her practice.

In this section we saw how Mirit positions herself in relation to her instrumental orientation as a mentor. In the next section, we are introduced to how Mirit construes her mentoring conversation as guided by her emergent insights.

6.4.2 Responding to Connections Between Theoretical Concepts and Practices 'in Action'

> *How do I make connections between theoretical notions and experiences that I observe in student teacher's actions? What strategies help me make those connections? What difficulties do I experience when trying to make those connections?*
> *What theories guide and ground my actions?*

thinking in practice

Mirit continues to share with us how she positions herself anew, more symmetrically in the mentoring discourse, and more responsive to connections between theoretical concepts and actions. Notice how she gradually construes these connections by structuring her actions in a patterned manner, considering moment and place, and guided by the developing interactions that she appreciates while reflecting on action (Adapted from Orland-Barak & Rachamim, 2009):

Indeed, in the conversation that followed I defined a concept and asked the mentee to say how it connected to the lesson. I also presented characteristics of pupils' behavior as referred to in various studies and challenged Chen to connect these to what had actually happened during her lesson. I also connected various incidents that occurred during the lesson and showed how they could be brought together in a more encompassing 'theory'. My goal was to show the mentee connections between classroom organization, discipline problems, and the needs of the teacher and the pupil as evidenced in outside 'scientific' sources. I wanted the mentee to extend her understanding of the problems I was raising by learning from outside examples that could help her to apply outside knowledge into the situation.

Analyzing and reflecting on the videoed conversations I learned that the connections to theory that I had made allowed for highlighting weak spots in the mentee's actions in a non-judgmental and less personally charged manner. How can I make connections between theory and practice keeping a more symmetrical conversation?

Driven by the above question, when I observed Chen's next lesson I was attentive to identifying an issue in her teaching that could be connected to the literature. I identified the issue of visuals. Between the first and the second conversation, after having reflected on the videoed meeting, I decided to look for articles that might assist her, on the one hand, in highlighting the issue to Chen and, on the other hand, in encouraging Chen to be more autonomous by asking her to read the article for the following session and think about ways of connecting it to her lesson. The experience proved to be very successful both for Chen and for me. I learned that exposing the mentee to different articles and theoretical sources can be beneficial if the mentee is granted the responsibility to make her own connections. I learned that it can lead to a reflective and symmetrical conversation, shifting the responsibility to the mentee, allowing her to examine her lesson from a different perspective.

Chen's learning from encouraging these connections was corroborated to me at the end of the year when she said 'I benefited very much from those times when you brought things from outside related to mentoring like the article you gave me . . .and you threw questions to think about during the week. . .

The grounded process of systematic articulation of her mentoring eventually led Mirit to a shift of conception about the dialectical relation between theory and practice in mentoring. Guided by reflection on action, she construes understandings about how to integrate outside theoretical sources with practical experiences, challenging the student teacher to connect between her actions and relevant concepts that emerge from these sources:

I learned to distinguish between theory that you create through action and theoretical sources which help the mentee to construct her own theories.

Mirit's case also illustrates how a mentor gradually shifts from articulating the difficulties encountered by her mentee as accounts of idiosyncratic behaviors to conceptualizing novices' learning and hardships as more generalizable cases reflective of novices in general. In the process, she moves from the use of local, personal language to a discourse characterized by the articulation of experience through the use of professional language. This positions the mentor in a less threatening or prescriptive discourse, encouraging the student teacher to examine her weak spots during the lesson without feeling personally threatened. Mirit's improvisation strategies were also featured by responses that carried descriptive rather than judgmental connotations. This form of challenge through supportive strategies of participation seems to have encouraged further scrutinizing and critical thinking.

Informed improvisation, through systematic articulation of practice, enabled Mirit to conceptualize how the mentee can be encouraged to monitor the direction of her own mentored learning and, at the same time, of how the mentor can create opportunities for connecting between the mentee's personal concerns with other major areas of professional learning that he/she, as expert, identifies as problematic and wishes to explore during the conversation. The process of systematic, monitored identification of categories of meaning that emerged from the analysis of the mentoring conversations helped Mirit to identify and 'name' recurrent patterns and personal modes of assistance that were shifting throughout the process. This led, in turn, to try new revised modes of action.

6.4.3 Encouraging the Mentee to Rationalize Action

thinking in practice

How do I create the right combination between encouraging the mentees to express feelings about their practice and analyzing that same practice?
How do I overcome emotional barriers and use them as occasions for learning?

The appropriate dose of challenge and support is crucial to good mentoring practices (Daloz, 1983). While improvising, the mentor must, then, be alert to moments during the conversation which invite for discharging (Heron, 2001) disturbing, critical incidents in teaching. This can serve as an important catalyst for further rationalizing on pedagogical issues at stake and for connecting vicarious experience with theoretical constructs. In the following account of assisting an intern, the mentor shares her insights of how she starts from the mentee's concerns, inviting her to share troubling issues and using those as a springboard for making conceptual connections between feeling, thought, and action. Notice how, in her articulation of the experience, she employs a less local and more professional language (Freeman, 1993):

My first systematic attempt to create a balance between guidance/control and facilitation of the mentee's own learning began during the second mentoring cycle. In the first mentoring conversation I invited Chen to share any troubling issues in her teaching. Chen raised two major questions: 'How does one handle discipline problems in the class and create an atmosphere of mutual listening? and, how does one handle kids with special needs? I decided to facilitate the conversation around these issues, beginning from where Chen 'is at' in relation to her voiced concerns. Yet, by contrast to my previous 'non-intervention mode', I used Chen's elaborations to develop broader issues of classroom organization and their connection to discipline problems, to receptive listening, and to pupils' special needs. I linked these concerns to my own observations of Chen's teaching in the classroom, where I had identified a significant gap between the way in which her class was organized (in rows) and her stated belief that 'learning is best promoted when pupils collaborate and learn from each other' (which called for organizing group work and seating arrangements in groups). Guided by these understandings, I asked questions that would challenge Chen to recognize the inherent contradictions between her classroom organization mode and her espoused ideas about effective and meaningful learning. As Chen articulated these emergent contradictions I further connected them to broader issues of classroom discipline, of creating a receptive listening atmosphere and differential learning. In doing so, I was attending to Chen's previous feedback regarding her expectations to guide her more and acting both as facilitator and guide – a combination which had surfaced from previous analysis of our mentoring conversations and which I was determined to work on.

Guided by the insights that she was gaining from systematic analysis of her practice, Mirit could construe informed improvisation, one which built on emotional and conceptual articulation of experiences. The process, in turn, prompted talk around issues that might have been unattended by the mentor but that are crucial for the mentee and her future development as a teacher. In doing so, she learned to promote learning opportunities that combine general intellectual with personal expressive, emotional aspects of the experience of learning to teach. This enabled her to improvise by connecting between person, environment, and actions – for further planning of specific mentoring strategies and modes of assistance (Orland-Barak & Rachamim, 2009, p. 607).

6.5 Responding 'on the Spot'

Creative mentoring, like creative teaching, can be conceived of as improvisational performance. As such, 'responding on the spot' emphasizes the interactional and responsive creativity of the mentor to connect experience, belief, and knowl-

Responding on the 'spot' by connecting experience, beliefs and knowledge

Intervening to mitigate conflicts

Foregrounding connections between cultural codes, values, strategic and pedagogic reasoning

Calling up on knowledge and procedures to demonstrate and direct action

edge as situations emerge 'on the spot' from unpredictable and 'unscripted' dialogue (Sawyer, 2003).

In sociocultural and social constructivist theory, meaningful mentoring is improvisational, open-ended collaborative talk, not structured in advance. Hence, the role of the mentor to respond in a way that mitigates conflicts, foregrounding connections between cultural codes, values and pedagogic reasoning. Likened to improvising ensembles, responding on the spot is heteroglossic, as the voices of the performers meld together through an action-response mode characterized by intersubjectivity (Ibid.).

Disciplined improvisation through informed responding on the spot can be described as 'a dynamic process involving a combination of planning and improvisation' (Brown & Edelson, 2001, p. 4), midway between ritual and the extreme improvisationality of everyday small talk. Mentoring sessions, like lessons, are then conceived as 'structured conversations' in which dialogue is largely improvisational, but within overall task and participation structures (Erickson, 1982). Effective mentors (like teachers) can use a wide range of degrees of structure, shifting between scripts, scaffolds, and activity formats as required 'in situ' (Berliner, 1987; Borko & Livingston, 1989; Leinhardt & Greeno, 1986), and flexibly employing strategic modes of thinking and acting. These shifts in themselves are improvisational responses on the spot which call up on knowledge and procedures to demonstrate and direct action geared to the unique needs of the participants.

6.5.1 Intervening to Mitigate Conflicts

What are the implications of avoiding confrontation?
What are the implications of trying to preserve a
static, nonconfrontational discourse?

thinking in practice

As mediators, school mentors constantly engage in mitigating conflicts, resolving here and now problems, and dealing with emergent tensions and disagreements between the school staff and the administration. Mentors' ways of improvising in such cases are usually informed by the school ethos, and by the mentor's own norms, codes of professional behavior, beliefs, and experiences. Avoiding or encouraging confrontation around a particular issue (successfully or unsuccessfully) is, to a large extent, informed by these norms, beliefs, and experiences. The following case depicts the complexities of responding 'on the spot' by connecting between knowledge, experiences, and beliefs.

The conversation excerpt below was brought by Raul, an Arab school mentor, to a conversation group of mentors. Raul tells the group that he was asked by the school principal to find out why so many teachers in the school do not take part in professional staff meetings in each of their subjects. Raul (the mentor) has summoned a meeting with all the subject matter coordinators in the school to hear from them what they think the problem is. Raul, like other examples of mentors in the Arab sector, is seen by the teachers of the school as the principal's 'right hand' man. This worries Raul a bit, since he knows that the teachers might not open up to him as would like to. On the other hand, prior to sharing the transcript of his conversation, Raul makes sure to stress that despite that he has an excellent relationship with the teachers. Conscious of his concern, he opens the conversation with a reassuring utterance:

Raul (the mentor):   *Let's begin. I want to say first of all that I am not here to judge, I am here to listen and help. There is no right or wrong. Let's all learn from one another.*

Raul tells us that he had carefully planned the beginning of the conversation and that he thought that being explicit about his motives would give him access to the group. Put differently, it would position him more symmetrically, making space for the teachers to 'discharge' feelings and expose authentic concerns and dispositions. In discursive terms, he would be construing a discourse of empathy rather than prediction and control, encouraging the mentees to discharge feelings in order to rationalize action. Explaining himself to others, indeed, allowed for open sharing of participants' feelings. Hassan, the math coordinator complains:

Hassan: *The math group does not collaborate with me. Everyone does what he wants. I cannot get them together and it's very frustrating.*

Responding 'on the spot' by connecting to Hassan's frustration, Raul poses a probing question (Heron, 2001), meant to trigger more responses from the rest:

Raul (to the rest):   *Why do you think this happens to Hassan?*

To which Abed, another coordinator, responds confrontationally:

Abed: *I think it's both the staff but also you Hassan, we sometimes need to look at ourselves too.*

Feeling threatened and probably insulted by Abed's assertion, Hassan queries:

Hassan: *What do you mean??* (in loud tone)
Abed: *I don't know but from my experience one needs to talk to teachers in the same level – eye to eye. Have them share. Teachers don't like to be treated condescendingly.*

In his utterance, Abed is implying that Hassan has a condescending mode of behavior with his teachers, and he is rather explicit about his criticism toward him. Abed's confronting comment gains escalation when Ahmed, another coordinator, joins in to support Abed, directing the group to consider an additional angle to Hassan's behavior:

Ahmed: *Wait a minute. I think it has also to do with the fact that you don't bring anything new to the meetings – you have to update them all the time to be a source of knowledge, inspiration and leadership.*

At this point, the conversation was escalating to becoming an 'attack' on Hassan – certainly not what Raul had predicted would happen when he asked the question *Why do you think this happens to Hassan?* – a question meant to engage participants in a less personally loaded discourse. But Raul could not predict how participants would respond. His utterance had been taken literally rather than as an invitation to discuss the issue of teachers' absence in a more detached, analytical manner. Failing to connect between feelings, beliefs, and knowledge 'on the spot,' Raul's evasive response hints at his limited kit of improvisational resources. Under such circumstances, he can only opt for an over supportive move, hence, breaking the escalation with a laconic 'good':

Raul: *Good, excellent. . .let's continue.*

Saluah, another coordinator, takes advantage of Raul's redirection of the conversation to discharge her frustrations as a novice on the issue:

Saluah: *I am new as coordinator and I feel like I am constantly pushing this heavy cart and I am constantly pushing and pushing from the back.*

Again, Raul praises and supports:

Raul: *This is incredible. You are sharing wonderful things. Who else. . .?*

Miriam, the English coordinator empathizes with Saluah:

Miriam: *As a coordinator for English I feel the same as Saluah.*

At this point, Raul pushes the conversation to invite suggestions for strategic action:

Raul: *Look; it's a hard feeling – this frustration you all mention. What can be done to change it?*
Hassan: *It's very difficult, especially because you have nobody to help you.*
Raul: *Who wants to say something to Hassan?*

Miriam: *Maybe you should talk to the principal directly and tell him what is happening with your teachers...*

Hassan: *What? Do you want me to be an informer?*

Whereas until now Raul had positioned himself rather neutrally and had almost been unheard in the discourse, Hassan's reaction prompts Raul to articulate an explicit educational stance on the issue:

Raul: *I do not agree with you at all. It's not being an informant, it's the duty to report.*

Raul, for the first time in the discourse, improvises by formulating a sound, executable judgment in the face of uncertainty. Whereas until now, he had adopted for an indirect, nonconfrontational mode of participation in order to mitigate conflicts, he now 'dares' to respond directly and unequivocally. Such a response, which can be potentially conducive to a new confrontation, is deeply rooted in the cultural borderlines that Raul is not prepared to cross: One's *duty* to report to those whom you are accountable to. His response 'on the spot' is, thus, of an inherently moral character, embedding a strong sense of professional responsibility. Not being able to remain indifferent to Raul's authoritative assertion, Abed responds back, voicing a fervent internally persuasive discourse:

Abed: *This is what YOU say...not the teachers ...what do you know? Do you know what goes on there...if they know that I reported something it's like being an informer in the eyes of the teachers.*

Abed challenges Raul's moral positioning on the issue. His provoking response could be taken up by Raul to enhance a more critical discourse around accountabilities and duties as they play out in leading roles at school. In the language of improvisation, it would entail challenging the 'here and now' meanings that various participants attribute to the issue, prompting their articulation of the underlying beliefs and thoughts, reflective of the norms and rules of behavior that they follow in the context of their occurrence. However, inattentive (or probably lacking the skills) to improvise in such a direction, Raul restricts himself to a procedural and almost technical response:

Raul: *Ok. Let's focus on what else to do ...*

The above excerpt illustrates the complexities inherent in improvisation while responding on the spot to emergent issues that have a controversial cultural grounding (such as loyalty to accountabilities and what constitutes professional duty). In our case, such complexities seemed to have obstructed in-depth handling of the issue at stake. The result, put bluntly, is a case of bad improvisation on the part of the mentor: For one, he does not manage to fully elaborate on the articulation of participants' concerns and frustrations (as he had pronounced at the beginning of the meeting). Furthermore, by preserving a nonconfrontational, instrumentally oriented discourse, he missed out on important opportunities for encouraging critical, in depth examination and reflection on emergent controversies. Such a disposition to entertain a consensual discourse was informed both by the cultural ethos of the school and by the mentor's personal ideological positioning in relation to his role.

6.6 Foregrounding Connections Between Cultural Codes, Values, Strategic and Pedagogic Reasoning

thinking in practice

What guides your decision to adopt direct confrontation in situations that are culturally loaded? How do you help the mentee handle resistances that are rooted in culturally sensitive issues?
How do I encourage the mentee to reflect on how the cultural codes of the environment might affect particular pedagogical actions?

Whereas the previous section portrayed a nonconfrontational mode of improvisation to mitigate conflicts, this section focuses on how mentors respond on the spot through strategies of intervention that challenge mentees' taken for granted values and pedagogical actions. As they construe direct confrontational modes of response, they confront the mentees with new connections between knowledge, experience, and beliefs.

In this conversation between a school mentor and a mentor of mentors, Iris (the school mentor) is sharing her unsuccessful experience in trying to work with some of the teachers on their attitudes toward the reform she wants to implement. Notice how her mentor construes her responses 'on the spot,' gradually surfacing possible contradictory connections between Iris' pedagogical actions, her strategic reasoning, and the cultural codes and values of the context.

Iris begins with an account of her problem, both pedagogically and personally:

Iris: *...in my school we are trying to implement a new reform at policy level which brings in very strongly the element of multiculturalism and multilingualism into our curriculum ...and I am having problems as the school mentor to work with some of the teachers on their attitudes towards the reform.*

Her mentor's response through a clarifying question 'Why *do you think that happens?*' somehow resonates with Raul's initial question to the group at the beginning of the conversation in the previous section *Why do you think this happens to Hassan?* Unlike Raul, however, the mentor omits the use of second person 'you' (*Why do you think that happens* [to you]?), shifting the direction of the conversation to the issue itself. Indeed, Iris accepts the mentor's invitation as she 'explains herself' by connecting pedagogical, personal, interpersonal, and cultural considerations:

Iris: *The school is Cherkesian, and they are a very closed group and com-*
           munity and there is a big problem in the community – on the hand, they
           want to preserve their identity and culture as Cherkesian and on the
           other hand they want to open to the world, to develop and the greatest
           difficulty revolves around the language: English is the international lan-
           guage, Hebrew, they all speak, Arabic is the language of religion and
           instruction and Cherkese is their mother tongue. And this creates lots of
           problems . . . . Teachers move from one language to another during the
           lesson, the textbooks are both in Arabic and in Hebrew which is fine but
           there is no set policy and that's what we want to decide together as a
           staff – arrive at an informed statement of language policy for the school.
           I must also say that teachers in the school are both Hebrew speakers and
           Arab speakers. I myself speak Arabic but my mother tongue is Hebrew.
Mentor: *It's very complicated. . .*
Iris: *Yes, we came to the conclusion that one of the problems of our low*
           achievements has to do with the languages. I am working with the
           entire staff and one of the teachers, who is a core figure in the school,
           refuses to participate and strongly disagrees to the whole idea and to my
           leadership. He does not cooperate; he is very knowledgeable and very
           appreciated by the school staff. He is Cherkesioan and it's very important
           for me to engage him in the project.

Connecting to Iris' appreciation of the situation, the mentor responds 'on the spot' through catalytic and cathartic strategies. These are meant to foreground a more comprehensive appreciation of the problem as a question of both personal, emotional resistances and resistances of a cultural grounding:

Mentor: *I understand from what you say that you want to recruit him for the*
           project but he is very resistant to the idea and that he has a very mean-
           ingful place in the school and he is also meaningful to you. What does it
           do to you his lack of involvement? How do you feel about it?

As corroborated in Iris' next move, the mentor's improvisation strategy indeed challenged Iris to 'discharge' inner controversies related to the fact that she was not Cherkesian.

Iris: *It's hard for me. First of all because he is Cherkesian and I am not – it's his*
          tradition and his language. He makes me feel very insecure . . .

In her appreciation of the situation the mentor's response toward Iris was direct and confronting: She was trying to lead a fundamentally cultural–ideological school reform in a context which was culturally and ideologically distinct from her own. This was the classic case of a mentor coming from the dominant culture to implement educational reforms on a minority group from a different culture.

Mentor: *I guess that the fact that he is Cherkesian and you are not makes you feel*
           uncomfortable – have you thought that maybe the source of discomfort
           might come from the fact that you are the one leading such a big and

meaningful project on languages and culture and you are coming from outside that culture? Maybe that's his source of resistance?

By contrast to Raul's efforts to mitigate conflict, the mentor improvises through confrontational strategies meant to destabilize and problematize. This creates insecurity but, at the same time, opens a challenging avenue for reexamination and introspection, calling for rethinking familiar modes of action.

Iris: *If so, then what can I do? You mean I should quit the project because I am an outsider? There are many advantages to being an outsider in this case – that's why I was appointed...*

Mentor: *True. I'm not saying you shouldn't be there. I'm only saying that this is something you need to think about – the implications of it for how certain teachers feel about your role as agent of change coming from 'above'. Are you prepared to enter into that terrain? I know it might put you in a vulnerable situation.*

Iris: *I'm scared that I will loose my say in the group. I have been working so hard to convince teachers into it and I think I have succeeded.*

Mentor: *But you are still very disturbed and bothered by this teacher's behavior. I am here for you, are you prepared to figure this out between you and me first? We can take roles – I can be the mentor and you will be the resistant teacher...*

Construing direct confrontational modes of response 'on the spot' demands of the mentor to be highly skilled in strategies of interaction and communication that combine the right forms of challenge and support. In Heron's terms, it would involve integrating informative interventions, whereby the mentor seeks to raise the mentees' awareness about a certain attitude or behavior by challenging them through direct feedback, whilst not making a personal imposition of ideas. It would also entail seeking facilitative interventions to release powerful emotions alongside seeking to develop and problem-solve by encouraging self-reflection, self-direction, and self-discovery – all of which affirm the worth and value of the mentee's qualities, attitudes, beliefs, and actions.

6.6.1 Calling up on Knowledge and Procedures to Demonstrate and Direct Action

Who do I approach in cases of professional misconduct?

thinking in practice

Responding 'on the spot' calls upon knowledge that is composed and enacted within the special constraints of the context. It also incorporates patterns from past action directed toward action, through continuous adaptation and appropriation of knowledge, beliefs, and goals to changing purposes, exigencies, and toward the establishment and maintenance of mentor–mentee relationships.

Consider how the mentor in this conversation responds to the mentee on the spot by calling up on familiar demonstration and simulation strategies and procedures in order to direct the mentee's future action. The mentee is a school coordinator who works with an entire staff of teachers. She shares with the mentor her problem in getting the staff together to meet regularly. She complains that many homeroom teachers do not come to the meetings. Unlike Raul's case, the mentor has not been requested by the school principal to intervene but rather been personally approached by Sarah (the mentee) to assist her.

Already at the beginning of the conversation, the mentor (Tal) construes a direct, thought-provoking question meant to encourage introspection and analysis:

Tal: *What do you think is the reason for such a small participation?*

Sarah's response *People have trouble coming back from far away. They have children* provides a quick, pragmatic response, far from being too introspective. Tuning in where the mentee is at, the mentor connects to Sarah by shifting to a more pragmatic positioning in the discourse, calling upon strategies of application:

Tal: *And what have you done in that respect?*
Sarah: *I don't force them to come but I tell them it is very important. But I can also understand them and I am very empathetic with them – maybe that's why they don't take it seriously enough ...*

Reading into what Sarah identifies as being her 'weak point', the mentor construes a response 'on the spot,' one which transcends the 'here and now' incident offering, instead, a broader outlook at her role as coordinator. At the same time, however, she is careful to attend to Sarah's practical need to find a solution to her problem. In doing so, she resorts to simulation as a strategy that both demonstrates and models for Sarah the kind of responses that she can draw on while encountering certain behaviors or spoken reactions. Notice how, while simulating, Tal improvises by calling upon her knowledge of mediation questions which are intended to educe intention, clarification, commitment and values:

Tal: *Now you better understand what it means to be a coordinator – it's a new ballgame, it's being in a different position with the teachers and adopting a whole new mode of interaction – it's not easy. But you really want to solve this problem do you? I understand that it's very important for you to have the teachers meet.*
Sarah: *Yes, but I know it won't work...'*
Tal: *Let's try a simulation. I will be the coordinator and you will be the problematic teacher. Let's start:*[the mentor begins the simulation]
Tal: *Tomorrow I am organizing the staff meeting straight after the workshop session so we can continue and then you won't have to come an additional day.*
Sarah: *But I have to leave straight after the workshop at 3:30! I have nobody to take out my daughter from school.*

Tal: *I understand your constraints – I have been wanting to talk to you about it. But there is also your active involvement as part of the staff – and staff meetings are part of it so I suggest you find an arrangement.*

Sarah: *I can't! I have no arrangement.*

Tal: *If you were asked by the principal to come to regular pedagogical meetings during the year – wouldn't you come and find an arrangement? Would you also say to the school to the principal that you can't because you have to take out your daughter from?'*

Sarah: *That happens only once in a while. Then I can arrange it with my husband.*

Tal: *So, I am not asking to meet every day. I'm asking to meet once in a . . .*

At this point, Sarah stands out of her role and says: *I'm willing to try talking to the teachers in that way but I'm sure it won't work.*

Sensitive to her expressed insecurity, Tal exhibits the right dose of challenge and support, modeling for Sarah a 'rationale for action,' that is, how she should articulate the educational importance of conducting regular meetings and how she should turn over responsibility for arranging meetings to the group.

Tal: *How about setting a date and a time. Tell the staff how you feel about it all. . .you can say that the meetings are important because you need to one, identify problems and needs together as a staff; two, that it is important to arrive at curricular decisions together so that everybody feels ownership and can contribute with their particular strengths to the group. Have them tell YOU how many meetings they would want to have, where and when.*

Toward the end of the conversation, Tal invites Sarah to appraise the whole experience, resorting to a question that triggers reflection and possible further application of the procedures used to demonstrate and direct action. Notice, how, in the last move, Tal is careful to grant the mentee the possibility of determining the kind of assistance and direction that she wants to pursue.

Tal: *So what do you take with you from our conversation?*

Sarah: *I am going to try to share with them how I feel and also to try to really find out what they need and would want to share in those meetings. I think I will try to have them become more in control of the content of the meetings . . .*

Tal: *When do you want to meet again?*

Sarah: *Before the meeting. I would like to write for myself some questions and maybe we can do a simulation again like what we did now?*

The above case underscores the intricate and highly conscious process of responding on the spot while improvising. Specifically, it portrays the synthetic and compositional processes of construing a response while resorting to strategies of modeling and simulation in mentoring. Advancing understandings coherently in mediated learning through demonstration 'in action' necessitates sophisticated improvisation skills to formulate sound and appropriate judgments.

That is, on the one hand, believing that there are multiple ways of thinking about a puzzle which are consistent with the right answer, and, on the other, learning to become puzzled by what others mean. This understanding of the particular dynamics of a learning conversation between mentor and mentee can, then, be transferred and applied to other teaching and mentoring situations.

In this chapter I have discussed the conceptual roots of Improvisation as a Domain of Praxis in Mentoring. The following *dimensions of praxical connections* between forms of practice and dialogue constitute the Domain of Improvisation. Taken together, they yield a discursive portrayal of the domain of improvisation in mentoring, as illustrated in Table 6.1.

- *Tuning In*

  Connecting emotionally and professionally to respond to contextual differences
  Translating behavior into here and now patterns and modes of assistance
  Composing through recurring patterns

- *Articulating teaching, learning, and subject matter*

  Analyzing practice systematically
  Responding to connections between theoretical concepts and practices in action
  Encouraging the mentee to rationalize action

- *Responding on the 'spot' by connecting experience, beliefs, and knowledge*

  Intervening to mitigate conflicts
  Foregrounding connections between cultural codes, values, strategic and pedagogic reasoning
  Calling up on knowledge and procedures to demonstrate and direct action

Chapter 7
Reciprocal Connections in Dyadic Interactions

*How are appreciation, improvisation and
participation reciprocally established in conversation
and how are reciprocal moments of learning created
through appreciation, improvisation and participation?*

*thinking in
practice*

7.1 Reciprocal Connections Between Appreciation, Participation, and Improvisation in Dyadic Learning Conversations

In this chapter I describe and interpret the concrete and dynamic meanings that improvisation, informed by appreciation and participation, take in the discourse of two mentoring conversations. The first dyadic conversation, between a novice mentor and a mentor of mentors, illustrates how reciprocal interactions are constructed to shape the process and outcomes of co-constructing knowledge, through intersubjective meaning making. The second dyadic conversation, between a mentor of English and a student teacher of English, shows how the kind of reciprocal connections established between appreciation, participation, and improvisation in a dyadic subject matter mentoring conversation yield particular forms of assistance and learning outcomes for both mentor and mentee.

7.2 The Dyadic Learning Conversation

Numenius said that Pythagoras gave the name of Monad to God, and the name of Dyad to matter (Chalcidius, in Kahn, 2001)

From a social constructivist perspective to learning, a dyadic learning conversation can be described as multiple forms of dialogues between 'I' (the mentor),

L. Orland-Barak, *Learning to Mentor-as-Praxis*, Professional Learning and
Development in Schools and Higher Education 4, DOI 10.1007/978-1-4419-0582-6_7,
© Springer Science+Business Media, LLC 2010

'thou' (the mentee), and 'it '(the subject matter) (Schön, 1987). In this metaphor-ical sense of teaching and learning as dialogue, the mentor tries to describe what he/she knows about the subject matter in a way that connects to the mentee's own understanding of that phenomenon. As Schön (1987) points out, 'a good learning conversation is somewhere midway between boredom and insanity.' That is, the basic core of a conversation is predictable and somewhat inert. It becomes dynamic and unexpected as we improvise, we become surprised and respond 'on the spot' with the possibility of new action and experimentation. The possible variety of responses leads to the realization that we can understand the same conclusion dif-ferently. This necessitates having what Schön (1996) calls the 'double vision of a coach,' aimed at encouraging the mentees to articulate what they learned, and by doing so helping them to understand how they arrived at that learning. This kind of loop learning (or meta-learning activity) entails encouraging 'objectivis-ing the experience' in a way that would enable standing back and reflecting on the process of learning gone through, during talk. In the process, both mentor and mentee reciprocally gain new insights and understandings of their respective practices.

7.2.1 Reciprocity in Learning Conversations

Reciprocity associates with notions of give and take, mutuality, interchange, and exchange. From a social constructivist perspective to learning, it suggests that knowledge is neither inside the person nor outside the world, but exists in the *reciprocal* relationship between persons in conversation. From a constructionist per-spective (Gergen, 1994), reciprocity replaces individual knowledge with knowledge as grounded in the relationship and therefore as created 'inter' – the views of partici-pants. Put differently, it is neither objective nor subjective, but rather intersubjective and interrelational (Kvale, 1995).

In mediated learning, reciprocity speaks to intersubjectivity (Wertsch, 1991; Engeström, 1995). Intersubjectivity is central to the establishment of interpersonal planes, created in joint activity, whereby influences are reciprocal between expert and novice partners in interaction. These eventually lead to the development of com-mon understandings of the purpose of the activity engaged in by participants (Tharp & Gallimore, 1988, p. 89).

During an ideal learning conversation, participants would engage in 'authentic conversation,' defined by Florio- Ruane (1991) as the dialogic process by which [they] create and negotiate knowledge with one another. As the mentor and the mentee appreciate each other's discourses and engage in mutual participation, they begin establishing common ground and negotiating knowledge through critical exchange of ideas on a common topic for discussion. In describing common ground, Florio- Ruane and Clark (1993) contend:

> The pursuit of common ground among conversational partners should aim at sustaining exchange of ideas ... not always trying to arrive at consensus but rather at articulating diverse views on complex subjects ... not to achieve consensus merely but trying to interpret the sense and meaning in one another's actions and words...(p. 6).

Hence, during a learning conversation, there are occasions whereby insights are gained inter – the points of view (Kvale, 1995) of the participants. These can be seen as instances in which participants enter into each other's frame of reference and establish a degree of intersubjectivity, which allows for opportunities to coconstruct knowledge in conversation (Bornstein & Bruner, 1989; Gergen, 1985; Greeno, 1997).

Appreciation and participation are then important conditions for establishing intersubjectivity and reciprocity, and for developing common ground as participants improvise 'in action.' But how does improvisation, informed by appreciation and participation, play out to enhance reciprocity and learning, through the coconstruction of knowledge? In the following section, I examine three instances of reciprocal learning in one dyadic conversation between a mentor of mentors and a mentor-mentee. I show how appreciation, participation, and improvisation are constituted reciprocally, through the conversation, to enhance learning.

7.3 Two Instances of Reciprocal Learning in One Dyadic Conversation

Let us look at two 'instances' of reciprocal learning, as they emerged in the discourse of one conversation between a novice mentor, Terry, and myself, a mentor of mentors. I elaborate on each of the instances as related to how appreciation, participation, and improvisation played out to yield occasions of reciprocal learning both for Terry and myself.

7.3.1 Reciprocal Learning to Construe Knowledge about Conducting Workshops

How does improvisation, informed by appreciation and participation, play out to promote instances of reciprocal learning in conversation?

The following excerpt, selected from a longer stretch of discourse, focuses on ways of conducting a mentoring workshop session. Terry begins the conversation by saying that she has realized that her workshop sessions had now *become more interactive and less question–answer ping-pong between* [her] *and the mentees.* I respond to her comment 'on the spot,' foregrounding connections between actions and concepts, (improvisation) as a way of helping her to articulate her response, using the language of mentoring:

L: *. . .so that means that the nature of your sessions is now closer to what we call in mentoring an authentic learning conversation, one which calls for natural, genuine interaction amongst peers. . .*

Tuning in to my comment, Terry validates and affirms my response, transferring it back to her own practice:

T: *That's really going to touch me . . . I can see myself in conversation with the teachers now very clearly . . .*

Terry's *appreciation* of my comment signaled to me that she had a disposition to continue *participating* in the elaboration of the idea. Thus, I was prompted to further *construe* my suggestion, connecting the idea with a practical suggestion. In doing so, I was sustaining my *participation* in the discourse, mediating person and context and *improvising* through new connections between experience and action:

L: *And you know what, now that you are saying, I think you might also want to have something that didn't work for you and share it with the teachers, so that you are sharing with the teachers also your SOS kit.*

My articulation 'in action' to Terry's response that she can share moments of failure with the teachers was an idea that I had never thought about before. In fact, as I wrote in my journal, after the conversation, I had never resorted to that strategy in my own workshop sessions, as a mentor of teachers neither had I shared with the mentees my personal stories of unsuccessful experiences. On Terry's part, my response foregrounded connections between the idea of authentic conversation and its actual realization during the workshop. In discursive terms, it enabled her to *construe* a concrete image of her new *positioning* in the workshop sessions and to *appreciate* how the concept could actually associate to the 'here and now' action:

T: *I would tell them my story through three questions: what did I plan, what did I do and what do I think happened?*

Until now, we were each *participating* and *improvising* in the elaboration of our own meanings regarding the organization of mentoring sessions, as the interaction developed 'in action.' Notice how, toward the end of the excerpt, the conversation develops to a joint, reciprocal *construction* of how conversation can operate as a means of assistance:

L: *You could also ask: what am I going to do about it? How am I going to change the situation that has been unresolved?*
T: *... You mean without spelling it out...*
L: *Right and that's your workshop*

Mutual *appreciation* of the relational and professional character of a learning conversation encouraged joint *participation*, as we appropriated texts from teaching and mentoring interdiscursively. In the process, we *improvised* 'in action' by calling up on knowledge and procedures to articulate new ideas of how mentoring workshop sessions can operate as learning conversations. For Terry, the outcome of joint meaning *construction* was a more informed understanding of the strategies that can sustain and develop a conversational discourse in mentoring interactions. For me, it was elaborating on the idea of sharing past experiences of the mentor as a way of getting the mentees to open up to each other in conversation.

7.3.1.1 Asymmetry of Roles to Promote Reciprocal Learning in Action

An important factor, contributing to the coconstruction of meaning in the above exchange, was the asymmetrical nature of our relationship sustained by recognition of expertise rather than by exerting power (Bruner, 1990). I, the mentor of mentors, felt comfortable pursuing my agenda (in this case, helping the mentee to think about her sessions more as conversations) because I thought that my input would be affirmed. Indeed, Terry was receptive to my suggestion and could envision how my suggestion would actually work and improve her own context. On my part, her *participation* prompted me, in turn, to *improvise* in the direction of jointly exploring new possibilities. That is, I knew I was learning from Terry as much as she was learning from me. In Baley's terms (1996), there was a disposition on the part of both partners to be excited about each other and to treat the other as a source for learning, and to respond constructively to each other, or in Noddings's terms (1991) to provide a constructive response.

7.3.2 Reciprocal Learning About Discourse Processes

Let us return to the development of the conversation, to illustrate another instance of reciprocity. Recapping the last series of moves, in response to my suggestion about what to ask, Terry further improvises 'in action,' suggesting questions for helping the mentees think about their moments of failure and frustration. My affirmation of her idea, *Right and that's your workshop,* triggers a new instance of mutuality 'in participation,' prompting Terry to articulate a new insight 'on the spot':

T: *And then they could work in pairs on the same questions, and then present some suggestions to me... Lily...!!! Did you know that this is where we were going to end up?*

Terry shares her excitement about the way in which our ideas had been generated, during the conversation. Her inquiry of whether I knew how the conversation would develop challenged me, in turn, to reorganize my ideas and articulate them by connecting between the structure and dynamics of our conversations, moving the conversation from talk on application to talk on conceptualization. Put differently, the new perspectives that she was gaining by *connecting parts to whole* prompted me, in turn, to suggest a new *construal* of the situation – how process operates in conversation:

L: *I had no idea...but come to think of it, let's see, look, I think we constructed this together and this is the real value of us talking together, you know?*

Not satisfied with my explanation, Terry prompts me to explain myself to her:

T: *What do you mean?*

Terry's response challenged me to articulate in a more explicit manner the nature of the two-way process of communication that we had managed to establish, whereby we had become receptive and open to each other's ideas and which had, consequently, enabled us to arrive at new insights. Discursively, we had entered into each other's Discourses and jointly *participated* in the *construction* of meaning, through *improvisation* in the here and now situation. In the process of 'explaining myself' to Terry, I was also able to suggest replicating a similar process in her own mentoring setting, as a kind of loop into our process of coconstruction:

L: *Because I couldn't have gotten to this point alone. I constructed it as I got responses from you, and your responses were not preplanned. And then, you constructed it through my responses… and this is what you might want to create in your own sessions with the mentees*

Not quite convinced by my response, Terry continues to probe by saying:

T: *This is really great, but you probably had something in mind to begin with and then…*

Her probing challenged me to *improvise* anew – this time using a different strategy for explaining myself to her. In the process, I was able to *appreciate* more clearly the *overt behaviors and underlying messages that play out* in the dynamics of mentoring conversations:

L: *I did have certain thoughts about what I had seen which I wanted to share with you and I even had certain points that I felt were important to get across, as feedback to your session…but, it was the way in which we listened and related to each other's comments and responses that made it possible to reach this point…*
T: *So, it's all about the group of teachers talking about their teaching, not just the material…*

Terry 's remark signaled that she gained a new *appreciation* of the learning conversation: A new perspective as to the type of situated experiences and processes that can be enhanced in mentoring.

At this point of the conversation, we had each arrived at new insights – a kind of co-constructed eureka – through joint improvisation as we reciprocally engaged in processes of *participation* and *appreciation*. Terry was discovering that the content of mentoring sessions can also allow for the sharing of teachers' experiences, as much as for the specification of general pedagogical and subject matter issues. For me, it was gaining insight as to how *improvising,* through 'explaining oneself to others,' can become a learning opportunity both for the teller and the listener.

Reciprocal learning was also developmental as *appreciation, improvisation,* and *participation* unfolded in action while the discourse progressed: From shared practical understandings of how a particular mentoring activity can be implemented, we eventually arrived at a more sophisticated co-construction of how discourse processes operate and evolve in mentoring conversations.

7.4 Conditions for Sustaining Reciprocal Connections in Action

Participation, Appreciation, and Improvisation were established and sustained reciprocally by a number of conditions. First, the genuine desire to arrive at a more informed understanding of an idea prompted participants to probe and push for clarity, without fearing the other's reaction, making space for expressing hesitancy and uncertainty. Second, the need to 'explain oneself to the other' enabled the reorganization of thoughts and ideas 'here and now.' Third, challenging positions by asking probing questions and being constructively critical about each other helped to reorganize ideas. In the process, there was safety to challenge positions, to express feelings of excitement and discomfort, to share uncertainties, and to being open to questioning deep-rooted assumptions and practices. Thus, appreciation of genuine listening and participation through constructive intent and safety played out to sustain improvisation. Responses were characterized by constructive intent, or in Bailey's (1996) words [creating] *a system by which participants signal that they are attending to and valuing that person's talk or actions* (p. 165).

7.5 Appreciation, Participation, and Improvisation as Reciprocally Established in Dyadic Subject Matter Mentoring

The nature of the reciprocal connections established between appreciation, participation, and improvisation in the discourse, eventually, directs the presence (or absence) of a particular form of interaction and orientation to mentoring. The following dyadic conversation between a mentor of English and a student teacher of English illustrates this point. In particular, we will see how, while reading the situation, the mentor is inattentive to certain voices inherent in the mentee's text. Unaware that she is silencing such voices while responding on the spot, she fails to fully connect experience, knowledge, and beliefs in her mediation of learning. Thus, although at the surface it might seem that she has tuned in to where the mentee is at, a deeper consideration of her moves surfaces intricate contradictions, at the crossroads between her appreciation of the mentee's text, her mode of participation in the discourse, and the strategies that she employs while improvising in action.

7.5.1 Silenced Voices and Texts in Conversation

> *thinking in practice*
>
> *What does it mean to genuinely listen to the mentee's text?*
> *What voices might be left unattended?*
> *What voices influence my choice of action?*
> *What inner dialogues do I conduct with the different voices in activity?*

The following conversation revolves around a student teacher's account of an English lesson that she taught in a comprehensive high school, situated in a major city in the South of Israel. The student teacher is an immigrant from the United

Kingdom and comes from an observant religious Jewish background. The mentor is an EFL teacher who is involved in both in-service and preservice mentoring programs.

Mentee: *When I planned the lesson for my 10th grade, I thought it would be a good idea to have a pre-reading activity, around the concept of friendship and loyalty –which was the main topic of the story they were going to read. I also prepared activities to introduce them to the key vocabulary of the passage. It was all planned, step by step. I began by asking them to get into groups and share with others an experience about being disappointed or let down by a good friend. I also had cards with different sayings about friendship and loyalty. I asked them to chose which card they identify with most and why. I could not predict what could have gone wrong when everything was so well planned, but it did . . .they started walking around. I heard boys asking girls if they wanted to become their 'friends' (as if insinuating other kinds of boy–girl friendship) and that they promised them they would 'be loyal' to them . . .I was appalled by their behavior!!! It got way out of my control and I was very embarrassed. In the High School I went to back in the UK, something like that would never have happened. There is a basic respect for the teacher and also between boys and girls . . . boys would never start with us in front of the teacher. . .*

Mentor: *From your story I see you wanted to prepare them as much as possible for the language and concept of the passage. . .*

Mentee: *Exactly, and look what happened . . .*

Mentor: *What happened?*

Mentee: *I wanted them to interact, to share opinions and ideas. . . it is such an important educational issue besides the language.*

Mentor: *But did they interact? Were they using the language? Were they communicating? Wasn't your purpose to develop fluency through the activity?*

Mentee: *Yes, they were using English. It's just what they were saying. I cannot accept that. I think they did not take me seriously . . .they were being impolite.*

Mentor: *Why?*

Mentee: *They were asking girls to 'go out' with them . . .*

Mentor: *And that insulted you.*

Mentee: *Very much. They were very disrespectful.*

Mentor: *I sense you feel deeply insulted.*

Mentee: *Yes and I think they don't accept my authority.*

Mentor: *Can we think of other possibilities together?*

Mentee: *Like what? It's quite obvious from their behavior, don't you think?*

Mentor: *Maybe it is less about your authority and more with the way in which they are used to talking about friendship . . . besides . . . don't forget it's a tricky age. Do you think you might want to open up the issue in class next lesson? You said before you had a good rapport with them after all*

> *...We can also think of another type of activity, less personal, which will make them interact and use the vocabulary...*

Mentee: *I'm not sure...I don't think I want to talk about these topics.*

Mentor: *I do suggest we try to build some activities together.*

Mentee: *If that's what you think...OK*

Let us examine what the above conversation is about:

The mentor's appreciation of the case is that the pupils' behavior might have more to do with being teenagers and with their particular 'teenage' language, rather than with their lack of respect for the teacher. This being the case, we might, then, on the 'surface' understand why the mentor construes, 'on the spot,' her line of questioning and suggestions for action.

But let us explore other possibilities, such as the complexities inherent in taking a direction which solely focuses on local issues of task organization and pupils' age and talk. For example, one could appreciate apparent gaps between the student teacher's cultural codes of behavior (as an immigrant coming from a strict orthodox background) and the secular context of the school, with codes of behavior that abide by more liberal orientations to education.

When examining the conversation, the mentor's questions and responses are seemingly geared to acknowledge the mentee's distress. As part of her mirroring strategies, the mentor paraphrases the mentee's feelings and experiences sustaining participation through cathartic interventions such as echoing and picking up on feeling cues (Heron, 2001), meant to access the mentee's thoughts and feelings of distress. But does the mentor *really* appreciate the controversies inherent in the mentee's text? Does the mentoring conversation lead both the mentor and mentee to examine their respective texts as reflective (or not) of the 'authoritative discourses' (Bakhtin, 1981) that dominate their thinking and actions? If this direction were to guide the mentor's appreciation of the mentee's distress, then improvisation could be geared to contesting assumptions about teaching, as shaped by the cultural codes that play out in the interaction. For example, when the mentee maintained that the pupils were being impolite to her, the mentor could opt for a response that foregrounds connections between cultural codes, values, strategic, and pedagogic reasoning. She could ask: 'How does your interpretation of what the pupils were doing as 'impolite behavior' reflect the way in which you were educated and the values that you stand for, and are not prepared to cross as an educator?' Following with a question, 'How might these values differ from the school population you are dealing with?' and, connecting back to subject matter teaching, 'How can we think of strategies (developed through fluency and accuracy activities in English) that can bridge between the two?'

When foregrounding new connections and interpretations, the mentor *appreciates* by *contemplating* how the mentee's traditional, orthodox background might bear an influence on the kind of assertions that she is making about her teaching and about the pupils' learning. Her participation in the discourse could, then, be geared to challenging the mentee to appraise her pedagogical practice anew, signifying her teaching as entrenched between the school culture she is confronted with (which is new to her both as a new teacher in the system and as a new immigrant in the country) and her own traditional orthodox background and educational upbringing. The mentor, on her part, could *appreciate* how her own assumptions about effective teaching and learning played out in the direction that she chose to undertake with the mentee: By foregrounding the situation as being a case of pupils' age, when confronted with such a task, she backgrounded possible exploration of the cultural and social codes that might influence the mentee's educational reasoning and actions. Alternately, the mentor could defy her own enacted orientation to mentoring. She could, for example, reevaluate the nature of the participatory roles that she undertook throughout the conversation (partly determined by the authoritative discourses of the college guidelines for student observation and evaluation) which guided her responses and mode of *improvisation*. This kind of inner dialogue between the different 'internally persuasive and authoritative discourses' (Bakhtin, 1986) would allow for an extended text to be *construed*, one which contests taken for granted expectations, ideologies, and courses of action.

Returning to my initial point at the beginning of this section, the kind of reciprocal connections that were created throughout the conversation did not account for appreciation of the controversies inherent in the mentee's text. As such, it did not allow space for a more critical and comprehensive construal of an appropriate strategy of assistance, in order to maximize learning from the experience. This was evident in the way in which the conversation ended – neither reassuring nor culminating in a new insight. Instead, the strategy offered by the mentor for future action did not consider too many options. We can conjecture that the mentee agreed to meet, because she had no other choice. After all, she was being evaluated as a future English teacher and the mentor's mandate, besides ongoing support, was to assess student teachers' progress during practice teaching.

The above cases underscore the dynamic and intricate forms and meanings that appreciation, participation, and improvisation take in natural settings of real-life situations. The manifold webs of connections that are expressed 'in action,' remind us that other than for analytic considerations, domains of praxis are interrelated and inseparably constituted in activity.

Chapter 8
Reciprocal Connections in Group Interactions

How are appreciation, improvisation, and participation reciprocally constituted in collaborative conversations?

thinking in practice

8.1 Reciprocal Connections Between Appreciation, Participation, and Improvisation in Collaborative Professional Conversations

In the previous chapter, I showed how appreciation, participation, and improvisation are reciprocally constituted to promote different forms and qualities of learning in dyadic conversations. In this chapter, I focus on two contrastive examples of group conversations. In the first example, I show how appreciation, participation, and improvisation are successfully constituted in the public space of group mentoring conversations, to enhance participants' learning. By contrast, the second example shows how devoid of a discursive, dialogic orientation, the group mentoring conversation remains static and underdeveloped, restricting its learning value for the participants.

8.2 Group Conversations as Contexts for Professional Learning

An examination of how teachers and researchers are challenged to rearticulate and reconstruct available and often conflicting discourses, including each other's, has implications for what it means to learn in a professional development community (Grossman, Wineburg, & Woolworth, 2001).

Professional conversations are conceived as social contexts for constructing and negotiating meanings; for creating spaces for participants to bring their practice under critical scrutiny; and for locating their voices in their experiences and in the experiences of others. Professional conversations help to articulate, analyze, and frame dilemmas and to solve pedagogical problems as they play out in different contexts (Clark, 2001; Cochran-Smith & Lytle, 1991; Darling-Hammond & Mc Laughlin, 1996; Florio-Ruane, 1991; Lieberman, 1995; Little, 1993; Olson & Craig, 2001). Professional conversations can also constitute important opportunities for the development of interpersonal reasoning (Noddings, 1991) and for 'pushing' participants to develop new ideas (Pfeiffer, Featherstone, & Smith, 1993). They can also function as valuable spaces for public expression, for crossing boundaries, and for authoring articles (Florio-Ruane, 1991).

As sites for the co-construction of knowledge, professional conversations draw on a view of learning and language as a social, communicative act, generated and constituted by dialogue and conversation. The process and content of professional conversations can, thus, be constrained and/or altered by the nature of the public space that is created by participants in conversation (Griffiths, 1995, p. 158). According to Griffiths (1995), an act of communication creates a public space. This public space is defined both by the purposes of the conversation and by the power relations that develop amongst the participants. Understanding how public space is established, therefore, necessitates attending to conversation triggers, rules, and rituals, that is, to the conventions that govern who may speak, when, about what and for how long. Griffiths further argues that successful communication is shaped by the degree to which participants share activities, experiences, and values. Thus, it is important to look carefully at what is shared by those who communicate. In her words: '...in so far as I want to make others understand me, I have to share a set of perspectives, or a set of activities with them. We have to negotiate these within the public-political spaces we create in any conversation' (p. 165). Taken to the domains of mentoring, public space would be constituted by forms of appreciation, participation, and improvisation in dialogue. This calls for examining how appreciation, participation, and improvisation are shared, negotiated, and deliberated in the public conversational space to support learning.

8.2.1 Conversation as Spaces for 'Dialogue' in Professional Conversations

An idea begins to live, to take shape, to develop, to find and renew its verbal expression, and to give birth to new ideas only when it enters into genuine dialogical relationships with other, foreign, ideas. Dialog is not the threshold to action but the action itself ... (Bakhtin, 1984, p. 72).

Professional conversation as 'dialogue' speaks to Bakhtin's (1981) concept of language as created in dialogue and of utterances as dialogically constituted, as people enter into conversation with one another. Of a sociocultural constitution, utterances embed a multiplicity of 'voices,' grounded in the speaker's past and present discourses, each carrying particular values and ideologies. These 'voices' constantly play out in the unconscious and implicit meanings that participants make of their experiences in conversation and are 'claimed' as they are uttered in conversation (Hicks, 1996, p. 52). Thus, any one utterance may also encompass not only the 'voice' of the person talking, but also the voice of the person the utterance is directed to, the voice of the addressee, as well as other voices gained from previous life experiences, from our history and our culture. Bringing together the notion of dialogism with action, Bakhtin claims that these voices are not self enclosed or deaf to one another. They hear each other constantly, call back and forth to one another, and are reflected in one another: *And outside this dialogue of 'conflicting truths,' not a single essential act is realized, nor a single essential thought* [expressed] (Bakhtin, 1984, p. 62.)

Dialogue-as-appreciation in professional conversations would express a fundamental orientation to the other, and a desire to be understood in relation to an 'Other' (Bakhtin, 1984, p. 64). As participation, dialogue in conversation constitutes the basis of dynamic relationships and encounters (Buber, 2000). A dialogic relation in conversation is, thus, a way of relating to one another in the fullness of each person's existence and in the fullness of differences amongst people. As improvisation, dialogue in the conversational space permeates one's external responses to others. It is inherent in inner and outer consciousness in action, and it is a way of relating to people and ideas that remain different from ours.

The notions of 'authoritative discourse' and 'internally persuasive discourse' are a key to Bakhtenian thought. Bakhtin (1981) conceives of the very bases of an individual's ideology as shaped by the struggle and dialogic relationship between authoritative discourses and internally persuasive discourses. Authoritative discourses constitute, according to Bakhtin 'the words of the fathers,' that is, the already acknowledged discourse by an authority that is hierarchically seen as higher:

The authoritative word demands that we acknowledge it, that we make it our own . . .quite independent of any power it might have to persuade us internally . . .it demands our unconditional allegiance [and] permits no play with the context framing it, no play with its borders, no gradual and flexible transitions, no spontaneously creative stylizing variants on it (Bakhtin, 1981, pp. 342, 343).

In contrast, in internally persuasive discourses, there is maximal interaction between one's word and the other's word, allowing for free creative development and for 'distinguishing between one's own and another's discourse, between's one's thought and another's thought . . . [until] thought begins to work in an independent, experimenting and discriminating way, [so that] there is a separation between internally persuasive discourse and authoritarian enforced discourse, along with a rejection of those categories of discourses that do not matter to us, that do not touch us' (Bakhtin, 1981, p. 345).

Adopting Bakhtenian concepts to interpret professional conversations implies identifying the polyphony of voices that participants claim, as they position themselves in relation to each other in dialogue. It also means distinguishing the discourses that shape these voices in conversation. Since voices are claimed through utterances, the utterance, then, becomes the main unit of language analysis, whose meaning is defined in relation to its position in the discourse.

8.3 Appreciation, Participation, and Improvisation as Constituted in Public Space: Learning in and from Group Mentoring Conversations

How do teachers collectively construct professional knowledge in conversation? The series of excerpts selected for this section draw on data from monthly conversations conducted in the context of an in-service professional conversation framework designed to support 10 mentors working with teachers in different educational settings. The excerpts illustrate how appreciation, participation, and improvisation operate 'in talk,' creating opportunities for participants to collaboratively construct knowledge about mentoring, as they challenge each other, reframe and articulate understandings, and analyze their practice. Throughout the conversation, the participants try to assist Michal, one of the mentor participants, to solve her dilemma. In the process, a polyphony of voices is claimed in the public space, informed mainly by authoritative discourses. At several points during the conversations, these authoritative discourses are debated and challenged, yielding the uttering of voices from more internally persuasive discourses (Orland-Barak, 2006).

> Now you've heard the story ... what would you do? ... honestly I've tried everything and nothing seems to work.

It is the middle of the school year. The group had begun meeting, since the beginning of the school year once a month. This is their fifth meeting. Michal is telling the group about the resistance that she is experiencing from one of her mentees, who refuses to cooperate and to attend the mentoring sessions regularly, despite the acute discipline problems that she claims to be having in her classes at school. As Michal tells her story, her tone of voice is pitched high, conveying her anxiety and discomfort with the situation: *Now you've heard the story [pause]...what would you do? [pause] ... honestly I've tried everything and nothing seems to work.*

Michal's utterance reinstates the typical Bakhtenian question of 'who is doing the talking?' Her utterance *I've tried everything* echoes a polyphony of voices from her own past professional experience with similar cases, which she seems to have (unsuccessfully) drawn upon, in trying to find a way to communicate with this teacher. At the same time, it reflects the voices of the persons the utterance is directed at – the other mentors in the group with other experiences whose appreciation might enrich her understanding of the situation. In her utterance she is, thus, creating a space for others to participate in a way that legitimizes their experiences and possible contributions to help her with the teacher. Her utterance 'what can I do?' implies an open invitation to participate by 'helping her out.' The conversation commences in the following way (Adapted from Orland-Barak, 2006):

(1) A: *Did the group know about the relationship of the class to that teacher* [the mentee]?

(2) M: *Yes, they knew.*

(3) B: *Was there anything else not 'functioning' with that teacher, the times she did come to the meetings with the group?*

(4) M: *Many times she was into herself, would not open to the group. . .*

(5) C: *Look, I explain this as a state of fear on the part of the teacher. She was confronted with a stressful situation, in terms of her status in class and probably didn't want others to know about it. It happened to me when I was a novice teacher so many times. . .*

(6) R: *As a counselor and coordinator, I have had similar experiences of people not showing up for meetings regularly. But everybody has her own problems and if you are part of a team, in order to sustain the team, I had to set boundaries.*

(7) N: *I also had that experience with Yehudit; she forgot the meeting altogether. . . I told her to do whatever is needed to cancel her plans and to come to the session. . .*

(8) B: *She deserves to be treated assertively, especially if it's a pattern that repeats itself apparently . . . this is our educational mandate and responsibility to nurture their growing into becoming professionals. . . .*

Michal's initial utterance initiates participants' appreciation into a polyphony of voices from various discourses, grounded in their own social and professional life experiences to provide the 'right' reading into her situation. Michal's appreciation that the teacher was often into herself and would not open to the group (4) is mediated by Cathy (5) who, in her attempt to explain the teacher's behavior, echoes the voice of participation based on her experience as a novice teacher. Her utterance *It happened to me when I was a novice teacher so many times. . .* surfaces her own reminiscences as a novice teacher and helps to signify the situation from the perspective of the status and vulnerability of novice teachers: *She was confronted with a stressful situation in terms of her status in class and probably didn't want others to know about it.*

This polyphony of participatory voices is meant to reexamine Michal's appreciation of the situation by shifting the focus of concern on herself and her resistance to trying to make sense of the case through the perspective of the insecurities that novices face. Cathy's assertion, *I explain this as a state of fear on the part of the teacher,* conveys a rather deterministic reading of the situation as mostly a case of being a novice. This is interesting because it reveals an intricate interplay between Cathy's empathetic appreciation of a similar situation (through the voices that she echoes from similar past experiences as a novice) and the implied authoritative discourse that seems to guide her appreciation, as if dictating 'how one should read into novices' behavior.'

Cathy's utterance is defied by Rachel (6) who, echoing voices from her professional discourse as counselor and coordinator, typifies the situation maintaining that *if one is part of a team, in order to sustain it, one must set boundaries.* Her utterance reflects a fixed, authoritative discourse regarding her appraisal of the meaning of working as a team, which seems to guide her practice. Thus, two competing participatory authoritative discourses seem to emerge – Cathy's and Rachel's. Interestingly, though, these do not challenge each other further in the conversation. Rachel's discourse, though, seems to gain support in the conversational floor both from Nava (7), *I also had that experience with Yehudit, she forgot the meeting alto-gether . . . I told her to do whatever is needed to cancel her plans and to come to the session . . .*, and from Betty, who voices a strong authoritative pedagogical discourse (8): *She deserves to be treated assertively, especially if it's a pattern that repeats itself apparently . . . this is our educational mandate and responsibility to nurture their growing into becoming professionals . . . .??* Both Nava and Rachel participate to affirm that mentors be explicit and assertive about the importance of attending the meetings, as part of their educational mandate *to nurture professional growth.* The utterances incorporate a polyphony of voices from authoritative discourses of men-toring and teaching: that the mentors' mandate is to nurture professional growth, that the mentors should be accountable to the nurturing of their mentee, and that team work is about setting boundaries. These discourses serve Nava, Betty, Rachel (and Cathy) to continue participating by making claims about the boundaries of their practice and about the ways in which commitment, responsibility, and accountability can operate to assist Michal.

Although the issue appeared to have been 'rounded up,' Meira, another par-ticipant, tunes in to defy the issue of boundaries and commitment that had been rather consensually accepted, until now. Her utterance is a form of improvisa-tion, connecting experience and knowledge anew. As such, it defies previous voices of accountability, reframing the issue in relation to her own experience of accountability toward Rutie, the project leader:

(11) M: *Yesterday I told Ruthie* [the mentor of mentors in the conversation group]
          that I wasn't coming to this meeting; she was very upset with me.
          Although I knew that I was right and my place was at school . . .

Until now, Michal, the mentor who had posed the problem and initiated the conversation had remained silent, which can be interpreted as if she was trying to 'register' the various voices of mediations from the floor. In her utterance, she restores her participation in the discourse, relating to others' voices:

(16) M: *The few times that she did come I told her, 'I am glad that you made it.' I*
          stressed how important it was for me and I expressed my satisfaction that
          she had done it for me.

The conversation continues as follows:

(17) J: *Why should they do it for you? This is a classic example of what happens*
          with novice teachers who are forced to come to meetings.

Liz, the group coordinator, defies Judy's utterance by raising a new controver-sial issue, inviting participants to take a stance, articulate their perspectives, and problematize the boundaries of their practice:

(18) L: *The situation is that the message that the meetings are voluntary at the*
          beginning of the year, but then, on the other hand, you are asking people
          to commit themselves to participating in order to keep the framework . . .
(19) N: *It's easier when it's voluntary than compulsory . . .*

(20) L: *But you need the participants the same as they need you ... in order to 'keep' you functioning as a mentor ... your rather drastic reactions to them not coming to the meetings comes out of your need to fulfill your role, or rather to establish your role in relation to them ...*

(21) N: *... but once you have joined, then, you are committed...*

(22) L: *Why?*

(23) R: *Because it is important to have a support group!*

Again, the group coordinator responds 'on the spot' to problematize voices that seem to convey rigid authoritative discourses in regard to the function and purpose of a support group:

(24) L: *Why? and what if the group is not 'supportive'?*

(25) R: *That depends on the mentor ...*

(26) L: *What makes you be so sure about that? What if you are left with only two teachers ...?*

(27) A: *Then the mentor is not O.K.*

(28) L: *The scheme that you created sends a somehow mixed message .... and who really needs who???*

Liz's invitation to critically examine taken for granted notions of what constitutes a support group in mentoring, indeed, prompts participants to engage in the critical uttering of more internally persuasive discourses:

(29) A: *This is what happens in 'home sessions.' We had never given it serious thought ...*

(30) J: *I can feel that I started with 8 and was left with three and that really shattered my self confidence. I have difficulty when teachers say to me: I forgot ....*

The conversation then gradually develops into scrutinizing the boundaries of the practice, in an attempt to conceptualize and articulate the new insights gained from the conversation, that is, as 'a case of something' in mentoring:

(31) N: *It's a question of the boundaries between being a friend and a mentor*

(32) L: *So, what was Michal's story all about?*

(33) H: *I see this as a question of wanting the mentees to model her own behavior*

(34) M: *Michal's story seems to be about empathy...*

(35) M: *I wrote it's about modeling and boundaries*

(36) M: *I focused my story on the mentee's resistance but now, I see it's more about my own resistances, maybe fears of being rejected and about my place or status within the group ... it's also about me, the teacher ...*

(37) L: *I agree, this could be rewritten, not as a story about the teacher you worked with, but about you ...*

Michal's final utterance (38), *I focused my story on the mentee's resistance but now, I see it's more about my own resistances, maybe fears of being rejected and about my place or status within the group ... it's also about me, the teacher...,* incorporates more intimate voices that expose personal dispositions, fears, and uncertainties. Her utterance also embeds the multiple identities that she manages as a professional and her positioning in relation to them. It carries voices stemming from what Gee (2001) would refer to as her nature-identity (stemming from one's natural state), from institution-identity (derived from a position recognized by authority), discourse-identity (resulting from the discourse of others about oneself), and affinity-identity (determined by one's practices in relation to external groups). As such, it condenses the collection of influences and effects from immediate contexts, prior constructs of self, social positioning, and meaning systems that become intertwined inside the flow of activity, as a teacher simultaneously reacts to and negotiates given contexts and human relationships at given moments. (Olsen, 2008, p. 139)

8.3.1 Learning in and from Group Mentoring Conversations

As we have seen in the above excerpt, appreciation, participation, and improvisation were constituted in dialogue, in the public conversational space, to promote learning from experience. As participants engaged to assist Michal solve her dilemma, some authoritative discourses were scrutinized, yielding the uttering of voices from more internally persuasive discourses. The insights that were coconstructed, in and from the group conversations, thus, reflected some of the internally persuasive discourses that emerged, as participants scrutinized, problematized, and critically examined the fragile boundaries of mentoring.

We now turn to a different, contrasting case of a group conversation. As we will see, despite its stated 'collaborative conversational setting,' the conversation neither adopts nor engages in discursive modes of participation that challenge new insights and understandings.

8.4 Mentoring Student Teachers: Missed Opportunities for Learning in and from Group Conversations

The following transcript is taken from a group mentoring conversation, following the observation of a History lesson given by a student teacher in an 8th grade class, in a Junior High School in Israel. The lesson revolved around the theme of the rise of Absolutism in France. It should be noted that the student teacher is an orthodox male doing practice teaching in a nonorthodox Jewish state school. The class is heterogeneous. The entire lesson (45 minutes), which was given by the student teacher, was conducted through frontal/lecture mode teaching, despite the fact that the teaching methods course at the university (specially geared to the teaching of History) stresses the integration of progressive, interactive methods of teaching, underscoring the relevance of content to pupils' lives and their prior knowledge.

During the lesson, the student teacher mentioned new concepts, dates, and names but did not introduce them, neither didactically nor through the use of any visual aids or communicative teaching techniques, to make the material more accessible to the pupils. The only visual that he used was a map of Europe which was hanging on the board. The lesson was observed by the student teacher's subject matter mentor (one of the History teachers at school) and three student teachers of History who work as a group, together with the pedagogical school mentor, and the university coordinator who is in charge of all the student teachers doing practice teaching in the various subject matters, at that school.

Following the lessons observed, the group meets regularly to discuss the lesson.

Aware of the unsuccessful implementation of the lesson (as insinuated by the school mentor to the university coordinator after the lesson had ended), the mentor begins the group conversation with a cathartic move:

M (Mentor):   *How did you feel?*

Probably expecting that the question would invite David (the mentee) to discharge feelings of discomfort about the lesson, the mentor is confronted with an unpredictably complacent answer:

D: (mentee): *Very well, I delivered the things I wanted.*

The mentee's utterance, *I delivered the things I wanted*, embeds a strong traditional text of teaching–as-delivering), evocative of his observant religious background which is strongly dictated by strict authoritative discourses of obedience to Jewish norms, rules, and traditions. At this point, the mentor does not challenge this text (e.g., by foregrounding connections between the mentee's background, his choice of language and consequent actions). Rather, he probes to trigger anticipation of similar scenarios:

M: *If you were to conduct the lesson for another parallel class tomorrow, what would you do differently?*
D: *I will activate the students more.*

The student teacher's utterance, is partly affirmed with an *O.K.*, but not further pursued 'on the spot' to foreground connections between the student overt behaviors and how these might possibly contradict the meanings implied in the notion of *activating pupils*. Instead, the mentor preserves his nonconfrontational mode of talk with a move that pushes for connections between the content of the student's response with his previous planning, which is a recurrent feature of teacher talk. Hence, talk revolves around the application of preplanned activities, backgrounding opportunities for informed improvisation to connect between persons, context, and content:

M: *O.K., and what did you implement from our feedback on the last lesson you gave?*
S (student observer):   *Summarizing the lesson in the end, defining goals, and not compromising too much.*

Again, although the mentor connects to the student's response, his probing question is framed conventionally, as if replicated from the traditional pool of preplanned (rather than improvised) questions that teachers are trained to ask in their teaching:

M: *What were your goals and did you achieve them?*
D: *My goal was to teach the background for the rise of Absolutism.*

From this point onwards, the mentor opens the public conversation by initiating a turn-taking ritual, one which invites participants to share their observations of the lesson. Notice the process of 'turn taking' that gradually unfolds. Each participant takes turns to give feedback on the lesson: The student teacher participants offer mostly supportive comments, while the school mentor and the university coordinator extend on connections between teaching, learning, and subject matter. Notice the structure of the utterance, suggesting the fixed ritual of turn taking and talk that is 'permitted.'

M: *O.K. Let's see what the others think. Amal, your turn to give feedback to David* [the observed student teacher]. *Remember the rules – first positive, constructive feedback.*
A: (Student observer): *The strong point of the lesson was his dynamics.*
M: *Amal, you are talking to him, not to me. . .so talk to him directly*
A: *O.K, Your voice was clear; you knew the subject well and had presence during the lesson. The points for improvement are that when you enter a class, you have to wait for the students to calm down and only then, you can start teaching. You started teaching when none of the students were listening and then, the theme of the lesson wasn't clear for them.*
M: *O.K. Thank you. And what about you, Celia?*
C: (Student observer): *The lesson was fine. You know the subject well, you've read the lesson plan in advance and you succeeded teaching everything you planned to teach during the lesson. In the beginning of the lesson, you didn't wait for silence and for the students' attention. The material you gave, in the beginning of the lesson, was too vague. During the lesson, you also turned your back to some of the students but you used the map well and let the students participate. It was very nice that you remembered the students' names. The lesson was just fine.*

At this point, the university coordinator intervenes. Notice that she takes up the conversational floor, without waiting for an invitation from the mentor to enter the public space (as was done with the other student teachers). This also seems to be part of the ritual: Rules of participation and intervention are not symmetrical but determined according to hierarchical roles and positions in the conversation (Fairclough, 1992). As we will see in the next series of turns, the conversation becomes closer to 'monological stretches,' led both by the mentor and the university coordinator alternately. As they elaborate on each other's feedback, they suggest, tell, offer pedagogical tips and develop ideas. Notice that throughout these lengthy stretches of turn taking, the David's voice is almost 'unheard.'

Ran (university coordinator): *I wanted to talk about the lesson's concept. In the last group meeting, we discussed the use of 'lecture mode' as teaching method in History lessons. During that discussion, you had had reservations about this kind of teaching and yet, this is how you conducted the whole lesson. You said that lecture mode is less activating for the students and that it's important to address them with questions, yet you hardly did that, during the lesson we observed. For example, at the beginning, you said that you would tell them [the class] what the king ate and you didn't get back to that. The lesson is a kind of story. Sticking to the story, withal its plots and dramas could have made it much more 'alive' for the pupils. What do you think?*

M: *Following what Ran [the university coordinator] said, I want to emphasize the kind of 'coloring' that you can give to the character of the king. For example, you could have directed the pupils to the king's picture in the book and ask them what they thought the king had eaten (he was large in size). This kind of 'spicing' attracts the eye, the ear, and the mind. . .*

Ran picks up on the mentor's comment to probe the student teacher's reasoning:

R: *Can you know, in the end of the lesson, what the students learned? How?*

The student teacher's reply embeds the same, recurrent traditional teaching text:

D: *I can't know. I could only know, if I give them homework or if Dan [the school mentor] gives them a quiz next lesson.*

Again, similarly to the mentor's move on previous occasions, Ran does not attempt to challenge the strong cultural texts reflected in the student teacher's language and which seem to direct his rigid views about good teaching and learning. Rather, he chooses a strategy which is more geared to the activity itself, trying to trigger connections between concepts and actions:

R: *Try to think whether you could have done something else, or an activity through which you could have felt or known what the students were learning, without having to give them homework or grades. . . For example, from what you studied in the didactics lessons, what could you have implemented in the class for that purpose?*

David's response, again, calls for confronting and challenging perspectives on the meanings inherent in certain notions to describe what he thinks *'should be done.'* For example, notice how in his expressed view, 'playing' connotes solely with dramatic effects, reflective of common narrow views of teaching-as-performance or teachers-as-actors as not serious work (Orland-Barak, 2003b) which slow down for the 'covering the material':

D: *I've learned that one should 'play' more with the students and not merely teach them with the mimics, with the visual aspect, with my alertness as a teacher, with my movement, and so I did. I was also afraid that I wouldn't be able to cover all the material that was planned for the lesson.*

At this point, for example, the mentor participants could engage in informed improvisation to dispute the student's authoritative discourses that dictate his interpretations of 'play' and of 'covering material' in teaching. Such views can be contested, for example, drawing on recent educational thought on performance as revealing of the idiosyncratic rules, roles, and rituals that participants engage in through performance in a particular educational culture (McLaren, 1986, 1988).

Amal, one of the other student teachers, seems to be prompted to show the connections that *she* has made in previous lessons:

A: *Last lesson I took the text and changed it into a riddle, I took it from the seminar course at the university.*

Amal's utterance is not further developed or mediated to affirm, validate, or challenge positions or inherent controversies. Rather, another chain of 'telling monologues' reemerges, as the mentor and the university coordinator seem to support 'each other,' probably as part of their Discourse as expert teachers and mentors, in the presence of the students. The student teachers are there, but not 'in there':

R: *The lecture mode does not allow for any of that, it's difficult to get to feel the class and what they are learning. This does not mean that teaching through lecture mode is completely undesirable. On the contrary, I have had excellent 'lecturers'...*

M: *The summary was the place to check what the students had learned, through higher order thinking questions. The 10 minutes of the summary were enough time to do that. It is a good feeling to stand in front of a class and lecture, but we must not fall for that, because, then, you have no possibility of knowing whether actual thinking is occurring. There is another kind of difficulty in giving an assignment, in order to check comprehension, but this is not the occasion to open a discussion on that matter.*

I identify with what the other students said. You demonstrated knowledge on the subject, you used your voice well, you played with your tones, you had movement around the class, which helped you keep the students alert. You didn't use the board enough. After writing on the board, you should take a step back and check whether the writing was clear. The pen you used was almost evaporating and the pupils seating at the back of the class couldn't see what was written on the white board. Only by 11.10 you 'announced' that you now arrived at the lesson's main topic. That means you took 15 minutes at the beginning of lesson for an introduction to the topic which is far too long. You mentioned names of places and many concepts – there was a place for writing them on the board. You used the map. I videotaped it and I will send you the film – You've neglected the side of the class that is close to the window. You should scan the whole class with your eyes; you shouldn't talk with your back turned to the students. It creates a situation in which some of the students can't hear you. In the end, you explained the term Absolutism.

The mentor continues to suggest to the student what he should have done. His utterance embeds a strong personalistic discourse of teaching, one which acknowledges the importance of building on pupils' prior knowledge and on establishing personal connections with the pupils. Yet paradoxically, such a discourse seems to be only partially implemented in his discourse as mentor:

You should have started from the students themselves. You could have asked them what they had known about the term, before you started explaining it. You handled well the discipline problems, you called the students by their names, so you made the relation with them more personal and warmer.

One of the pupils mentioned his visit to the Palace of Versailles. What did that pupil actually want and need? The attention of the class and your attention! How often does one get to talk about having been in the exact place you are learning about in history lessons! He was just waiting to be asked to talk about it and to get your feedback! It was missed because you didn't pay attention to him long enough – he must have remained very frustrated about it. These moments are so important for the pupils and it's important to be attentive to them.

To sum it up – you have presence in the class; you'll be a good teacher.

In the above utterance, the mentor integrates straightforward suggestions about what to do through directive and prescriptive language, meant to clarify, expand, and apply. The differences that evidence between his talk about teaching and his enacted discourse as mentor suggest something about the situated character of teachers' professional identities (Flores & Day, 2006) as well as about the manifold positionings and identity constructions that play out while enacting various professional roles in one domain (Blumenthal, 1999; Day, 1999; Orland-Barak, 2002). In a similar amalgam of prescriptive, directive, and clarifying acts, but interweaving conceptual with directive language, Ran suggests:

Ran: *In a story, the storyteller doesn't take for granted that the listeners have the background, so when telling the story, he makes sure that certain concepts and background knowledge are made clear and exposed through all kinds of literary devices – take that to your lesson: You used many different concepts and you assumed the students were familiar with them. Not all of them were, so some could not follow the story.*

M: *If you look at the pupil's history book – How can you make a use of that?*

The mentor's last utterance finally manages to engage the student teachers back in the conversational floor, although David, the focal 'subject' for whom the conversation was initially intended, is still silent.

C: *You might choose a certain section and focus on it by reading it aloud dramatically, or you can use a certain concept which is explained in the book and develop it into a simulation.*

A: *If we ask pupils to read parts of the chapter for homework, they will not do it. If we don't make it compulsory they won't read. You should pick an interesting section and make it into interesting activities in class.*

Student teachers' procedural talk about what works is common amongst novices (Rust, 1994; Berliner, 2001). In this respect, Amal and Celia are no different. Following that line of reasoning, the mentor elaborates on roles, pedagogical perspectives, and procedures:

M: *It is important to look inside the book backward and forward. The book has a certain sequence, a certain logic. It's important to learn about that logic and to introduce it to the students – what have we done and learned so far? Where are we headed? Our role is to revive the story that appears in the book.*

The book is written in a language that most students in the class find difficult –
newcomers, learning disabilities etc. and therefore, the book should be at the
background.

Breaking the prevalent, practical-pedagogical orientation of the conversation,
Ran, rather unexpectedly, pushes for new connections between knowledge, beliefs,
and actions. In doing so, he instantiates a more academic discourse:

Ran: *It's important to take all that's been said here and to examine it against what*
        each one of you [pointing to the student teachers] *brings to teaching from*
        your beliefs, background, and experiences as pupils.

His utterance triggers a new turn in the conversation, finally opening the public
space for scrutinizing and introspecting into ingrained assumptions, and for collaboratively attending to voices that had remained silent, until now. Indeed, such
a direction briefly restores the student teachers' voices in the conversational floor,
in this direction: Coming from different backgrounds (an Orthodox Jew, two Arab
Muslims, and one Arab Christian doing practice teaching in a Jewish secular High
School), Ran's invitation seemed particularly relevant for the kind of dilemmas and
conflicts that might surface in such a context:

D: *I must mention that the class gave me a good feeling about me coming from*
        an orthodox background, teaching secular classes. This gave me a good feel-
        ing which doesn't always happen in other classes, because of the way I dress
        [traditionally].
A: *It happens to me as well, coming from the Arab sector, I also feel very welcome*
        in this class although my mother tongue is not Hebrew. Last year pupils used
        to laugh at my accent and it wasn't easy during periods of tension and war
        with some classes.

David and Amal's utterances convey strong messages of estrangement, resonat-
ing with Schutz' (1970) notions of belonging. Ran uses them as opportunities for
further exploration and articulation of feelings, dispositions, and future action:

R: *Does teaching Jewish students, as an Arab student teacher, affect your teach-*
        ing? And David, does teaching secular students differ from orthodox schools?
        And what do you take with you from the experience?
A: *The mentality is different. In an Arab School there is no addressing the teacher*
        by name. There is a stronger discipline – the discipline is the guiding principle.
        In a Jewish School, you'd find more liberalism.
D: *Here, the relations with the students are closer than in religious schools. I*
        also take that with me – I take with me the more personal relations with the
        students.

For the first time in the conversation, students begin to speak from a more
internally persuasive discourse. This also opens a space for challenging each other
intellectually, as reflected in Celia's following utterance:

C: *If we already began talking about different perspectives, I wanted to say that*
       at several points during the lesson, there was place for showing the pupils that
       certain facts have been interpreted differently by different historians.

Celia's comment could have developed into a challenging conversation around competing positions, mediated at the crossroads between the personal, the ideological, the cultural, and the pedagogical. The mentor could, for example, encourage the student teachers to reexamine perspectives on ingrained assumptions and pedagogical stances on curricular issues or promote connections between curricular content and relevant pedagogical strategies.

The opportunity was, unfortunately, missed. For one, David's reply to Celia, *That's true, but as I said, I was afraid I would not cover the material I was expected to cover during the lesson...*, restored the conversation to managing procedural aspects of time and planning. Since such a view had not been directly put into critical scrutiny, David probably felt reaffirmed about his conception that in a successful lesson, one 'must' cover all the material planned. It seems, then, that the long monologues of 'telling' and 'suggesting' had not really touched him. It had now become evident that his silence throughout most of the conversation had little to do with new possible perspectives that he might have been 'absorbing' from the 'floor,' and more to do with the absence of a dialogic platform for contesting his ideas about teaching and learning History. Although initially, the mentor had voiced his discomfort about the lesson, the conversation ended in a consensual and over-supportive atmosphere, leaving David quite satisfied with his performance. As the title of this section implies, valuable opportunities for learning in and from group conversations were missed, as the discourse, embedded in fixed rituals, developed into detailed elaborations of technical-pedagogical suggestions, devoid of in-depth exploration of potentially controversial issues that had begun to emerge throughout the conversation.

8.4.1 Turn Taking Over Collaborative Discourse: Missed Opportunities for a Learning Dialogue in Group Conversations

The above conversation sustains Griffiths' assertions: regarding knowledge construction in the public space, but from the perspective of the missed opportunities to advance and share activities, experiences, and values: It suggests how group mentoring, devoid of discursive and dialogic features, actually constrains the quality of the public space created by participants in conversation. Characterized by technical rituals of turn taking which seemed to have backgrounded opportunities for more discursive elaborations of assumptions, beliefs, and enacted pedagogies, important potential learning dialogues were missed on the way. Discourses were unchallenged and ingrained beliefs and educational stances toward teaching, learning, and subject matter remained unarticulated; the conversation was featured by 'subjects' and 'objects' of talk, but there was *no* inter-subjectivity; there were 'I's,' 'Thou's,' and

'It's,' but no 'I–Thou–It' relation in dialogue (Buber, 2000); there were practices of mentoring, but not discursive practices; participants took turns in collaboration, but there was no collaborative turn taking; they talked about 'the other' but not to each other. The conversational floor was envisioned as a learning space for collabora-tively reflecting on the student teachers' experience, through symmetrical talk that acknowledges the value of distributed expertise, that is, novices and experts shar-ing and coconstructing knowledge (Clark, 2001; Tillema & Orland-Barak, 2006). In practice, however, the rituals of turn taking, including the kind of talk allowed for (or not) yielded a discourse which was predominantly characterized by the agendas and pedagogical stances brought forth by the leaders. These discourses shadowed, eventually, the reflective, integrative, and conceptual talk that could have developed in conversations that are grounded in distributed expertise (Clark, 2001).

Reciprocal connections between Appreciation, Participation, and Improvisation were, then, absent from the conversational floor. Devoid of mediation between per-sons, context, and content, it was inattentive to what went on 'at the backstage' of the conversation, and how it could have affected the kind of discourses that were prior-itized. The 'backstage' of the conversational scene, uttering a polyphony of voices, sheds light on the various stances that participants eventually adopt in relation to each other, to their practice, and to others' practices. Reading into these discourses could underscore, for example, the strong influence that cultural groundings have on the articulation of student teachers' visions of successful teaching and of teaching subject matter. By accessing student teachers' worlds as learners and as members of an ethnic group, the mentor could appreciate the recurrence of particular utterances and interpretations as reflective of their unique experiences, stories, and culture. David's utterances would, then, be signified anew while critically examining and becoming aware of the value systems that direct the meanings that he attributes to his actions.

Chapter 9
Toward the Design of a Curriculum on Learning to Mentor

The curriculum is never simply a neutral assemblage of knowledge...

It is always part of a selective tradition, someone's selection, some groups' vision of legitimate knowledge. It is [always] produced out of the cultural, political, and economic conflicts, tensions and compromises that organize and disorganize a people... (Apple, 1996, in Cochran-Smith & Demers p.263)

Apple's seminal work provides a conceptual foundation for the challenging task of translating the praxical, discursive character of mentoring practices into a set of principles and procedures for a curriculum on learning to mentor. The three Domains of Praxis developed throughout this book call for a curricular stance, as Apple would suggest, that has a dialectical, moral, ideological, and political grounding. The remaining three chapters of this book try to stand up to this challenge:

This chapter begins by presenting the foundations that underlie a curriculum based on the three domains of learning to mentor-as-praxis. These are, then, reframed to suggest deriving principles for *learning* to mentor, with a focus on what these foundations *mean* for expected processes and outcomes. The deriving learning principles are translated, in turn, into assertions underlying the design of appropriate settings, conditions, and tasks.

Chapter 10 offers concrete examples of working methodologies for accomplishing these principles. Chapter 11 considers paradoxes, ambivalences, challenges, and difficulties that might emerge while implementing and appropriating such methodologies.

The goal of this chapter is to suggest principles of design and procedure that can serve as a basis for the design and implementation of a curriculum for learning to mentor-as-praxis in teacher education. I find it important to stress that the principles presented in these chapters are regarded as dynamic, tentative frameworks open to scrutiny and meant to invite innovative, creative thinking.

L. Orland-Barak, *Learning to Mentor-as-Praxis*, Professional Learning and Development in Schools and Higher Education 4, DOI 10.1007/978-1-4419-0582-6_9, © Springer Science+Business Media, LLC 2010

9.1 Foundations for Learning to Mentor-as-Praxis

> Learning to mentor calls for the acquisition of three interrelated domains
> of knowledge: Appreciation, Participation and Improvisation in a variety of
> dialectical connections at the crossroads between forms of dialogue and forms
> of practice.

- Learning to mentor develops readiness to improvise, appreciate, and participate in the complex webs of professional, social, and cultural relations that characterize the practice.
- Learning to mentor entails the acquisition of practices to improvise, appreciate, and participate in the complex webs of professional, social, and cultural interactions.
- Learning to mentor enhances critical pedagogue roles and agency.
- Learning to mentor embeds integrative, conceptual, multidisciplinary, and interdisciplinary processes of learning.
- Learning to mentor is construed dialectically through encounters between academic and professional discourses and social and cultural settings.
- Learning to mentor calls for ongoing processes of repositioning and reconstruction of knowledge in dialogue.
- Learning to mentor entails acquiring a professional language for communicating in different cultural settings and social contexts.
- Learning to mentor is sustained in community and through activity.

9.2 Professional Learning-as-Praxis

The above foundations underlying a curriculum for learning to mentor-as-praxis call for a social constructivist orientation toward learning and learning experiences that values dialectical processes, while encouraging a view of *professional learning* as dialogue between three interrelated settings of learning and discourses of practice: theoretical learning in practice, practical learning in practice, and academic learning at the university.

9.2.1 Theoretical Learning in Practice

Professional learning underscores the importance of developing what can be referred to as *theoretical learning in practice* (Bulterman-Bos, 2008). Theoretical learning in practice would account for the *conceptual processes* that shape professional learning in practice, such as attributing and designating, ethical and professional reasoning and judgment, reflection on dilemmas, and ramification of concepts. These conceptual processes are inherently theoretical, in that they engage the learner in reciprocal inductive and deductive sense making of practice and in triggering thinking at levels of principles, pattern recognition, metacognition, and justification of decision making in practice (Ibid.).

Theoretical learning in practice occurs and develops in conversation through clarification processes; is embedded in situations in context; connects inductive and deductive processes with procedural and conceptual knowledge; is intrinsic in personal examples stressing historical processes of the discipline; and leans on practice and is mediated in practice. It also entails identifying, establishing, and articulating one's own personal space in the practice; forming personal norms of professional behavior in dyadic, triadic, or group mentoring relations; being aware how feelings, thoughts, and actions operate in the relational mentoring space; and articulating thoughts and reactions to stressful situations.

9.2.2 Practical Learning in Practice

A dialectical conception of professional learning also includes aspects of *practical learning in practice*. Constituted in dialogue, a praxical approach to practical learning in practice would enhance appreciation of theories in action, improvisation while thinking 'on one's feet' as you do, making decisions 'in situ,' and activating intuitive thinking and heuristic strategies simultaneously while thinking about doing. Practical learning also calls for participation through contextual thinking or thinking in and through cases, participation and improvisation through multi-dimensional thinking by connecting between environment, persons, and actions, by thinking through exceptional, unique cases rather than through generalities, and by building repertoires of general and unique cases. It also entails improvising while integrating skills simultaneously in action, considering how contextual factors play out for solving problems.

9.2.3 Academic Learning at the University

Academic learning at the university *involves appreciation of* the growing body of knowledge that has developed in the field of mentoring through exposure, critical inquiry, and dialogue. A praxical approach to academic learning would, thus, consider how research agendas and recent theorizing have been shaped by historical processes to influence the direction of the field and the character of relationships that define the practice. It also examines how emergent insights from the literature can operate as tentative interpretative lenses to make sense of the 'here-and-now' context of practice. Academic learning, thus, promotes critical dialogue between theoretical notions grounded in research and contextual insights grounded in practice – toward the development of a personal, educational theory of mentoring 'on' and 'for' professional action. Critical examination of the encounter between the

general and the local suggests wearing multiple interpretive lenses at the crossroads
between global theorizing and local considerations, while scaffolding and accessing
a mentoring text.

9.3 Principles Underlying Professional Learning-as- Praxis

Professional learning, conceived of as continuing dialogues between the three interrelated settings and discourses of learning discussed above, is, then, sustained by
the following principles:

1. Any kind of learning occurs in the context of interactions that attend to relations
   between subjects [I], objects [Thou], and content [It].
2. Learning calls for a simultaneous focus on what is learned, how it is learned,
   and why it is learned.
3. Learning occurs at the meeting between processes of appreciation, participation, and improvisation.
4. Any learning experience involves varying degrees of appreciation, participation, and improvisation.
5. Learning is recursive and integrative, combining person, text, action, and
   context.
6. Learning processes integrate knowledge, skills, and reasoning through
   perspective-taking.
7. Any kind of learning would call for personal involvement, social awareness,
   and conceptualization of processes.
8. Learning always builds on prior learning.
9. Learning involves the mentor in the construction and development of learning
   products and outcomes, toward maximum ownership of learning.
10. Learning engages the mentor in critical self scrutiny of ideologies, beliefs, and
    dispositions.
11. Learning processes and outcomes sustain the passage from role modeling to
    self modeling of one's own actions in new contexts.
12. Learning encourages connections between personal interpretations and contex-
    tual constructions.
13. Learning engages in the articulation of personal experiences that are then con-
    ceptualized into personal theories, working principles, and practical procedures.
14. Learning is construed through the analysis of personal and collective decision-
    making processes toward their integration into a personal rationale for future
    action.
15. Learning stresses encounters and dialogues between Discourses and the profes-
    sional languages that they represent.
16. Learning embeds clarifying ambiguities and exposing contradictions.
17. Learning is sustained and enhanced through exploration of the learner's
    personal and professional history.

18. Learning is situational and enhances communal processes of meaning making.
19. Learning is nonlinear, distributed, and interconnected.
20. Learning is directed toward both personal and collective meaning.

9.4 Principles Underlying the Design of Learning Settings and Tasks

The multifaceted, dialectical connections underlying the character of professional learning call for the design of learning environments that allow for initiating, sustaining, and evaluating learning in, on, and from experience. Specifically, such environments should

- encourage tasks that examine appreciation of similarities, differences, and contradictions between participants' roles as teachers and as mentors;
- provide opportunities for critically reflecting on how systemic factors shape the nature of participation;
- create frameworks of participation for mentors to share their own stories of practice as teachers and as former mentees, through which they can collaboratively reflect and reframe their thinking and possible misconceptions of practice;
- expose mentors to situations that challenge their ingrained beliefs and assumptions, prompting them to examine instances of dissonance between their educational agendas as teachers and as mentors;
- provide ample opportunities for exposure to and observation of multiple mentoring settings at different stages of the process, in order to build a repertoire of contrastive cases for future participation and improvisation;
- provide opportunities for practicing mentoring in authentic contexts of participation and through formalized processes of academic supervision in practice;
- encourage tasks that combine the use of authentic texts with academic texts;
- encourage loop learning strategies and tasks;
- be designed around inquiry-based tasks and tasks that connect between 'being, doing, thinking, and feeling';
- promote tasks that encourage the articulation of practice;
- promote tasks that call for collaborative and communal processes of participation through meaning negotiation and dissemination of joint products of such collaborations;
- advance tasks that promote improvisation and participation strategies through systematic analysis of practice, creative, and divergent thinking, and the development of cultural sensitivity;
- promote tasks geared to the development of appreciation skills that assist in identifying the conditions that play out to shape a particular mentoring situation.

9.5 Constructivist Frameworks in Academic Settings

The above principles speak to the design of frameworks that follow constructivist, dialectical, and communal approaches to adult learning (Zellermayer & Munthe 2007; Craig & Deretchin, 2009). These frameworks, designed around the integration of academic texts with authentic texts from the field, constitute challenging and yet safe spaces for making sense of the process of developing expertise when professionals move from one role to another within the same domain. The dialogic nature of such frameworks allows for solving problems and burning issues, for constructing understandings about differences and similarities across mentoring practices, and for making sense of the dissonance brought about by experiences of distress in the passage from teaching to mentoring. As such, they draw on the potential of teacher inquiry communities 'structured to foster deep intellectual discourse about critical issues [for becoming] spaces where the uncertainties and questions intrinsic to teaching [and mentoring] can be scrutinized. Given the moral, cultural, and political character of mentoring, it is important to provide professional inquiry contexts that are safe and challenging for dealing with the conflicts and tensions brought about by competing discourses. These spaces can encourage mentors to scrutinize authoritative discourses and articulate, instead, more internally persuasive discourses. In these conversation-reflection spaces, participants can establish links between their work as mentors and their work as teachers and reflect on their educational agendas as teachers and as mentors (Orland-Barak, 2005).

The various courses and partnerships described below reflect the growing recognition that effective teacher education occurs when academic and professional practices are integrated in one course (Calderhead & Shorrock, 1997; Clark, 1995, 2001; Kagan, 1993). The courses also reveal a new direction to upgrade the status of mentoring by demanding a formal background of academic and professional studies as a requisite for selection or for functioning in the role of mentor. This implies that mentors would have to go through these kind of courses at some time during their work in order to get an official recognition.

The orientation of these professional courses follows a view of the mentor-as-reflective practitioner and researcher into his/her own practice, stressing the need to develop a common professional language, unique to the practice of mentoring. It also advocates recent views of knowledge and learning as co-constructed in professional conversations (Clark, 2001; Mullen, Kochan, & Funk, 1999), and action research models of inquiry based on collaboration and reflection on action, whereby mentors are invited to share and analyze their field experiences and narratives of practice (Connelly & Clandinin, 1990; Diamond & Mullen, 1997; and many others). To this end, mentors are invited to document their experiences through portfolios, cases, journals, and stories of critical incidents in their practices. These are brought to the course sessions, often constituting the main working texts through which connections to more theoretical concepts are made.

Let us turn to a few examples of how such constructivist academic settings have been translated into professional and academic courses (Adapted from Orland-Barak 2003a, p. 195–198).

Example One

Mentoring Skills and Practices

This academic course is an elective course offered as part of a two-year Master's program at the Faculty of Education in a major university in the northern region of the country. The course allows practicing in-service mentors eligible to undertake the general Master's program in Education, to specialize in Mentoring during their two years of study (four yearly hours of courses on mentoring). The special track accredits them with a formal certificate as qualified mentors, granted by the Ministry of Education, in addition to the general Master's degree. The course is designed as a case-based pedagogy course. At the beginning of the year (the first four weeks of study), participants are asked to read a number of articles selected by the course professor, on the area of Mentoring and Mentored Learning. During the sessions the participants are encouraged to connect between theoretical ideas and their practices. The discussions in class focus on the connections between the research literature on mentoring and the context of mentors in their practice. The mentor participants also write cases about their practice and present them to the rest of the group. To illustrate the genre of case writing, two published cases are analyzed and discussed during the sessions, with a focus on what constitutes a case as compared to other narrative modes (such as journal writing and autobiographical writing), and on how cases can be used as working texts during mentoring sessions. These preliminary sessions lead to a class activity around the construction of guidelines with reflective questions to frame the writing and presentation of the mentors' cases in class.

Example Two

Mentoring of Mentors' Course

Cosponsored by the Ministry of Education and the Faculty of Education at a major university, the professional conversation group for the 'mentoring of mentors' (MoM) was designed to provide ongoing support to 10 mentors of novices in their first year of teaching in the northern region of Israel. The focal group consisted of 10 in-service mentors of teachers from different disciplinary backgrounds and levels of expertise. The group met regularly, once a month, in the company of the project leader and an academic researcher and facilitator. The sessions aimed at encouraging the mentors to voice dilemmas and stories from the field, and at collaboratively reflecting on their participatory roles as mentors and as teachers, in order to construct more informed understandings about their roles and about the practice of mentoring. The MoM model constituted one component of a more comprehensive project designed to assist first year teachers (Strahovsky, Marbach, & Hertz-Lazarowitz, 1998). The larger mentoring project was unique in that, contrary to disciplinary-oriented models, it focused on supporting the novice teachers on general aspects of their induction into teaching. This 'existential' rather than disciplinary/subject matter approach to in-service mentoring was based on the contention that first year teachers share similar concerns about their practice, namely concerns about basic survival needs and socialization into the profession that transcend any kind of disciplinary affiliation. In order to facilitate assistance, at this level of survival in the system, the mentors were released and excluded from administrative and physical hurdles such as having to deal with policy-making, contacting with principals, interventions within the schools, and observations of the teachers in their classes (all of these were assigned to the person leading the project). This brought up the image of the mentor as 'off-site,' that is, one which deals exclusively with the clinical support of the mentee to the exclusion of managerial and organizational aspects of mentors' work. The stories that mentors shared with the group revolved around dilemmas of participation in competing agendas, the consequences, and implications of using particular strategies of improvisation and on the perspectives adopted by participants while appreciating a particular case.

Example Three

Action Research Course for Mentors of English Teachers

This two-year action research course was organized by the English inspectors of the north of the country in coordination with a major university. The objectives were to familiarize mentors, coordinators and, at a later stage, teachers with a new national English curriculum. The course was organized around bi-monthly meetings. The first meeting of the month was usually a general lecture given by experts on content areas that connected to the new curriculum. The second meeting of the month focused on the implementation of the materials via hands-on tasks following a systematic action research cycle: Defining a particular problem, investigating its sources in the theoretical and practical field, suggesting an informed plan of action, implementing the plan, and documenting and reflecting on the outcomes for future revised action. As a course requirement, participants were asked to construct group portfolios that represented their process of learning about the new curriculum. The portfolios were submitted to the course leaders at the termination of the course.

Example Four

Learning the Practice of Mentoring

Similarly to Mentoring Skills and Practices (Course One), the course is given as a two-year course in a major university and is funded by the Ministry of Education. In contrast to Course One, the current course does not constitute part of an academic track toward a Master's certificate, although it accredits mentors with a formal certificate as qualified mentors, granted by the Ministry of Education. The two-year course is designed around a major conversational component (similarly to the previous courses) interspersed by guest lecturers on different topics that relate to the practice of mentoring as shaped by various systemic conditions. As a requirement for the course, mentors are asked to read relevant professional literature, to present cases of practice and to present their professional histories as mentors to the group. During their presentations, they are encouraged to employ various mentoring strategies they find suitable for the particular ideas they wish to present, considering the unique systemic and interpersonal features of the context. The discussions following the presentations focus both on the process (i.e., the strategies that mentors used for activating the group) and on the content of the stories and cases (Table 9.1).

Table 9.1 Mentoring courses in constructivist academic settings

The courses	Participants	Design
Mentoring of Mentors course	10 mentors of graduate university novices (interdisciplinary)	**Support framework for mentors. Collaborative conversations around stories from the field Academic course towards accreditation.**
M.A course for mentors	20 mentors (interdiscipli- nary). M.A students	**Case - based pedagogy. Two year action research model.**
Action Research course for mentors of English teachers.	Mentors and coordinators of English (Disciplinary)	**Course for the dissemination of a new English curriculum**
Professional course for the accreditation of mentors	20 in-service mentors (interdisciplinary)	Two year course towards a certificate. Based on conversations, cases and workshops.

9.6 Course Design: Rationale

The rationale for the design of programs for learning to mentor draws on and is consistent with the foundations and principles of learning specified above. As such, it stresses the following goals, outcomes, and prerequisites.

9.6.1 Goals

1. To encourage mentors to identify personal overt choices and preferences as indicative of covert, idiosyncratic ideologies, and cultural codes.
2. To enhance the appreciation of connections between mentors' covert ide-ological and moral considerations and overt forms of communication and pedagogical reasoning.

3. To foreground relevant connections between cultural codes, values, and strategic and pedagogical reasoning in a particular mentoring context.
4. To develop strategies for interacting and responding appropriately in different mentoring contexts.
5. To develop in the mentors a professional perspective and stance toward their role which enables them to locate their mentoring practices in the wider context of the school and the community.
6. To foster in mentors general intellectual capacities commensurate with the developing professional role of the mentor, under changing circumstances of their future careers, and, in particular, the capacity to conceptualize and theorize.
7. To expand trainees' range of academic experience in a variety of content areas while reflecting on connections between theory, practice and experience.
8. To expose trainees to a variety of experiential contexts and field experiences that allow for connecting between theoretical concepts and experiential insights to develop a subjective educational theory as mentors.
9. To critically examine the professional continuum of life-long learning and development of expertise across a profession.
10. To develop a professional language of mentoring.

9.6.2 Outcomes

Specifically, mentors would be expected to demonstrate the following competencies of *Appreciation*:

- To recognize and confront gaps between the mentor and the mentee's codes and norms of behavior
- To reframe perspectives on ingrained assumptions and ideologies
- To typify the mentoring context and signify emergent cooperative breakdowns
- To take perspective by making educated conjectures and connecting the parts to the whole
- To recognize role boundaries
- To evaluate educational interventions as rooted in moral stances
- To reframe perspectives on resistances as rooted in contradictory values
- To reframe rigid views about effective pedagogical practices
- To signify contradictory and competing accountabilities
- To contemplate in order to build repertoires of practice
- To anticipate contradictions of interest in forms of support
- To make educational construals for future use

Mentors would be expected to demonstrate the following competencies of *Participation*:

- To validate and affirm interactions
- To carry out agency

- To appropriate mediation tools to reconcile between different texts
- To recognize culturally diverse texts and privileged and rejected discourses
- To mediate professional learning guided by a sense of commitment and responsibility
- To exhibit activism informed by an ethics of care
- To negotiate contradictions in interaction
- To deal with conflicts of loyalty and commitment while carrying out agency
- To attend to culturally valued texts in potentially intimidating interactions, forging awareness of the core values that direct the mentor in his/her construal of a professional self
- To appropriate texts from teaching, mentoring, and leadership interdiscursively
- To engage in validating and affirming reciprocal communal learning as a way of empowering autonomous professionals to lead innovation and change at the workplace.

Mentors would be expected to demonstrate the following competencies of *Improvisation*:

- To connect emotionally and professionally to respond to contextual differences
- To translate behavior into here-and-now patterns and modes of assistance
- To compose activity drawing on recurring patterns of action
- To analyze practice systematically
- To respond to connections between theoretical concepts and practices 'in action' in the context of mentors' work as well as in broader contexts of the practice.
- To encourage the mentee to discharge feelings toward rationalization of action
- To intervene to mitigate conflicts
- To foreground connections between cultural codes, values, and strategic and pedagogic reasoning
- To call upon knowledge and procedures to demonstrate and direct action

Given the dialogical and embedded character of positioning and construing within the different domains of praxis, the above outcomes would be evidenced interrelatedly and inclusively in activity.

9.6.3 Selection of Participants

The passage from being a teacher of children to becoming a mentor of teachers, as I have tried to show, does not occur naturally. Rather, it is a highly conscious and gradual process of reorganizing and reconstructing beliefs and understandings that the novice mentor holds from other professional experiences in order to make sense of the new context of mentoring (McIntyre & Hagger, 1993; Orland, 1997). As such, it is important to develop a set of prerequisites and criteria for the selection of mentors. Given the multifaceted, multidimensional, and complex character of the practice, it would be rather limiting to assume that being close to what Berliner (2001) defines as an expert teacher is enough of a consideration for recruiting potentially successful mentors. Beyond expertise, it seems imperative to consider qualities that go beyond cognitive skills and abilities, to include those of emotional intelligence, such as the degree of participants' 'reality testing' (Bar-On, 2000), empathy and disposition to, and active involvement in self inquiry and reflection. If so, criteria that touch upon some of the tendencies identified in Smith and Strahan's (2004) prototype of expertise in teaching might be applicable to expert mentors as well: A sense of confidence in themselves and in their profession; the ability to develop relationships with teachers; contributing to the teaching profession through leadership and service; and showing evidence that they are masters in content areas (p. 365) (In Orland-Barak, 2005).

9.7 Evaluation of Professional Learning

9.7.1 Principles Underlying Authentic Assessment

We assess what we teach: This is a basic principle in any kind of informed assessment scheme, whether formative or summative, school-based, university-based, or practice-based. A discursive, dialogical perspective to learning to mentor-as-praxis calls for an evaluation of professional learning that is congruent with the approach, orientation, processes, and modalities of work espoused by the relevant program. In tune with Wiggins (1989), assessments should reflect professionals' intellectual work, and they need to be characterized by active engagement, exploration, and inquiry on the part of the student being appraised. Hence, the notion of *authentic assessment* is particularly relevant and reflective of the context sensitive and process-oriented curriculum suggested in this chapter. In the context of teaching, Darling-Hammond (2000) characterizes authentic assessments as those that sample the actual knowledge, skills, and dispositions of teachers in teaching and learning contexts; require the integration of multiple types of knowledge and skill; rely on multiple sources of evidence collected over time and in diverse contexts; and are evaluated using codified professional standards.

A praxical view of learning to mentor, embedding a constructivist pedagogical orientation would, then, call for an orientation to the assessment and evaluation of professional learning which embeds similar characteristics to those of *authentic assessment in teaching*:

- It is formative, that is, it focuses on process and development of learning over time. This implies that participants are assessed at various points throughout the course, each time with a focus on how they have progressed in a particular area as compared to the previous time.
- It employs a variety of modalities for assessing ongoing progress. Different modalities would include processes such as observations, conversations, interviews as conversations, simulations, written reflections, accounts of field experiences, etc.

- It draws on a variety of contexts and genres for assessing competence and performance. Contexts of learning would, thus, integrate academic learning, theoretical learning in practice, and practical learning in practice. Genres for assessing in such contexts would include combining the use of cases, portfolio, story, academic texts, transcripts of mentoring conversations, video, visual triggers, etc.
- Feedback is based on a collection of evidence from multiple sources. This means that the final assessment should attribute relative weight to all the different sources of evidence, including different contents, contexts, and development of processes.
- It is both an individual and a collective process. That is, assessment criteria and evidence need to be construed as a group process, through peer assessment and/or self assessment.
- It is representative of the areas of knowledge competence and performance in each of the three domains of appreciation, participation, and improvisation.
- It includes authentic performance tasks that reflect the embeddedness, complexity, and situatedness of real-life mentoring scenarios. This suggests that assessment tasks should integrate simultaneous performance in a variety of competencies and skills – as close as possible to how they would present themselves in authentic activity.
- Criteria for assessment are transparent and negotiated amongst participants. That is, participants should be familiar with and take part in the process of developing criteria for assessment.
- It is dynamic and considers performance in a variety of contexts. This implies that assessment criteria would identify a core of basic competencies alongside distinctive criteria that attend to specific expectations and/or constraints of different mentoring context.
- It attends to specific products of learning. In other words, in addition to its formative character, assessment is oriented toward an end product evidence of learning.

9.7.2 Authentic Assessment Tasks in Academic Courses for Mentors

Let us examine some examples of authentic assessment tasks that abide by the above principles, as part of an academic course for mentors.

Appraising Expectations Over Time

During the first mentoring session the course professor hands out a series of open-ended questions that invite participants to write their expectations of themselves during the course, of the group, and of the course leader. The completed handout is folded and given to the course leader in an envelope with the participant's name. The envelope is kept closed until the end of the course.

During the last session participants open the envelope, reread their initial assumptions/expectations and revise them according to new insights they have gained throughout the year – with a focus on conceptualizing the nature of their shifts over time as well as of their development as shaped by the different encounters with academic learning contexts, with theoretical learning in practice, and with practical learning in practice.

Appraising Evolving Concepts of Mentoring

In addition to the questions around expectations, participants are asked to address five questions regarding their initial concept of mentoring: (1) What are the main dilemmas of a mentor? (2) What is possible to achieve in mentoring? (3) What is not possible to achieve in mentoring? (4) What are the skills and strategies that mentors need to acquire? (5) What are the main questions that concern mentors?

Similarly to the first set of questions, responses are collected in an envelope and then reopened and revised at the end of the course.

The two components of self appraisal focus on the conceptualization of the learning to mentor process over time, with an emphasis on participants' articulation of their evolving constructions of their professional image.

Assessment of Concepts Over Time

In addition to the process of developing a professional image, self assessment tasks can focus on the development of content knowledge. One example is the evolving 'dictionary of notions' that participants compile, revise, and extend throughout a course. At the beginning of the course the course leader hands out a comprehensive list of notions to be covered during the year. In the middle of the semester participants are asked to select, amongst the notions covered, those that are particularly relevant for them and provide an informed explanation of their meanings to the rest of the group. Participants repeat the process at the end of the course. In addition, they are required to add new notions to the list as they emerge from experiences, readings, and/or the learning conversations. They are asked to elaborate on the new notions, showing their relevance for particular activities and experiences, as well as their connection to other theoretical sources.

Another example is asking students to fill in an alphabetic list with concepts that were discussed during the sessions. Students are, then, asked to choose the most relevant concept for them and create a collaborative activity for the group around the concept, drawing on relevant theory and practice.

Assessment of Mentoring Over Time

Participants are asked to submit ongoing reflections on recorded mentoring sessions every month. The guidelines for reflection are constructed together between participants and the course leader and revised/extended/refined as new insights are gained over time. A final metareflection on the whole process is submitted at the end of the year. This is handed back to the student with emergent questions to deepen and refine reflection on particular issues identified by the course professor.

Chapter 10
Records of Mentoring Practices

> Experience is the richest source of adult learning; therefore, the
> core methodology of adult education is the analysis of
> experience
>
> (Knowles, 1978, p. 31).

Knowles' call for attending to experience as core to professional learning in adult education goes back as early as 1938, when John Dewey developed the concept of 'experiential growth' as core to the development of school children, teachers, and professionals in general. Indeed, to date, much of adult education underscores problem-solving and inquiry-oriented pedagogues that address the social development of the learner and the quality of his/her total experience. The prevalent view is that adult learning is more effective when it is relevant to the participants' 'vicarious experiences' (Stake, 1988), to their daily dilemmas, concerns, and stages of professional development (Knowles, 1978; Hunt, 1978; Brundage & MacKerarcher, 1980), and when it allows for adult learners to share these experiences with other colleagues in conversational frameworks that are both challenging and supportive (Florio-Ruane, 1991; Connelly & Clandinin, 1995; Clark, 1995; Rust & Orland, 2000).

10.1 Constructivist Pedagogies

Experiential learning speaks to constructivist pedagogies, which advocate that knowledge is created and not received (Von Glasserfeld, 1996), and socially constructed and mediated by discourse, rather than transferred by talk (Vygotsky, 1962). In this vein, learning is an active process of making sense of the world (Dewey, 1933; Rorty, 1980) and requires open-ended, challenging, and meaningful tasks that engage the learner in multiple perspectives on the issue at stake (Fox, 2001; Korthagen & Vasalos, 2005). Programs also advocate creating spaces for sharing experiences with other colleagues in evolving 'dialogues of practice,' as a way of organizing content to make it meaningful for professional practice (Gudmundsdottir, 1991). In these spaces, participants' schemas can be reconstructed to develop more encompassing and complex gestalts about the connection

L. Orland-Barak, *Learning to Mentor-as-Praxis*, Professional Learning and
Development in Schools and Higher Education 4, DOI 10.1007/978-1-4419-0582-6_10,
© Springer Science+Business Media, LLC 2010

between theory and practice (Korthagen & Kessels, 1999). Thus, the discourse of constructivist pedagogy speaks to a framework for thought and action which is dialogically constituted, as people enter into conversation with one another (Bakhtin, 1981), embedding a multiplicity of discourses, grounded in participants' past and present discourses, each carrying particular values and ideologies (Fairclough, 1992; Gee, 1996; Miller-Marsh, 2002; Elbaz-Luwisch, Moen, & Gudmunsdottir, 2002).

The above features, underlying constructivist pedagogy, operate as a conceptual platform that informs the design and implementation of appropriate teaching methodologies, and modalities of work, tools, and processes of learning.

How does the rhetoric, advocating constructivist discourses of practice in teacher education, play out 'in action'? How does it translate to particular methodologies of action? Chapters 10 and 11 elaborate on the use of a variety of methodologies, drawing on 'records of authentic practice' that reflect constructivist approaches to adult learning. Chapter 10 describes and examines different modalities of work grounded in constructivist approaches to professional learning: Case study, portfolios, critical incidents, video, action, research, and the use of visual texts. Chapter 11 takes the reader into the affordances and limitations of constructivist teaching methodologies for particular contexts of mentoring and mentored learning.

10.2   Using Cases in Academic Learning

> ...Case writing involves more than recall. Teachers and their collaborators are reconstructing and constructing their experiences and understandings. What emerges is often new understanding that was not available to the writer at the time of the original experience (Shulman, 1992, p. 19).

Case-based instruction reflects a view of learning as a contextualized and local activity, embedded in a particular site, time, and space and shaped by the multiple field dilemmas that practitioners manage in their practice (Moje & Wade, 1997). In preservice education, cases are used as instances exemplifying theoretical principles, maxims, and norms (Shulman, 1986), and for preparing prospective students for the context complexity of classrooms, providing context-bound knowledge of specific scenes and situations that they are likely to encounter and problems around which they will be required to frame and resolve (Carter, 1988; Harrington & Garrison, 1992). Their incorporation, as selected teaching cases, often constitutes an integral component of teacher preparation programs.

Unlike their use in preservice education, cases in in-service education programs reflect more narrative traditions of personal and collaborative story writing, as catalysts for professional growth and change (Kagan, 1993). The primary 'cases' used in these contexts are, thus, authentic stories from the field, written by participants and sued as working texts in staff development programs. The following is an example of a university course that was designed as a case-based graduate pedagogy course for mentors as part of their M.A. program (Adapted from Orland-Barak, 2002).

10.2.1 Process and Content

During the first weeks of study, students were asked to read academic articles selected by the course professor, on the area of Mentoring and Mentored Learning. During the sessions, participants were asked to identify the theoretical notions and major questions addressed in the articles. These were then examined in light of their own cases. For example, when students read about the notion of reciprocity in mentoring, they were asked to identify the forms and meanings that reciprocity takes in the unfolding of their case. The discussions in class focused on establishing connections and surfacing emergent gaps between recent trends in research on mentoring and the context of their practice. Students were also given two published cases to read as samples of possible ways of writing cases. These were analyzed and discussed during the sessions with a focus on what constitutes a case, on the boundaries of a case as compared to other narrative modes (such as journal writing, autobiographical writing), and the ways in which cases can be written, presented, and dealt with as working texts during mentoring sessions. These preliminary sessions led to a class activity around the construction of guidelines with reflective questions to frame the writing and presentation of the mentors' cases in class. In addition, the group designed a framework for evaluating the presentation of the case and for reflecting on the experience following the discussion in class. The guidelines were negotiated in class between the group and the course professor. The ten weeks that followed focused on the writing of the participants' cases and their presentation to the rest of the group.

The original cases, written by the mentors, were collected before they were presented to the group. During the sessions, some participants took turns in writing protocols of the sessions. The course professor also maintained a journal to include reflections and field notes related to what she thought the participants were learning, to the dynamics of the conversations as opportunities for learning, and to points or issues that she wished to stress in the sessions that followed. Following the presentation of their cases, participants were required to submit a paper focusing on their learning from the experience as related to the guidelines for evaluation and reflection.

10.2.2 Insights Gained

10.2.2.1 Reframing Perspectives, Recognizing Gaps, and Validating Interactions

An academic context for 'learning from experience,' through the writing and sharing of cases, constitutes an important opportunity for developing competencies in the domains of appreciation and participation, in the context of academic learning. As participants shared their cases with the group, they were prompted to reconstruct their initial readings of the stories, often reframing perspectives and ingrained assumptions about the case. The cases allowed for typifying collective stories of

practice, as invoked by the different social and professional Discourses of participants. The writing and sharing of cases enabled mentors' to reframe perspectives
on resistances and to signify competing accountabilities as they interpreted experience anew through collaborative meaning-making. At the end of the year group
interview-as-conversation one of the mentors commented:

> One of the things that was most difficult for me was having to put my experiences on paper,
> bearing in mind that it had to describe what I went through in terms of the situation and . . .
> convey a certain conflict that I have about my practice. It was kind of exposing myself to
> the group, beyond the plot itself . . . and it was interesting for me to realize, as I was writing
> the case, how, by deciding what to include and what not, I could see the case with different
> eyes . . . and I kind of found that challenging . . . .

10.2.2.2 Recognizing Boundaries and Signifying Accountabilities

Mentors used the writing of cases as an opportunity for articulating conflicts of
mediation between personal understandings and values, and the external requirements of the job as elaborated by policy makers, administrators, teachers, and
inspectors. The conversations around the cases also allowed for recognizing boundaries and for signifying accountabilities as they compared practices across contexts.
The mentors' stories were about genuine conflicts and dilemmas in their practice,
depicting the real story rather than 'heroic Hollywood plot and stories portraying a
preferred identity' (Convery, 1999; Connelly & Clandinin, 1990).

10.2.2.3 Representing Experience Publicly

Writing for an audience in an academic setting encouraged the participants to make
their private cases public. In trying to convey their perspective to an audience,
within the constraints of a case (as compared to more lengthy registers such as
journal writing) and within the time limitations of the course sessions, the mentors were encouraged to elaborate a concise 'scene' that described and interpreted
their actions, feelings, and thoughts. Said that, many participants found the imposed
constraints of time and length somehow problematic:

> . . .Translating the real experience into a short case felt to me like reducing my actions,
> feelings and thoughts into a two page document . . .

10.2.3 Constructivist Principles in a Pedagogy of Cases

A pedagogy of cases, in the context of academic learning, engages mentors in critical self scrutiny of the ideologies, beliefs, and dispositions that are surfaced through
the cases that they choose to share. In the process of constructing the case for an
audience, participants are encouraged to make connections between personal interpretations and contextual constructions. The variety of cases presented stressed new
encounters, dialogues, and communal processes of meaning-making, challenging

participants to clarify ambiguities, to articulate a rationale behind action, and to conceptualize personal experiences into personal theories of practice.

The task guidelines for writing a case, sharing it with others, and engaging in critical conversation around the case (see task details below) encouraged examination of roles and provided opportunities for critically examining how systemic factors shape the nature of mentors' work, for articulating practice and for examining instances of dissonance. The academic framing of the course also allowed for participants to critically scrutinize their cases, integrating field experience with theoretical insights from the course literature. The fact that participants were assessed on the basis of the depth of their reflections and on their ability to problematize practice encouraged them to 'think deeper' and to write cases that generated confrontation, disagreement, and challenge for the participants:

> ... knowing that I was going to be evaluated, not on the basis of a right or wrong action but on what I learn from it, really forced me to look for a way in which my case could raise questions and even disagreement on certain issues...

Five Levels of Case Analysis

- **Informative diagnostic:**
  What happened? What did I do? What developed as a result of the case?
- **Contextual:**
  What leads me/prompts me to tell the story?
  What caused the situation?
  How does it relate to other incidents from my professional experience?
- **Emotional:**
  What does it do to me?
  How do I feel?
- **Interpretative:**
  What can the case teach me about mentoring?
  What can I learn from the case?
- **Deliberative:**
  What will I do if I find myself in a similar situation in the future?

Guidelines for Case Discussions

Questions jointly constructed by the group

Content of the case:
What dilemmas/conflicts surfaced in your case?
What was common to other cases?
What did your case reveal about:
   Personal theories?
   Practices? Skills?

What did you chose to stress in your case?
What did you chose not to stress? Why?

Personal and collective value
Why was the case brought to the audience?
   (to get reactions/to stress success)
   (to stress failure/to teach others)
   (to learn about oneself?)
How did the story develop in light of the reactions?
What can I learn from the case about myself? Others?
How does it connect to other cases?
What determined the choice of case?
What is this a case of . . .? in relation to my practice and my role?

Guidelines for Evaluation of the Presentation of Cases

(1) Organization:
   Approach . . . .
   Role of the narrator . . . .
   Role of the audience . . . .
   The process of presenting the case . . . .
(2) Guidelines for reflection on the cases:
   I learned that.....
   I thought that....
   I wonder about....
   I was surprised that. . .
(3) New questions:
   I changed my ideas about . . . . I connected to . . . .
   I was reminded of . . . .
   I discovered gaps . . . .
   I was surprised to hear that . . . .

10.3 Using Critical Incidents

Critical incidents are those occurrences that let us see with new eyes some aspect of what
we do. They make us aware of the beliefs and assumptions that underlie our instructional
practice (Newman, 1990, p. 17)

A similar channel to case study is the use of critical incidents as a constructivist pedagogy. A critical incident can be very generally described as an event or
events that are of particular significance to the professional life of the writer/person
(Tripp, 1993, Flanagan, 1954). These events are usually surfaced at the intersection

between moral and pedagogical dilemmas (Orland-Barak, 2003b), while mentors act upon relational, deliberative, and critical roles (Valli, 1990), in their interactions with mentees. Critical incidents can, then, reveal how mentors' pedagogical reasoning operates alongside their strong sense of moral obligation toward the well-being of the mentee.

10.3.1 Process and Content

The professional course, conducted at a major university in the north of Israel, was designed to provide ongoing support to a team of ten mentors selected to assist university graduate teachers in their first year of induction, into teaching both in Jewish and Arab schools (Strahovsky, Marbach, & Hertz-Lazarowitz, 1998). Mentors were encouraged to function as facilitators, collaborators, cothinkers, and as support figures to the mentee.

Participants working in the intervention project were given ongoing support through regular monthly meetings, in the company of the project leader and a facilitator/researcher. The purpose of the support sessions was to encourage the mentors to voice their dilemmas from the field. In addition to providing an open space for participants to freely share burning issues and dilemmas, the mentors were invited to write and share stories about memorable critical incidents in their practice.

The writing of critical incidents was as an open-ended process, in order to ensure maximum freedom for participants to include the critical or memorable incidents that they wished to write. To this end, general guidelines for the form and content of the stories were provided and phrased as open-ended questions in order to preserve the open nature of the task. Participants were also encouraged to respond to two prompts: (a) Give the story a name and (b) What does the story reveal about your practice of mentoring? (Orland-Barak, 2003b)

The following questions were the guidelines for the writing of critical incidents:
When writing your story, the following questions might guide your thinking:

(1) Why did I choose this particular story?
(2) What important details and information about my context do I need to include?
(3) Who was involved? What happened?
(4) What did I think then? And now?
(5) How did I feel? And now?
(6) What did I do?
(7) What is this a case of in my mentoring?
(8) What did I learn about myself?
(9) What did I learn about mentoring?
(10) What new questions has this story raised?

10.3.2 Insights Gained

10.3.2.1 A Channel for Articulating Moral Stances

The writing of critical incidents constituted an authentic platform for articulating moral stances as mentors, toward administrative, educational, and professional matters. The incidents underscore mentors' supportive roles as carers and as moral agents to their mentees in critical situations. Values that they cherished as experienced teachers, such as integrity, care and caring, and responsibility and commitment, were transformed into mediation tools that instructed and directed novices about 'what ought to be done' in diverse critical incidents.

10.3.2.2 Participation Through Traditional Images of Support

As mentors shared their stories of critical incidents, they were able to draw commonalities in their perception of roles in such situations. For example, they realized that in critical incidents, where their mentees' well-being was at stake, they all acted upon more traditional images of the mentor as 'the wise experienced teacher,' sharing their personal vision and understanding of the situation through less symmetrical and more prescriptive forms of intervention.

10.4 Using Portfolio in Academic Learning

> ...Constructing a portfolio was a meaningful learning experience for me: It was the first time, both as teacher and mentor, that I could test in practice what I learned in a seminar course and explore its relevance to my situation almost in real time. (Mentor, portfolio entry)

The use of portfolios to record and evaluate professional learning from experience is well documented in the literature of teacher education (Farr Darling, 2001; Loughran & Corrigan, 1995; Tillema, 1998). Hence, the decision to introduce the portfolio as a tool in teacher education is influenced by the recent views of reflective practice, systematic engagement, and documentation of action as evidence-based practice (Tillema & Smith, 2000). Accordingly, practitioners are encouraged to document reflection through portfolios, as catalysts of professional growth and change and as primary working texts in staff development and mentoring programs. Thus, many in-service mentoring programs are structured around opportunities for mentors to develop reflective practice. In the two courses presented in this section, participants were asked to construct and present a portfolio as a way of documenting the learning. The portfolio as a tool for documentation of experience allowed for engaging in reflective processes at cognitive, emotional, and metacognitive levels (Wade & Yarbrough, 1996; Loughran & Corrigan, 1995) (Adapted from Orland-Barak, 2005b).

10.4.1 Process and Content

The two in-service courses reflected different orientations in the use of the portfolio in academic learning. In each course, the criteria for using portfolios were based on different answers to the following questions:

- What purpose does it serve?
- Who determines what goes into the portfolio?
- What is the degree of specification for the kind of evidence?
- How is the evidence organized?
- What are the forms of participation in the construction process?
- What is the involvement of the course leader?
- How is the portfolio presented?
  (Zeichner & Wray, 2001)

10.4.1.1 The 'Product Portfolio' Course

The 'product portfolio' course for in-service mentors emphasized the use of the portfolio as a tool for representing the 'products of learning' of a new national English curriculum. The course, mandated by the English Inspectorate in the northern region of Israel, was intended to equip mentors to disseminate the new approach to language teaching in schools.

In tune with the new curriculum's requirement that portfolios be used as tools for alternative assessment in teaching, the in-service mentoring course required mentors to compile a collaborative professional development portfolio as evidence of their learning throughout the year. In terms of purpose, the portfolio aimed at documenting mentors' learning of the new curriculum.

The guidelines for the writing of the portfolio entries were given in advance by the course leaders. These included:

- A cover letter
- Lesson plans and assessment performance tasks, according to the new curriculum
- Records of the mentors' meetings with teachers on the new curriculum
- Reflections on the process of learning.

Although participants were required to document their learning process sequentially throughout the course, the mode of presentation of evidence was left to the participants. In terms of participation in the construction process of the portfolio, participants were encouraged to construct group portfolios to be presented at the end of the course. Thus, participants chose to collaborate with each other either

on the basis of prior professional or personal contacts, or on the basis of relationships that grew out of their participation in the course. Collaboration in the process
of constructing entries was not, however, stated as an aim, since the sessions were
not structured to allot time for participants to share their entries or to actually construct the portfolio in class. Thus, the course leaders were not actively involved in
the process of constructing the reflective group entries. At the end of the course,
the portfolios were presented as 'final products' to the rest of the group. As a result,
mentors got accreditation for the course. By contrast, the 'process portfolio' adapted
to a different type of in-service course.

10.4.1.2   The 'Process Portfolio' Course

The 'process portfolio' was seen by the course leaders as an opportunity for mentors
of student teachers to become acquainted with the portfolio as an innovative form of
practice, for collaboratively experimenting with the process of writing a portfolio,
as a loop into learning about its uses, and for consequently disseminating it as a tool
for assisting and evaluating student teachers, throughout their practice of teaching
at school.

The conversations on the use of portfolios provided a basis for the mentors to
begin constructing their own portfolio as a form of 'learning by doing.' As the
semester progressed, sections of the portfolios were presented to the whole group
during the sessions and participants gave feedback to each other in the process of
constructing, analyzing, and evaluating the entries.

> The content of the portfolios was left to the participants' discretion. After a
> number of deliberations, it was decided by the group that they would include a
> section entitled 'sentence completion' to create a shared framework for exam-
> ining each other's entries. The sentence completion format entailed completing
> sentence beginnings such as:
>
> - I learned that. . .
> - I was surprised to hear/read that. . .
> - I do not agree with. . .
> - I would like to. . .
> - I have changed my mind about. . .

Regarding the organization of evidence, participants could decide on how they
wanted to organize their learning. In relation to forms of participation in the construction process, mentors were asked to construct individual portfolios during
the course, and the entries were brought to the sessions and shared with participants throughout the course. Thus, in contrast to the 'product' portfolio, the
sessions were structured to promote collaboration by allowing participants to negotiate meanings and, as a result, revise their entries. The course professor, thus,

functioned as mediator during the sharing of the portfolio entries and intervened to assist participants in the process of creating their reflective entries. The portfolio was submitted to the course professor at the termination of the course. Unlike the 'product portfolio,' the 'process portfolio' was not formally assessed. Its completion was seen as part of the requirements of ongoing participation in the course.

Table 10.1 compares the 'process' and 'product' portfolio based on Zeichner and Wray's (2001) framework of the conditions of portfolio use (Orland-Barak, 2005).

Table 10.1 Process and product portfolios: A comparison

Conditions	Process portfolio	Product portfolio
What purpose does it serve?	To document mentors' process of learning to construct a portfolio.	To document mentors' learning of a new curriculum.
Who determines what goes into the portfolio?	The mentors together with the course leaders	The course leaders
Degree of specification of the kind of evidence	*Semi-open*: To 'reflect' on the process of learning to construct a portfolio. Completing open statements such as: I learned that . . . . I changed my mind about. . . I am concerned about. . . I was surprised to learn . . .	*Standardized specifications*: * lesson plans according to the new curriculum * specification of sessions with the mentees * adaptation of materials according to the new curriculum * integration of the new concepts and terminology into the lessons * observations of teachers using the new curriculum in class * reflections on the process
Organization of the evidence	Open	Chronological organization of the learning process throughout the year.
Forms of participation in the construction process	Individual portfolios constructed during the course. Entries shared with participants during the course.	Group portfolios constructed at the end of the course. No process of sharing of entries during the year.
Involvement of the course leader	Course leader functioned as mediator during the sharing of the portfolio entries and intervened in the process of creating reflective entries.	No active involvement. Course leaders did not intervene in the process of creating reflective entries.
Presentation	Submitted to the course leaders at the termination of the course.	Submitted to the course leaders at the termination of the course.

10.4.2 Insights Gained About Processes and Products in Portfolio Writing

10.4.2.1 Collaboration Toward Joint Meaning-Making

In the 'product portfolio,' the mentors shared and negotiated meanings toward the production and presentation of a team portfolio. In the process of joint construction, they validated and affirmed interactions, recognized culturally diverse texts, engaged in validating and affirming reciprocal communal learning, connected to each other emotionally and professionally, and analyzed practice systematically toward a final product. The articulation of the process of collaboration that participants engaged in was then used by the mentor of mentors (the course professor) as a loop learning activity for gaining insights into similar processes that mentors can trigger in their own contexts. Hence, the activity provided a learning setting for demonstrating processes of appreciation, participation, and improvisation through communal learning. The infrastructure of engagement (Wenger, 1998) toward the instrumental goal of constructing and presenting a group portfolio sustained a rich, communal learning process.

10.4.2.2 Taking Perspective and Analyzing Practice Systematically

The two tasks of constructing a process and/or a product portfolio suggest that the quality of reflection resides less in the use of different types of portfolios to address different purposes, and more in the *collaborative process of participation* in constructing a group portfolio. Such a process can become a powerful learning opportunity for participants to critically and systematically articulate their practice and for gaining new perspectives as they reflect on how they negotiate emergent contradictions individually and collaboratively in the group. Participants' positive dispositions toward constructing a portfolio as an opportunity for development suggest its potential for professional learning and development in the context of academic learning.

10.4.3 Constructivist Principles in the Use of Portfolio Tasks

The task of constructing a portfolio underscores, by nature of its design, a constructivist approach to professional learning: It calls for attending to the dynamic connections between what is learned, how it is learned, and why it is learned; it encourages the integration of knowledge and perspective taking; it requires personal involvement and conceptualization of processes building on prior learning; and it involves the mentor in the construction and development of learning products and outcomes, toward maximum ownership of learning. As a collective activity, the task challenges participants to analyze personal and collective decision-making processes toward their integration into a joint collaborative products and personal rationale on and for future action. The task guidelines for writing a portfolio, for sharing the process with others, and for evaluating process and outcomes provided a guided yet open-enough framework for representing idiosyncratic as well as partici-patory understandings of the practice of mentoring. Mentors also perceived the task of documenting their learning and of working toward a final written product as an upgrading of their professional status. As with the pedagogy of cases, the academic framing of the course encouraged participants to engage in critical reflection, inte-grating field experience with theoretical insights from the course literature. It also allowed for establishing crucial connections between field work and academic work, initiating and sustaining important dialogic spaces between knowledge grounded in field experiences and knowledge grounded in the academia. The final assessment of the portfolios also provided a positive and challenging incentive for participants to scrutinize and introspect into their roles and practices.

10.5   Using Visuals in Academic Learning

Writing paints pictures with words, while drawing speaks with lines and colors . . . Cultural research encourages to give to the concept 'text' a wider meaning in order to include visual images in it (Mitchell & Weber, 1996, p. 304).

The integration of verbal with nonverbal modes of expression has gained pre-dominance in the field of teacher education as a way of representing experience. Visual techniques, specifically the activity of drawing lines, have been used to explore the memorable persons, concerns, and events that teachers attributed to their professional careers. Images and drawings are used as a way of understanding teach-ers and teaching (Denicolo & Pope, 1990; Pope & Denicolo, 1986; Radnowsky, 1996; Mitchell & Weber, 1996; Orland, 2000; Beijaard, Van Driel, & Verloop, 1999; Conway, 2001; Johnson, 2002; Ben Peretz, Mendelson, & Kron, 2003) and for engaging participants in the representation of critical passages in their profes-sional careers. Nonverbal reflection evokes a kind of semantic memory (Linton, 1979) that allows for conveying the 'gist' of participants' perception of their devel-opment. It also speaks to Vygotsky's nonverbal mediational tools through which the learner through assisted performance advances through his/her zone of proximal development (Lantolf, 1994). Thus, visual representations can constitute a comple-mentary nonlinguistic mode for constructing qualitatively unique understandings of how the visual and the nonvisual mutually define and support each other while repre-senting learning from experience (Radnowsky, 1996, Johnson, 2002). They suggest a creative platform for uncovering participants' views and thoughts and function as metaphoric tools for articulating emotional and rational aspects of experience integratively.

10.5.1 Process and Content

Draw your concept of mentoring and of a mentoring conversation

One of the major components of the Master's university course entitled Mentoring Skills and Practices was the focus on mentoring conversations.

Participants (experienced and prospective mentors) read academic research and professional literature on the topic, encouraging connections between conceptual notions and mentoring conversations which they were asked to record from their own practical work. As a trigger for initiating the topic around the second month of studies, participants in two different courses were asked to portray their concept of mentoring (in the first course) and of a mentoring conversation (in the second course). They were asked to use any geometric forms, lines, or pictures that best conveyed their ideas. After drawing their graphic representations, mentors volunteered to share their representations with the rest of the group. Participants were also asked to write a brief paragraph explaining the significance of the graphic representation. The activity lasted for almost an entire three hour class period.

10.5.2 Insights Gained

10.5.2.1 Recognizing and Confronting Gaps

The visual representations prompted participants to convey a holistic image of what participants' practice 'looks like and feels like' (Orland-Barak, 2000). Their use stressed the potential of nonvisual modes for enhancing processes of appreciation, as participants uncovered ambiguities, reframed controversies, and confronted realistic and idealistic perceptions of their professional experiences (Orland, 2000; Orland-Barak & Klein, 2005).

Nonvisual representations, as complementary written and oral texts, helped participants to confront gaps between ingrained assumptions and ideologies and their actual performance in that practice. The activity also encouraged the appreciation of dominant narratives of accountability, challenging mentors to recognize the privileged and rejected discourses that play out in their actual participation in the mentoring conversation (while analyzing the written transcription of the mentoring conversation and comparing it to the visual representation). Reflecting on how these dominant narratives play out in their attributions (through the visual representation), on the one hand, and in their talk, on the other hand, assisted to foreground connections and gaps between experience, action, beliefs, and knowledge. As such, the activity calls for becoming aware of modes of improvisation as informed by how mentors appreciate the often contradictory discourses embedded in their work.

10.5.2.2 Creating a Multivoiced Text for Typifying Mentoring

The visual representation, the annotations, and the verbal transcription of the conversations created a kind of multivoiced text, embracing a multiplicity of perspectives (Lather, 1992) that allowed for appraising mentor's pedagogical practices by typifying and signifying conflicting professional identities, codes of behavior, and moral stances toward mentoring. Confronting these two can, then, constitute a unique mirror into participants' appreciation of their practice. It can also unveil the presence or trace of one discourse within another (Fairclough, 1992; Lewis & Ketter, 2004) while becoming aware of how mediation and support play out in participation. This can lead to more dynamic rearticulations of otherwise stable discourses, bearing transformative potential for participants (Fairclough, 1992). The value of including the nonverbal representations along with the verbal sources lies, therefore, in the potential of their combination for surfacing conflicting and often incompatible discourses embedded in appreciation, participation, and improvisation at the meeting between academic and practical learning.

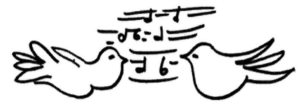

Annotation: *a mentoring conversation creates harmony between the mentor and the mentee. At the beginning they are strangers to each other and at a later stage they are able to 'sing' together. Both the mentor and the mentee have wings, that is, each of them has the opportunity to fly in her own way at the end of the collaborative relationship.*

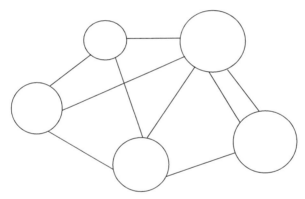

Annotation: *each of the participants in the conversation listens, thinks, reacts, contributes, and learns from the other. Each participant is at the same time a mentor and a mentee.*

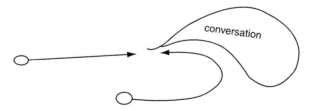

Annotation: *each comes from her own path, often parallel, not really equal, and at this meeting point the conversation begins to emerge.*

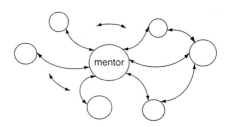

Annotation: *the illustration conveys the relationship between the mentor and the mentees and amongst the mentees. The cyclical dynamic form [of the illustration] shows that everything revolves around the mentor, who is a kind of leader, someone who leads processes in her group.*

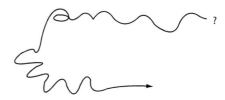

Annotation: *the conversation begins with a question or request. The mentor or the mentee relates to this question and the other listens. The dialogue develops into ups or downs, into an unknown route with different possibilities until reaching the target that can suit any of the two sides (Adapted from Orland-Barak & Klein, 2005).*

10.5.3 Using Visuals to Construct Knowledge

Tasks that encourage the use of visuals allow for constructing a qualitatively different understanding of experience, one in which the visual and the nonvisual mutually define and support each other. As a constructivist methodology, it helps construe one's 'story of action' (Clandinin & Connelly, 1987; Goodson, 1992), as shaped by prior learning and experiences, combining person, text, and task. In the process, participants become active interpreters of their own experiences, bringing forth a holistic and impressionistic integration of the forms and meanings that they attribute to their roles and practice. Of a constructivist nature, the task allowed for personal involvement and social construction of meaning, encouraged deep introspection and analysis, and generated talk around complex constructs, perceptions, and feelings.

Creating and sharing the different lines and interpretations constituted a process of construction and reconstruction, exchange and negotiation of practical and experiential knowledge. The activity encouraged participants to reconstruct the varied, dynamic but also cyclical and repetitive patterns of practice. As the participants explained their lines to each other, they were consciously engaged in the transformation of their thinking from a visual to a verbal mode. In the process of explaining their visual representations to others, they engaged in the construction of new understandings of their appreciation of and participation in the experience:

> It is in this explaining to others that we come to a clearer understanding ourselves of how we are thinking about ideas and actions. We learn from listening to ourselves explain to someone else how we are thinking about ideas and actions. In that explanation we relive the experience . . . and in reliving the experience we create the opportunity to reframe and reinterpret that experience in ways that [might] impact subsequent thought and action (Pfeiffer, Featherstone & Smith, 1993).

10.6 Using Video in Theoretical Learning in Practice

Video as a medium for reflection on experience has been, since the early nineties, a commonly used methodology in teacher education. Video is being used in the context of community learning, as a reflective additional tool to journal writing (Pultorak, 1993), as a tool for encouraging thinking aloud processes by mentors (Hatton & Smith, 1995), and as an integral component of action research projects in teacher education (Sherin & Ham, 2004). Video is also widely used for stimulated recall techniques (Bloom, 1953, Kagan, Krathwohl & Miller, 1963, Leikin & Dinur, 2003).

The integration of video triggers both reflection on action and delayed reflection, offering important advantages for enhancing learning to teach and mentoring processes: It allows for monitoring learning by providing new angles of observation on action. It also encourages participants to reflect, to examine themselves critically, and to understand teaching and learning in new ways (Sherin, 2002; Sherin & Ham, 2004). It also helps shifting from a focus on the teacher to a focus on the learner (Hammer, 2000; Richardson & Kile, 1999). From the perspective of mentors, it allows them to reflect on and for their actions (Conway, 2001) during a mentoring interaction, enabling the development of new insights about their mentoring styles (Sherin & Ham, 2004) and helping them to reframe their practical knowledge. Delayed reflection is also regarded as an important opportunity for encouraging detachment from the immediate experience, allowing for deeper analysis and reflection on the thoughts and actions that guided particular classroom actions – a kind of 'outside– in' perspective to action (Bengtsson, 1995; Eraut, 1995).

In the context of theoretical learning in practice, I describe an action research model, for mentoring student teachers, which used video as a tool for reflection, and whereby one of the authors functioned, both as a mentor and researcher. The action research-mentoring model entailed cycles of reflection on action that encouraged different modes of reflection, including the use of video as an opportunity for delayed reflection, both for the mentor and the mentee.

10.6.1 Process and Content

The mentoring action research model that was developed draws on the notions of reflection on action, delayed reflection, and reflection for action and is based on Korthagen's (1995) intervention conversational ALACT (action, looking, awareness, creation, and trial) model. The ALACT model is spiral and consists of five intervention stages: action defined as confrontation with concrete situations which require action, looking at or looking back on a situation (analysis and introspection into and back on the situation), awareness of essential aspects (to critical points in the situation), creation of alternative solutions or methods of action (creating alternative actions and methods of action), and trial of possible courses of action. The adapted model, which drew on the ALACT model, entailed two interrelated cycles of action: The intervention-mentoring cycle and the second-order action research cycle.

The *intervention–mentoring cycle* is a four-stage action research model of mentoring adapted from Korthagen's (1995) intervention model:

(1) The mentor observes the student teacher's lesson. The lesson is video recorded.
(2) The mentor and the student conduct a mentoring conversation following the observed lesson and video recording of the conversation.
(3) The mentor and the student teacher watch their respective video recordings: The mentor watches the video recording of the mentoring conversation and the student teacher watches the video recording of her lesson.
(4) The mentor and the student teacher engage in a mentoring conversation around their respective video watchings. The conversation is also recorded in video.

The *second-order action research cycle*, conducted by the mentor–researcher, aimed at gaining insights into the impact of the intervention–mentoring action research model on the student teacher's and the mentor's learning respectively. The process engaged the mentor–researcher in the analysis of the recorded mentoring conversations to identify mentoring actions that promoted and/or hindered the student teachers' learning. The analysis guided the mentor as to the kind of strategies, behaviors, and orientation that would best promote the student teacher's learning. It also served the mentor as a mirror for becoming aware of predominant dispositions and behaviors that characterized her mentoring style (Adapted from Orland-Barak & Rachamim, 2009).

10.6.2 Insights Gained

10.6.2.1 Connecting Concepts to Actions in Theoretical Learning on Practice

Delayed reflection encouraged appreciation through contemplation of pedagogical practices as a way of building repertoires of practice. It also triggered the mentor's awareness of how she mediated persons, context, and text, and how she appropriated texts from teaching and mentoring in order to establish and sustain the mentor–mentee relationship in participation. Reflection on action and for action through video helped the mentor to shift from a focus on herself and her own performance as a mentor to focusing on what the mentee was learning from her intervention. In the process, she became attentive to her language of practice while responding on the spot and to the kinds of connections that she articulated between theoretical concepts and actions observed. These understandings are conducive to more informed and meaningful ways of improvisation while tuning in to the mentee and while responding on the spot to articulate insights about teaching and learning gained from the conversation.

On the part of the mentee, examination of her personal teaching through multiple modes of reflection and over a time span empowered her reflective thinking, advanced her responsibility toward her own learning, and raised her awareness of teaching. It also reduced her initial resistance toward mentoring, contributed to stressing the advantages of reflective teaching, and, as a result, encouraged her to adopt a more reflective stance toward her own teaching.

10.6.2.2 Tuning in to Compose New Modes of Assistance

Analyzing her own mentoring through systematic reflection on and for action led the mentor to important insights about modes of improvisation that call up on knowledge and procedures to demonstrate and direct new action. Examining her discourse led her to new insights about how to appropriate mediational tools, in order to frame and reframe the novice's learning process, affirming interactions that would connect between her personal concerns and experiences with extant pedagogical orientations and strategies. In doing so, the mentor learned to participate in a discourse that grants the mentee the opportunity to determine the direction and focus of assistance, hence, encouraging her to shape her own mentored learning.

While the mentee gained deeper understanding of her own teaching, she began exploring her ingrained beliefs about classroom organization, management, and differential learning, as they play out in the situated context of her teaching. As the mentor gradually tuned into the mentee's concerns, she learned about ways of encouraging the mentee to voice those concerns, as she gradually began to decide by herself how she wanted to explore these concerns and issues throughout the conversation. This determined the direction of learning that the mentee wanted to pursue and, at the same time, allowed for the mentor's ongoing guidance and 'say.' The process is reflective of how multiple voices are acknowledged and constituted in authentic dialogue (Bakhtin, 1981; Buber, 2000).

This double-loop examination allows the mentor to systematically analyze her practice as he/she learns to appreciate the mentee's process of learning by getting ongoing feedback on his/her mentoring from the mentee (Orland-Barak & Rachamim, 2009; Leikin & Dinvr, 2003).

The possibility of delayed reflection and examination of experience allowed for promoting discursive practices of appreciation, participation, and improvisation. Specifically, it engaged the mentor in reading the mentoring situation by making educated conjectures and connecting the parts to the whole; in appraising pedagogical practices by reframing rigid views; recording appropriate modes of support by making educational construals for future use; tuning in by translating behavior into here-and-now patterns and modes of assistance and composing through recurring patterns; articulating teaching learning and subject matter by analyzing practice systematically, responding to connections between theoretical concepts and practices 'in action' and encouraging the mentee to rationalize action; and responding on the 'spot' by connecting experience, beliefs, and knowledge while calling upon knowledge and procedures to demonstrate and direct action. From the perspective of the mentee, observing the video led her to become aware of her weak spots and acknowledge mentoring as a channel for learning rather than as an evaluative activity.

10.6.3 The Use of Video in Constructivist Pedagogy

The model draws on a constructivist perspective to learning endorsing the dynamic construction of meaning through constant reinterpretation of observed experience. Its cyclical, reflective, and hermeneutic grounding made the technical organization of the framework complex and time consuming. It included videoing the lesson, recording the mentoring conversations, and delivering them to the mentee the same day or the day after, to give her time to watch her lesson in between the meetings. This demanded allotting time beyond regular school hours.

Despite the above, the mentoring model that integrated video recordings, watching, delayed reflection on and for action, and conversations around these reflections constituted a particularly beneficial reflective mirror for the construction of knowledge: It allowed the mentor and mentee to distance themselves from the 'here-and-now' experience and appreciate initial emotionally charged reactions to their actions in a more 'factual mode.' For the mentor, it highlighted her appreciation of the gap between her espoused conceptions about mentoring and her realized actions and for reconstructing her envisioned roles and actions in informed improvisation. For the mentee, it raised her awareness of her beliefs and actions, surfacing connections between theory, beliefs, and actions that she had not been aware of in her teaching (Orland-Barak & Rachamim, 2009).

10.7 Using Story

Story is everywhere. No culture, no civilization, no human group has ever been found that does not use story as its basic and usual means of communication (Chambers, 1983, p. 20)

Writing personal stories is seen as a powerful channel for teachers' professional growth (Connelly & Clandinin, 1990; Diamond, 1994; Elbaz-Luwisch, 2001; Goodson, 1992; Kelchtermans & Vandenberge, 1994; Kooy, 2006; Olson & Craig, 2001; Polkinghorne, 1988; Shank, 2006; Schatz Oppenheimer, 2005). The personal and unique ways in which novice and experienced teachers interpret their experiences through story underscore their value for the individual teacher (Elbaz, 1983; Conle, 2001; Bullough, 1989; Clandinin, 2001; Connelly & Clandinin, 1986; Goodson & Hargreaves, 1996; Witherell & Noddings,1991) and for forwarding a view of reflective professionals who are actively engaged in the process of reorganizing and reconstructing their knowledge about the classroom (Clark, 1995), their relationship with pupils, their concerns about teaching, and their relationships with colleagues (Butt & Raymond, 1988).

From the perspective of mentoring novice teachers, examining the 'plots and dramas' that shape novices' practice using literary devices through the genre of story writing can open a window for accumulating knowledge (Josselson, 1996) into initial teaching experiences that often remain 'inward,' unarticulated (Kagan, 1992). These experiences can be interpreted as 'thinking big with small stories' allowing for conceptualizing the local and the particular as broader issues of identity of 'self and other' (Georgakopoulou, 2006). The use of story engages participants in introspective activity which 'takes the human image from the self to the culture instead of imposing a human image from the culture onto the self' (Baldwin, 1977, p. 28). It also allows for 'telling our own stories [as] a way to impose form upon our often chaotic experiences' (Grumet, 1988) and as a way 'to nourish, encourage and sustain ourselves' (Howe, 1984, cited in Cooper, 1991)

10.7.1 Process and Content

The framework of story writing was implemented in the context of a national 'contest of novices' story writing' in Israel (2004–2005). First year teachers (K-12) from all educational sectors in Israel (Jewish and Arab, secular and conservative) were invited, by the Ministry of Education and Culture, to compose a story that documents and mirrors their first year of teaching experience. The task entailed composing a story that reflected the novice's experiences in his/her initial encounter with teaching, learning, and education, in the school setting (i.e., encounters with pupils, teachers, principals, parents, subject matter, etc.). The purpose of the contest was to gain situated understandings of the 'plots,' 'dramas,' and 'heroes' that novices describe and voice through the genre of story writing. Gaining more informed understandings of the nature of novices' first year experiences in the Israeli educational context could, then, guide further design of a mentoring support framework for first year teachers, based on the insights gained by 'listening and introspecting into novices' inner world' (Schatz Oppenheimer, 2005) as voiced through their stories.

Seventy stories were received in response to the invitation, out of which ten were selected and compiled into a published booklet entitled Novices in Story' (Zilberstrom & Schatz Oppenheimer, 2005, in Hebrew).

10.7.2 Insights Gained

10.7.2.1 Assuming a Perspective

The activity of authoring allows for meaning and values to be expressed in dynamic form, as the narrator operates out of a point of view and shapes values into forms (Clark & Holquist, 1984, p. 10). From the perspective of the audience of educators, by discussing stories of classroom experience, participants increased their appreciation of the situational dynamics of teaching and learning, to make these worlds more susceptible to re-creation (Kooy, 2006). Conversations about stories can also lead to different readings by different readers. Furthermore, encounters between the narrative world offered by the writer (or speaker) and the existing imaginative repertoire of the listener can be of a strong moral impact (Conle, 2006).

10.7.3 Insights Gained

The genre of novices' stories offer a kind of case study literature that can be integrated into teacher education curricula, at preservice and in-service levels. Specifically, it offers a pedagogical-methodological framework of analysis, framed by the particular rules and conventions established for story writing. Adopting categories from literary analysis (i.e., headings, names, motifs, plots, and metaphors) and content categories of teacher's professional lives (i.e., persons involved, roles, functions and accountabilities, didactic and pedagogical agendas) can encourage novice teachers to examine the meanings embedded in the lived experiences recounted in written stories. Participants can, for example, be encouraged to write their own stories, using some of the above literary and content categories to develop their ideas, to express their feelings, and to articulate controversies and dilemmas that they wish to convey in their stories.

The guidelines can help certain participants who need an initial prompt for writing, especially, when the content revolves around unresolved complexities or around a particular dilemma or classroom situation which is particularly emotionally charged. Professionals can also be guided to identify recurrent or salient categories in a particular story (a recurrent motif, name, or theme) and to discuss the possible implied messages about teachers and teaching vis-à-vis examination of how these connect to their personal experiences of being a teacher and doing teaching.

An analytical framework provides an outsider perspective based on content and literary categories that allow for 'digging into' the details, intricacies, and 'multiple players' entrenched in the stories. This kind of outsider literary perspective to analysis and interpretation also allows for examining how parts combine into a whole, or how a series of events eventually develops into a rich plot about teachers and teaching.

In addition to the external categories of analysis, novices can explore both accurate, detailed examination of the 'parts' and how they combine into a 'whole' (the outsider perspective), with open, inductive, associative processes of meaning-making, grounded in the personal experiences of the interpreters (the insider perspective). Such a combination would enable both involvement with and detachment from the teaching event, attending to the interrelationship between cognition, emotion, and action in constructivist-narrative modes of meaning-making (Bruner, 1986, p. 178). Examining the stories from these two interrelated external and internal perspectives can encourage student teachers to scrutinize between the general features of the story (in order to typify it to other similar present or future stories) alongside engaging in 'educated conjectures' about how the particular features of the story might differ when transferred to another teaching context. For mentors, attending and examining these stories as evidence of their mentees' lived experiences can encourage discursive practices of appreciation and participation as they typify their mentees' context of teaching; observe pedagogical practices through their stories; assume diverse supportive roles as they recognize culturally diverse texts and privileged and rejected discourses; and intervene as cothinkers and carers.

In our work with student teachers, we tend to make generalizations about their functioning with a predictive stance toward future success (Guyton & McIntyre, 1990). Driven by this legitimate concern, we often tend to overlook the importance of stressing the singularity of each teaching context. Encouraging activities that push for identifying singularity, alongside generality, can offer a channel for enhancing prospective and novice teachers to read into their experiences and into the experiences of others with this dual focus in mind and become teachers and researchers in [their] own lives (Cooper, 1991).

10.8   Modalities and Processes of Knowledge Construction

Let us, now, zoom in to illustrate the step-by-step processes of knowledge construction that play out in the organization of particular activities described in the above sections. Put differently, how does the course professor or 'mentor of mentors' actually construe a 'plan' in order to encourage participants to engage in constructivist processes of appreciation, participation, and improvisation? The following examples focus on such modalities and processes in the three settings of learning described in earlier sections of this chapter: (1) Academic learning, (2) Theoretical learning in practice, and (3) Practical learning in practice.

10.8.1   Appreciation, Participation, and Improvisation in Academic Learning Tasks

As mentioned in earlier sections, translating constructivist pedagogy into a postgraduate university seminar entails the use of methodologies that encourage participants to establish praxical connections between theoretical concepts and their daily practices, prompting them to adopt a critical stance toward these practices. Hence, participants are required to write cases/stories/critical incidents of their daily practices which are then presented to the rest of the group. These texts are analyzed, scrutinized, and connected to relevant theoretical literature, with a focus on how the process can enhance competencies in appreciation, participation, and improvisation in the education of mentors.

In addition to the use of narrative devices, I have also integrated the use of participants' authentic mentoring conversations as working texts. Mentors are required to record and transcribe a genuine mentoring conversation from their own practice which is then used as a main working text during the sessions. During the course sessions, mentors are encouraged to organize mentoring activities around their own mentoring conversations (creating a simulation of mentoring the group). As part of the process, they are asked to organize tasks for the group that focus on particular aspects of their text that they wish to explore, as they relate to burning issues from their mentoring practices and to relevant issues from the theoretical readings on mentoring. The mentoring conversation texts brought to the floor are examined through various theoretical lenses as they emerge from the readings and as they play out in the simulation 'in action' of the mentoring activity. The process eventually engages participants in dialectical modalities of appreciation, participation, and improvisation as related to what actually happened, how it connects to and generates new local theory, and how it informs new understandings about what was acted upon.

Following the mentoring activity that they organize around their text, I encourage a discussion that focuses both on the process of mentoring the group (as led by the presenters) and on the content of the mentoring conversation text that was used during their simulation. This kind of 'loop' into both the process of mentoring the group, and the content of the authentic mentoring text is theoretically grounded in the constructivist assumption that experiencing and introspection into the experience are complementary meaning-making processes (Kivinen & Ristela, 2003).

Throughout the discussion, my role is to provide a model for facilitating a process of coconstruction of meanings. Thus, I use probing and confronting questions to 'push' the group into surfacing dissonances between taken for granted assumptions about mentoring, the 'here-and-now' mentoring conversation that developed during the simulation, and the transcribed mentoring conversation text that was brought to the session.

In the process, I make connections to theoretical models and concepts, encouraging the construction of new understandings through these interpretative lenses.

I try to demonstrate the examination of multiple perspectives on a particular issue and to provide opportunities for adopting a critical stance toward practice, conveying the message that constructivist learning is about asking better questions rather than getting clear-cut answers. The following two sequences illustrate the step-by-step process of developing appreciation, participation, and improvisation processes in academic learning tasks. The first sequence is structured around the reading of an academic text and its connection to the here-and-now context of mentoring. The second sequence focuses on the use of loop learning strategies around the presentation and mediation of a field text.

Sequence One: Connecting academic texts to the 'here-and-now' context

A selected list of core academic readings is provided by the course professor. Each participant selects an article from the list (or may suggest other relevant articles from published journals, upon approval of the course professor). The first two sessions are devoted to introducing a general overview of the literature.

- Every session, a different participant takes over the first part of the session (40/45 minutes). During that time he/she has to trigger talk around the major concepts and questions called for by the article, acting as the mentor of the group. In the process, he/she has to engage the group in a learning conversation around the major concepts using any strategies of mediation. The idea is to create a simulation of a group mentoring session around subject matter (in this case the contents of the article).

  The mentor of mentors (in this case the course professor) observes and writes comments and feedback on the process (i.e., the strategies used) and on the content (i.e., the major concepts) discussed.

- During the second part of the session, the course professor mediates a learning conversation around the *content* and *process* of the session observed. Participants, having taken the role of mentees, are now encouraged to voice their feedback to the 'mentor' from the perspective of their participation as mentees. The process is framed by a set of initial prompts. These questions are mainly geared to enhance participants' *appreciation* of the mentoring situation as they appraise and observe pedagogical practices, articulate their readings of the situation, and record appropriate modes of support.

  How did the 'mentor' advance my learning?
  How did he/she block participants 'learning? When and Why?
  What was predominant in the mentor's behavior?
  What Discourse/s do I recognize in the mentor's behavior and talk?
  What were the predominant characteristics of the discourse created in the group?
  What did I learn about mentoring having been in the role of the mentee?

- The mentor, at this point, is asked not to respond but just listen and record insights from the floor.

- The course professor, then, presents his/her feedback paying special attention to *appreciation processes* such as identifying emergent gaps between the mentor's espoused views about mentoring and the language of mediation that he/she uses and/or *improvisation processes* such as articulating connections between the concepts developed in the academic text and how these played out (or not) in the mentor's mediation. He/she also encourages participants to make connections between the 'theoretical concepts' presented in the article and the idiosyncratic meanings that they take in their particular contexts of participants' mentoring, focusing on emergent contradictions, dilemmas, and constraints brought about by the situated nature of their mentoring interactions (*domain of participation*). Comparisons across contexts while mediating persons, context, and content are also encouraged (*domain of participation*).
- During the third part of the session, after having taken in the input from the conversational floor, the mentor is encouraged to address the following questions:

What assumptions guided you in the choice of your strategies? How were these assumptions congruent (or not) with how you acted (as revealed through the participants' comments)?
What did you learn about yourself from the feedback that you got from your mentees?
What did you learn about the mentee's perspective?
What did you learn about mentoring?
What do you take with you?

Sequence Two: Connecting a field text to the 'here-and-now' academic context

- A selected list of core academic readings in the area of mentoring and mentored learning is provided by the course professor.
- Each participant selects an article from the list (or may suggest other articles from published journals upon approval of the course professor).
- Each participant must also select a field experience (in the form of a case, story, excerpt, etc.) that he/she would like to share with the class.
- Each participant, in turn, has to present the field case to the group, focusing on how the particular case might illustrate some of the concepts developed in the article. Similarly to the previous process, one participant takes over the first part of the session (40/45 minutes) and acts as mentor of the group. The 'mentor' has to use strategies of mediation inviting participants to propose interpretations of what the case is about (see guidelines for conversation around cases in earlier section). Participants are also prompted

to make connections between the field experience and the main concepts highlighted in the focal academic article.

- During the second part of the session, the course professor leads the conversation using loop learning strategies to surface processes of *appreciation, participation*, and *improvisation* that played out in the discourse. For example, focusing on forms of improvisation, he/she draws participants' attention to how the mentor tuned in to participants, how connections between concepts and actions were articulated, and how the mentor called upon knowledge, and procedures to direct action as she responded on the spot. The mentor also encourages the articulation of processes of appreciation that became apparent during the session, such as how participants appraised pedagogical practices and reframed perspectives as they interpreted the case. In the process, he/she 'freezes' particular moments of interaction during the conversation to draw participants' attention to how they negotiated emergent contradictions, how they validated and affirmed interactions, and the extent to which they engaged in reciprocal communal learning (forms of participation).

- In the third part of the session, participants are encouraged to articulate the forms and meanings that the content or the main ideas of the academic texts played out both in what the mentor said, did, or responded throughout the session, and on the relevance of the main concepts of the article for understanding the field text brought by the mentor. The course professor, then, focuses on how the main ideas of article can be used as new interpretative lenses for conceptualizing 'what the case is about.'

It seems important to stress that the critical examination of practice in the context of a one-semester academic course, which included participants from a variety of cultural and ethnic groups, was not devoid of threats and expressions of resistance. For one, it took time for participants to feel confident and safe to scrutinize each others' practices, engage in exposing inner contradictions, and begin voicing more internally persuasive discourses. This is further elaborated in Chapter 11.

10.8.2 Academic Supervision in Practice

10.8.2.1 Structure and Content of the Course

The course Academic Supervision in Practice stresses the importance of integrating a component in the program which attends to deliberation, reflection, and conceptualization processes of mentoring practices. The four hour yearly academic course is structured around activity in three complementary practice learning settings: (1) a workshop session, once a week, with all participants, at the university (2) observation and reflection of the videoed workshop sessions, and (3) a practicum field experience where mentoring activities of different kinds and for different kinds of populations are observed (see syllabus below).

Course Syllabus

The *process of learning* throughout the course entails the construction of meaningful interactions, engaging participants in 'rituals of practices' (Wenger, 1998) through recurrent patterns of work and activity in three different kinds of practice settings:

Weekly reflections on the videoed session: The session is recorded in video into the e-learning site of the course. Students are asked to write reflections on the videotaped session through guided questions (see syllabus below).

The practicum field experience: Students observe and participate in variety of field experiences across contexts, populations, processes, and content foci (see syllabus below).

Rituals of practice are also established through a *structured sequence of activities* that take place in three different practice settings:

During the workshop session: The workshop session begins with an opening activity that invites students to connect to the content of the session, usually through personal connotations and associations, and creates an initial platform for focusing on particular strategies and processes.

The middle of the session is led by the students, each in turn activating the group through mentoring strategies and practices that encourage connections between emotional, cognitive, and social aspects of the particular selected experience. The end of the session invites participants to briefly reflect on the experiences mediated by their colleagues, encouraging them to voice the prominent issues that left a strong impact emotionally, cognitively, interpersonally, and so forth.

Weekly reflections on the videoed session: Participants watch the video of the session and write their reflections on the video following a suggested structure for documenting delayed reflection on action (see syllabus below).

The practicum field setting: Participants observe mentors in the field and are encouraged to reflect on the experience through observation tasks designed by the course professor in collaboration with participants during the workshop sessions. Participants are also expected to engage in mentoring activities and reflectively document the experience (see syllabus below).

The process of learning in the three contexts of academic supervision in practice acknowledges the active and dynamic character of meaning-making in practice. Such a process is characterized by decision making 'in situ'; intuitive thinking; heuristic strategies and simultaneous thinking; thinking about doing; contextual thinking and thinking in and through cases; discerning actions as reflective of cultural backgrounds; connecting between environment, persons, and actions through multidimensional thinking; juggling with integrated skills simultaneously; and thinking while doing (Orland-Barak & Wilheim, 2005). To attend to these aspects, active learning in practice occurs at three levels:

1. *Personal*: The practices and experiences encourage participants to share their personal voices and concerns by trying to develop a trusting and safe learning environment to develop their personal subjective theories (Kelchtermans & Vandenberghe, 1994) about mentoring through critical reflective processes.
2. *Collaborative level*: Special emphasis is paid to the co-construction of meaning in social activity and conversation. Participants mediate each other's learning as they share their experiences and work together on different field tasks. The collaborative level underscores the importance of establishing professional sisterhoods amongst participants (Evans, 2000) and of learning through distributed expertise (Clark, 2001).
3. *Expert–Novice level:* whereby each mentor participant regularly meets with the course professor, a mentor of mentors. The mentor of mentors mediates the novice's learning through loop learning strategies for analyzing practice.

Course Syllabus: Academic Supervision in Practice

Course Description

The course aims at engaging the student in informed mentoring activity in a variety of authentic contexts and settings of professional learning, at the university and outside the university.

The following questions frame the orientation of the course:

What is mentoring and how does my concept of mentoring develop over time?
What characterize different contexts of mentoring? What is shared and what is unique?
What processes and products characterize mentoring practices across contexts?
What characterizes a learning conversation in different contexts of mentoring?

Processes

Students will learn in two modalities:

- a reflective/experiential session at the university
- active participation in and appreciation of diverse mentoring contexts and settings of mentored learning (observations and partial involvement in

workshop sessions; mentoring conversations between mentors and student teachers; dyadic and group mentoring in schools, centers for professional learning).

Students will engage in metalearning processes around their field experiences and of the reflective/experiential sessions at the university. They will also engage in active participation in organizational change processes that call for mediation processes in the department, at the faculty.

Course Requirements

1. Active participation
2. Ongoing readings connected to field experiences
3. A series of reflective tasks to be submitted on an ongoing basis
4. Monthly portfolio entries on reflections around videoed mentoring sessions.
5. Dictionary of concepts

Guidelines for Portfolio Reflections

While reflecting on the session/s consider any of the following:
   I learned that. . .
   I thought that. . .
   I was unsure about. . .
   I was surprised to discover. . .
   I have changed my mind about. . .

Guidelines for Reflective Inquiry Field Tasks

Reflective inquiry field tasks are geared to self-regulated professional learning. The different inquiry tasks are structured around observations, interviews, conversations, and activities carried out in the field where mentoring practices take place. The student can chose amongst several options:

(1) Observing the Beginning of a Mentoring Process

Purpose: To expose the student to a variety of processes and interactions that can take place at the beginning of a mentor–mentee relationship.

Guidelines for action:

1. Arrange for a series of meetings with the mentor/s you are about to accompany in the field. The meetings should allow you to take part in a variety

of settings and modalities of mentoring and to be able to compare and contrast across contexts.
2. Jot down relevant issues that you would like to focus on during your field experience.
3. Share your points of interest and focuses of observation with your mentor.
4. Prepare a blueprint of tentative points for a contract that you would like to establish with your mentor. These points are shared, revised, and finally compiled into a joint contract between the mentor and the student mentor.
5. Register the insights that you are gaining/have gained from observing different kinds of interactions.
6. Share your insights with your mentor to develop new and more informed questions for the following meeting.
7. Engage in constant reevaluation of your insights as you engage in new activities in different contexts and settings.

(2) Observing the End of a Mentoring Process

Purpose: Exposure to ways of rounding up and concluding a particular series of mentoring sessions/meetings/dyadic relationships.

1. Arrange for a series of meetings with the mentor/s to take part in a variety of activities that focus on concluding a particular mentoring interaction in various settings, modalities, and contexts.
2. Register the insights that you are gaining /have gained from observing different kinds of interactions and strategies.
3. Share your insights with your mentor to develop new and more informed questions for the following meeting.
4. Engage in constant reevaluation of your insights as you engage in new activity in different contexts and settings.

(3) Observing a Feedback Process in Mentoring

Purpose: Exposure to different processes of assessment and feedback as they play out in mentoring relations.

Guidelines:

1. Read a selection of articles in the area of feedback.
2. Document your insights about how feedback plays out in different situations:

   - During an educational intervention,
   - While managing resistances that emerge during feedback,
   - While documenting a daily/weekly activity plan,
   - In critical incidents,

     – When conducting sessions with a group of learners,
     – When focusing on cognitive/emotional/social skills.

3. Conduct an interview with the mentor, before giving feedback to focus on plans, conditions, and relevant content to be discussed.
4. Write down the standards for a successful feedback process.
5. Observe feedback processes in mentoring conversations.
6. Considering the observation, share and summarize your conclusions with the mentor observed.

(4) Observing Processes of Learning in a Community of Learners

Purpose: Exposure to social processes of knowledge construction.

1. Read selections of articles in the theme of communal learning.
2. Document your reframing of perspectives on communal learning and note down a suitable process of cooperative learning for the group you have been accompanying.
3. Conduct an interview with the mentor about his/her perception of learning processes in groups:

    a. Contents he/she finds easier to work on with the group and the reasons.
    b. Contents he/she finds difficult to work on with the group and the reasons.
    c. Characteristics of communal learning in the group.
    d. Characteristics of individual learning in the group.
    e. A comparison between communal learning processes in different groups.

4. Conduct an interview with a group of student teachers about their perceptions of mentored learning processes (refer to the categories in paragraph 3)
5. Observe diverse group learning activities:

    a. Engaging in constructive questions.
    b. Analysis of topics and connections to the broader themes.
    c. Conceptualization, principle generalizations, processes and implications.
    d. Inductive and deductive processes.
    e. Dealing with inaccuracies and misconceptions.
    f. Communal processes – persons involved and ways of involvement, different social roles in the group.

6. Consolidate your comments and conclusions.
7. Share your findings with the mentor and discuss their implications.

(5) Observing Mentoring Processes

Purpose: Exposure to a range of mentoring processes.

1. Record your ideas about mentoring based on your previous experiences.
2. Coordinate with the mentor the anticipated mentoring meeting and produce a list of categories for observations.
3. Create an agreement with the student teachers and receive their consent for observation.
4. Observe a mentoring conversation and focus on the categories you have selected for observation. Record recurring events and new emergent categories that you find relevant.
5. Document your findings from the structured observation in light of the categories you have produced and the evolving themes that emerged during observation.
6. Summarize your conclusions and insights.

Guidelines for Creating a Concepts Glossary

1. Choose 10 concepts in mentoring, to which you have been exposed during the course.
2. Define and describe those concepts as you have experienced them during the course and in the field observations.
3. Turn to the professional literature and find the theoretical basis and relevant explanations for the concepts you have chosen.

10.8.3 Appreciation, Participation, and Improvisation in Theoretical Learning in Practice

The following excerpt illustrates a sequence of discourse in which a mentor mediates theoretical learning in practice. As described in earlier section 9.2.1 of the previous chapter, theoretical learning in practice refers to the conceptual processes that are developed in professional learning in practice, such as attributing and designating ethical and professional reasoning and judgment, reflection on dilemmas, ramification of concepts, and inductive and deductive processes. The example is situated in a different educational context of mentoring: Nursing Education. Specifically, the excerpt illustrates how the nurse mentor employs modalities of appreciation, participation, and improvisation as she mediates learning, assumes diverse supportive roles, tunes in and articulates learning processes, responds on the spot, and observes and appraises practices. In the process, student nurses engage in theoretical learning in practice.

10.8.3.1 Clarifying, Reframing, Reconstructing, and Being in Experience

Orit is a nursing mentor in a pediatric department in a small hospital in the north of Israel. She mentors a group of six nursing students during their six-week clinical experience. The nursing students are in their third year of nursing studies, at the Cheryl Spencer Department of Nursing, at the University of Haifa. The goal of pediatric experience is to acquire relevant knowledge, skills, competence, and a world view of pediatrics care. The mentor is a highly qualified staff nurse who was trained and certified to be a nursing mentor. Orit mentors the nursing students by accompanying them during their clinical practice. She observes and guides them in taking care of sick children and their parents, performing caring interventions and carrying out clinical procedures safely, making the proper clinical decision, managing stressful situations, and building appropriate interpersonal relationships with the children and their family.

The mentoring conversation sessions usually take place either at the pediatric department or in other relevant locations in the hospital (X-ray Unit, Emergency Unit). Orit plans most of her mentoring sessions in advance, considering the department routine, the children clinical conditions, and the student's educational outcomes and experience. During the morning session (the opening of the day), each of the students is asked to take care of one sick child and his/her family. The students must examine the child and gather the relevant information in order to make clinical decisions and to plan the appropriate intervention to the child and his family. The student, then, is expected to describe the child's clinical condition and justify his/her clinical decision to Orit. Orit asks the student questions and leads the conversation in order to identify the student's level of appreciation of the case. The student is also asked to write a 'care plan' for every sick child that he/she is supposed to take care of during practice. In writing the plan, the student has to integrate several bodies of knowledge (pathology, medicine, nutrition, pharmacology, etc.) and to name, label, and conceptualize the clinical condition of the sick child, matching it to an appropriate treatment. The morning sessions are characterized by focusing the attention of the student to relevant details and concrete actions that will enable the student to deliver safe and proper care. The closing session of the day is intended to deepen the clinical knowledge of the student and encourage him/her to conceptualize his/her 'lived' practice. During the closing session, Orit and the students reflect on a particular event and on the interactions that revolved around the entire experience, throughout the day and during other mentored learning sessions. The content of the learning sessions revolve around the schedule of the department's routine.

The following is an excerpt from a conversation conducted between Orit and the students in one of the closing sessions: Orit shows the student two X-rays of two patients (with different diseases of the gastrointestinal system). They are discussing the differences between them. While everyone is looking at the X-ray photos, Orit says:

Orit:	As we said, this is colitis as opposed to Crohn's disease. We see that this is dotted only in the large intestine and Crohn's, usually, can be decorated throughout the intestine in segments, but the disease itself started from the mouth to the rectum. It's throughout the digestion system. We will talk and I will demonstrate how it's seen. How do we actually define the IBD (Inflammatory Bowel Diseases)? How do we see the diseases in practice?
Student 1:	Malabsorption of the intestinal. Adhesions of intestinal.
Orit:	Basically, we defined these two diseases as inflammatory bowel disease as a chronic illness of intestine. We call it- 'runs in the family'
Student 2:	Especially in Crohn's disease.
Orit:	Yes, in Crohn's, if one of the parents is ill there is a 9% chance that the child will get Crohn's . . . But it's not always the case. . ., we have seen a mother with Crohn, the father was healthy and the child was also healthy.
Student 3:	Isn't an autoimmune mechanized?

Let us examine how Orit clarifies, reframes, and reconstructs being and doing in experience. First, she engages in a discourse that triggers students' memory of being in the experience (the conversation they had had in one of the sessions). She reframes those experiences by connecting them to content/disciplinary knowledge in Pathology, Radiology, and Medicine. In the process, she clarifies facts and details, naming and labeling relevant concepts and reconstructing them into a coherent model or distinguishable pattern.

Orit constructs the discourse, using several modalities of improvisation: First, she demonstrates the radiology and pathology notions of the diseases: Using a real X-ray of a real patient, she makes use of authentic evidence from the department to explicitly represent the relevant notions that can be attributed to the disease. She also compares two X-rays from different diseases. This process enables Orit to match the theoretical, pathological, and medical knowledge of two diseases to the signs and symptoms of two different patients by showing resemblance and dissimilarity, and by merging scientific facts with real cases from the department. The discourse is characterized by mutual participation to affirm and verify interactions between Orit and the students.

Let us turn to another example from Orit's mentoring sessions. Following the above conversation, a few days later, Orit and the students are having a closing mentoring session and the issue that is being discussed is the care of pain in Pediatrics.

Orit:	We can say that it's hurt like a mosquito bit, it's a small sting. We have to say that it's going to hurt, not to say it's not going to hurt

	because there is no correlation between what that happened in reality and what that we are promising to him. O.k.? Then, try to avoid it. It is helpful if we use anesthesia to reduce pain, to improve mobility and movement. The child can participate in the treatment and mobilized himself. This can prevent complications that might cause immobilization, and can reduce the guilty conscience of the parents. We can also see differences in the parent's attitude to the boy and the girl. To a boy, they will say 'you are a man and you can deal with it'. To a girl, they will say: no, she can't.
Student:	*For instance, Arabic patients tend to demonstrate pain less than other patients, like they can suffer more or they tend to complain less than the others. I have seen some patients at the Internal Medicine Department whose pain was 5–6 and they did not complain, but other people from a different mentality, when they have pain of 1–2 degree, they complain and exaggerate.*
Orit:	*Sometimes a child can say that he is under severe pain, can scream and go wild and we just go to call for a doctor and when we are back, he is already calm and playing. In the past, it was very common (even in our department), that care-giver treated children as if they suffer less from pain. The belief was that because children are small, it's less painful for them. And babies don't feel any pain at all. Those were stigmas that were commonly widespread, until the recent years.*

Orit elaborates on one of the interventions that the students have observed, in the department, by connecting experience, beliefs, and knowledge, hence improvising to develop awareness of forms of appreciation and participation. She starts her explanation by articulating her experience of how to handle the situation, describing her behavior and integrating it with her personal clinical rationale. Composing through recurrent patterns, she makes sure to stress that her experience is based on caring for numerous children, sometimes not according to a clinical principle that she has learned or that is written in the text book. This serves as a good strategy for exemplifying the integration of theory and practice and implementation of theory in practice, that is, responding to connections between concepts and actions.

Orit also appropriates texts from her own practical knowledge by giving personal examples, encouraging the students to bring their own examples as a way of developing their appreciation of the cases, through practical knowledge based on their personal clinical experience. Creating a conversational space for sharing distributed expertise and for sustaining professional learning, the mentor participates to promote a practical discourse of nursing that is embedded in thinking and talking 'in' and 'through' action.

10.8.4 Forms of Appreciation and Improvisation in Practical Learning in Practice

Continuing in the context of mentoring in nursing education, let us, now, consider an example of mentoring aimed at developing practical learning in practice, with a focus on managing, applying, and doing in action and through experience. As we examine the mentor's moves, we can clearly identify an apprenticeship of observation orientation, meant to develop habits of work, techniques, and performance skills. This practical aspect of learning calls for a less dialogical/discursive mode of appreciation, participation, and improvisation, confining mostly to improvisation strategies that call upon knowledge and procedures to demonstrate action, and to appreciation strategies that build on repertoires of successful practice.

10.8.4.1 Managing, Applying, and Doing in Experience

Debby is a nursing mentor in internal medicine department, in a small hospital. Debby is a certified mentor and, like Orit, works with six nursing students for a period of eight hours a day, three days a week, for two consecutive months. The learning arrangement is the same as in the Pediatrics Department described above:

Student:	*What to do with the hydrocortisone?*
Debby:	*We have to stop with the cortisone it's almost finished and to start with prednisone. Now, she stopped the steroid treatment and start p.o., the doctor wants 40 mg in the morning and 30 mg in the evening and now, we will see what the doctor's instructions are and we will carry them out.*
Student:	*I am not carrying out the instructions.*
Debby:	*Not the instructions*
Student:	(to the patient): *I am going to change your pants.*
Debby:	*What are you doing with the needle?*
Student:	*I am hanging her, when we change the antibiotics, we will use it. If we start a new intravenous line, we need a new needle.*
Debby:	*Let's go out and see the set. Let's look at the date and we will put the last date 12.2.' We need to change the bad sheets.*
Debby:	*What do you do? Mark it*
Student:	*I need to mark down that the patient has a lot of mucus.*
Debby:	*Does the patient need to get prednisone today? Write it down.*
Student	*How much cortisone did the patient got today? Why you determine that? There is no need to administer the drug to her? If I give it to her today is it critical?*
Debby:	*It's a good question, let's go and find out. We will go to the doctor and ask her what to do – should we or should we not administer the*

> *drug this morning? In the evening, we will find out what to adminis-*
> *trate. I would prefer it if you would ask the doctor if to administrate*
> *prednisone 40 mg in the morning once a day and write it down in*
> *bold for tomorrow.*
> Student: *Where do I write the time and the date?.*

At the beginning of the morning shift, in the Internal Medicine Department, there are usually several interventions and procedures that the nursing staff is supposed to be in charge of and accomplish. These tasks require a strict and explicit schedule, synchronization of actions and tasks, a plan to-do list, and adjusting guidance and regulation to the patient's dynamic medical conditions. In her mentoring, Debby deals with actual and immediate care processes, letting the student carry out some of the customary routine interventions that the nursing staff does every morning (administering drugs, reporting of normal and pathological findings). Debby's educational goal is to demonstrate to the students her operational habits and procedures, in specific caring tasks that are part of the local standard and routine of care in internal medicine department. Debby's routines are specific practices and actions that connect to common clinical phenomena that she comes across in her daily work in the department. One example is when Debby asks the student to write the date on intravenous equipment. The goal of this action is to monitor the timing of changing sterile equipment in used one, and the reason is to prevent infections. Debby participates in the operational routine together with the student, backgrounding any kind of talk around goals or clinical reasoning behind the actions and instructing the student, instead, on the specific details of the acts itself.

Devoid of conceptualization, the experience leads to clear-cut, straightforward, and precise talk between Debby and the student around the action itself. Debby also exemplifies the daily managerial behaviors that include strict and explicit sched-ule planning. She also demonstrates the synchronization of actions and tasks – the sequence of tasks that has to be rescheduled as a result of the physician's instruc-tion, department routine, and the patients' conditions. The student has three different practical tasks to perform simultaneously: One task is to write down and report about the patient's pathological findings and decide if the particular medical situa-tion requires immediate attention of the physician, as it displays a deterioration of the medical situation of the patient. Another task is to continue the drug treatment as planned and to change the equipment. Another task is to make sure that the right changes in the drug treatment are been carried out comprehensively.

During the same morning session, Debby continues to take care of her patients while being accompanied by two nursing students. The excerpts below are taken from the conversation that took place while she was visiting the patients:

> Debby: *Where should we mark the changes in the drugs, besides the nurs-*
> *ing notes? On the patient's bed chart. You erase the cortisone and*
> *write the changes what and how much we are administering to*

> the patient. Now, you have to report, what is the problem of the patient?
>
> Student 1:   Addison Syndrome and she has hyponatraemia from the Addison.
> Debby: How much natrium?
> Student 1:   126.
> Debby: Does she have fever today?
> Student 2:   36.7c (98.06 degree Fahrenheit), I did not check again because of the blush cheek.
> Debby: Let's report it.
> Student 2:   I will write that she needs help.
> Student 1:   The urine bag is full, do we need to change and start collecting urine?
> Debby: We need to empty the collection and we will start tomorrow morning. What do you do with all the urine after you empty it? Write it down.
> Student 1:   I wrote it already.
> Debby: Very good.
> Student 2:   Why is it related to fluid?
> Debby: It is not related.
> Student 2:   Hyponatraemia
> Debby: Permanent dialysis it's four hours. We can see some E.C.G. changes.
> Student 1:   They have to go to a special clinic to do pre dialysis blood test, will they do it?
>
> Debby: How much sugar in the test?
> Student 1:   172
> Debby: Did you write it in the chart?
> Student 1:   I will write it in my notepad and later I will write it in the chart.
> Debby: O.K. now, let's hook up the patient to the E.C.G. device. Left lag in direction and. . . .

As can be seen, Debby is working together with two nursing students as they perform some of the clinical tasks. In the process, Debby verbalizes her automatic thoughts and actions to the students. Such verbalization focuses solely on the psychomotoric dimension of the action, devoid of its cognitive, emotional, or social dimensions. The emphasis is on psychomotoric skills, aimed at constructing instrumental and functioning details. Even when the name of a disease surges during the conversation, it is not developed into a theoretical discussion of the disease but refocused into a live demonstration of the symptoms of the disease.

Debby, thus, improvises by attending to the particular actions, connecting them to broader bureaucratic procedures to expose the students to the local routines of the department. Such form of participative action does not make space for medical, pathological, or pharmacological discussions. To this end, the pathological findings are important only in that they must be reported as a checklist of right actions, but not as an opportunity for integrating different kinds of knowledge and conceptualizing processes, in this case, connecting, for example, between signs of fever and the symptom of a blush cheek.

The demands and intensity of the clinical situation combined with the responsibility for two nursing students probably prompts Debby to assume as directive, supportive role which is strongly directed by an ethics of care toward her patients. Participation in the learning conversation between Debby and her students has no predetermined order or guidelines which could direct to specific consequences or consolidate clinical principles. Rather, the process entails thinking as you do, is immediate, connects to doing 'here and now,' and is attentive to stimuli that emerge in the minute-by-minute action.

10.8.5 Appreciation, Participation, and Improvisation as Shaped by Theoretical and Practical Professional Learning

Debby's case exemplifies 'in vivo' the centrality of mediating both theoretical and practical learning in the authentic practice environment. In this setting of learning in practice, the three domains of appreciation, participation, and improvisation acquire unique forms and meanings. Student nurses' professional practical learning is, thus, mediated in a way that would allow for coping, managing, and reacting to 'real' patients, to dynamic and to unique clinical situations, to the constraints of the ward schedule, and to patients' expressed needs, lacks, and wants.

During mentored learning in practice, the student is encouraged to apply knowledge and skills, to perform caring interventions in action, and to identify and reframe daily routines and events into clinical cases and concepts. Professional learning in the practice environment entails, then, developing appreciation of the procedural details of the workplace's culture: The norms and language of behavior that characterize the patient's unit as well as the surrounding physical environment with its particular structure, clues, responses, reactions, and sounds. Such amalgam of stimuli and responses must be 'absorbed' by the student nurse and 'filtered,' through relevant mediation processes, to form a coherent and authentic portrayal of the dynamics, variability and multidimensionality of the nursing clinical setting.

To attend to the above, Debby takes the nursing students through a kind of 'absorption journey' which requires maximum integration and 'intake' of the multifaceted opportunities for learning, provided for by the here-and-now physical and human environment. The 'journey' is not structured or directed by any predetermined guidelines or checklists that accommodate to a particular stage of learning or hierarchical model or taxonomy. Rather, it develops ad hoc in the here-and-now reality of emergent clinical situations, and it is gradually construed as the students are encouraged 'to think on their feet' by making conjectures or by suggesting informed solutions to particular clinical 'stimulus.'

Learning to mentor in professional learning in practice, thus, calls for acquiring a less dialogical and a more action-oriented discourse of appreciation, participation, and improvisation. Such a discourse is grounded in the specific case or event, aiming at equipping the students with tools for decision making in situ. Through assisted performance, the mentor demonstrates how he/she connects between the specific features of the environment, the persons involved, and the actions to be undertaken, in order to develop practical skills and knowledge in action.

Chapter 11
Constructivist-Dialogic Pedagogies: Lessons From the Field

11.1 The Ideal of Constructivist Pedagogy: What Should Go Right. . .?

Constructivist methodologies, enacted in the context of academic-professional learning, are indeed, a viable channel for translating a praxical orientation to learning to mentor to an actual pedagogy of action. Faithful to the Aristotelian notion of *phronesis* – a practice that requires skill, character development, and openness to confronting the particularities of a given situation (Benner, 1984) – pedagogies of learning from experience (Dewey, 1933) speak to the notion of 'practice-based evidence' (Eraut, 2004) (as opposed to evidence-based practice).

In the context of learning to mentor, it implies that mentor participants generate and use evidence from their practices, taking the responsibility for inducting their mentees into generating such evidence. Practice-based evidence enables participants to construe their own situational understandings of Appreciation, Participation, and Improvisation as they engage in systematic reflection of emergent professional relationships, in establishing meaningful connections between theory and practice, and in providing a rationale for action. In the process, they develop a stance toward mentoring that is both affective and intellectual (Eisner & Powell, 2002); integrating practical, ethical, critical, and transformational dimensions; and leading the practitioners toward more informed understandings of their practice (Cochran-Smith & Lytle, 1993; Van Manen, 1991).

Constructivist pedagogies, such as the ones described in previous chapters, allow for voicing multiple perspectives and articulating educational assumptions and ideologies; for managing concrete pedagogical problems, dilemmas, and conflicts that emerge in different teaching contexts; and for attending to the challenges brought about by competing agendas and educational reforms in the field.

L. Orland-Barak, *Learning to Mentor-as-Praxis*, Professional Learning and Development in Schools and Higher Education 4, DOI 10.1007/978-1-4419-0582-6_11, © Springer Science+Business Media, LLC 2010

.2 Facing the Real: But. . .What Can Go Wrong??

Let us now consider the less 'ideal' side of
constructivist pedagogies. In doing so, it seems
important to engage in critical dialogue
of two major kinds:

thinking in practice

- Dialogues around the ethics and appropriateness of 'imposing' reflective con-structivist approaches, mainly rooted in western cultures, on cultures in which reflection at more critical levels is often at odds with participants' culturally ingrained images of learning and teaching. It also raises judgmental questions as to the implied hegemonic proposition that educators are not 'reflective enough' and should therefore 'be trained' through particular modes of thinking and reflection (Fendler, 2003).
- Dialogues around constructivist discourses that push toward critical, multiple per-spectives to understanding action, within an educational context, characterized by school reality that prioritizes single evaluation of performances.

11.2.1 Ethics and Appropriateness of 'Imposing' Reflective Approaches

An important insight gained from constructivist learning settings calls our attention to ethical controversies and dangers that might arise when pushing participants into becoming too personal in their reflections on action. Although a personal approach can challenge certain students, it can also block others, who gradually become extremely resistant. A constructivist pedagogy 'imposes,' to a great extent, pro-cesses of inquiry that not everybody might feel comfortable with, especially within the time constraints of a one semester-course, and when introduced to students from different backgrounds and traditions who will find it difficult to engage in a reflec-tive, self-scrutinizing process of reflection on their practice. For example, in the Israeli context, such students would be Jews, Christians, Druzes, or Moslems raised in more traditional, orthodox cultures. Thus, we need to 'watch' for those students who, even at a more mature stage in their professional careers (graduate students and experienced teachers), might not accommodate to on-going reflection on action. These students might ultimately find themselves opening up Pandora boxes in their personal lives and being left with a feeling of unfinished business once the course has terminated. Eventually, sessions that focus on personal aspects of the experi-ence (through the sharing of critical incidents, cases, or stories) should not cross the border into becoming therapeutic sessions (Orland-Barak, 2004).

It is also important to offer students the possibility of introspecting into the underlying assumptions, beliefs, and past and present experiences that shape the orientations that they adopt toward a particular aspect of their practice. One strategy adopted for encouraging reflection at personal levels without giving students the feeling that they have to expose personal matters to others is allotting time for engaging in reflective writing during the sessions at the university, which they can then chose to either share or not with others during the session. Thus, students are encouraged to reflect on the personal motives that led them to explore a particular issue in their practice, but they are not compelled to expose their personal reflections in their actual reports if they choose not to. This calls for exhibiting cultural sensitivity through discursive practices of appreciation, participation, and improvisation that grant recognition of culturally diverse texts and privileged and rejected discourses, that attend to culturally valued texts, that connect emotionally and professionally to respond to contextual differences, and that foreground connections between cultural codes, values, and strategic and pedagogic reasoning.

11.2.2 Constructivist Discourses in a Problem-Solving Context

Constructivist pedagogies engage the learner in constant questioning rather than arriving at 'neat' solutions to problem-solving processes (Green, 2002, p. 130). Said that, it is important to keep a balance between encouraging questions and arriving at tentative solutions. This would imply that sessions should combine constructivist modes of teaching (by encouraging students to generate theory as they articulate concepts and questions that emerge from their projects) with more controlled forms of teaching, allowing for a 'rounding up' and converging into a sum up of the notions that emerge during the sessions (Orland-Barak, 2004).

It is also important to bear in mind that if the structure of a course in graduate education program is inherently different from the rest of the program, students will find it difficult to adapt to. In the face of uncertainty, students are faced with either abandoning the process, becoming cynical about it, or eventually learning to adapt (Straker & Hall, 1999, p. 429). To this end, it is important to provide ample 'negotiatory spaces' during the course, that is, allotting time for students to question, probe, and scrutinize the introduction of a new form of discourse (Carson, 1997).

In graduate and in-service contexts, pedagogies of co-construction, in academic settings, can be complex, paradoxical, and ambiguous to both the course professor and the student participant. Inquiry into these contexts surfaces emergent tensions between two rigid discourses: One is the course professor's constructivist discourse which often reflects a more relativistic epistemology (Fox, 2001) and pushes toward articulating dilemmas and co-constructing meanings grounded in 'here and now' conversations. Such discourse also prioritizes intellectual over interpersonal confrontations and multiple perspectives over evaluation of performances, assuming that ingrained traditional, mandated approaches can shift to more constructivist practices, when participants talk the language of constructivism during the sessions. The other discourse, however, is the participants' more deterministic discourse, pushing toward clear-cut answers and solving problems, and expectations to evaluate performance and to confront interpersonal issues. These tensions have been proved to be similar in a variety of cultural contexts such as Israeli, North American, British, and Finnish (Orland-Barak, 2005).

11.2.3 What Can Go Wrong in Constructivist Pedagogy in Academic Mentoring Contexts?

> *How do I model my ideas about good mentoring in my own work with students?*
> *What are the consequences for students learning?*
> *What kind of resistances might it create? To what extent am I sensitive to different voices and discourses of practice represented in the sessions?*
>
> **thinking in practice**

The strategy of generating a grounded theoretical discussion out of the immediate 'here and now' situation, in an academic setting, is neither conventional nor easy to implement. It requires of the course professor to be particularly attentive to issues that emerge 'on the spot' and how these might connect to theoretical notions discussed in class, as a way of encouraging a discourse that is generative of new insights. More so, it becomes a particularly complicated endeavor when the 'recipient' student population is mentors of teachers who function as agents of change appointed to disseminate defined agendas and curricula, very often through predominantly 'top–down' modes of intervention.

Let me share snapshots of what can go wrong in constructivist pedagogy through a personal incident (Adapted from Orland-Barak, 2005c):

Orit, a successful veteran mentor of teachers of literacy had, since the beginning of the year, displayed signs of resistance toward the constructivist case-based nature of our sessions at the university. When Orit presented her case in class, participants were invited to relate to the case. As part of the constructivist tradition of developing an open-ended discourse that would challenge participants to critically surface dilemmas around the case, the group was invited to ask Orit questions regarding her case. Orit, for her part, was encouraged to document the questions that came from the floor, and use them as a springboard for reflecting on her practice (similar to the process detailed in the previous chapter). This procedure was meant to develop appreciation by conveying the message that questions need not always be 'answered,' but can be used as triggers for reexamining ingrained assumptions. This also implied diverging from the traditional question–answer mode and from the need to 'prove yourself right,' or to arrive at the best possible solution. In the spirit of probing and challenging (modeling, to a great extent, my own improvisation modes), the group had asked questions: Why did you choose to share with us a successful case of your practice? How does your case reflect your assumptions about agency? and so forth. For me, the constructivist course professor, participants' questions evidenced, indeed, that they were learning to appreciate, participate, and improvise in ways that attended to a more critical discourse of practice. Although the strategy of assembling questions from the audience, documenting them, and using them later on to raise dilemmas of practice, rather than solutions to a problem, had not been an easy process to induce, raising such questions constituted 'good news' of their development as critical, activist pedagogues.

Not for Orit, though. As people asked questions, Orit gradually raised her anxiety about the situation, to the extent that she began getting resistant and even aggressive toward the whole process. At a certain point she stopped everything and voiced her fervent disagreement to the whole process 'protesting' that she was not learning much from the entire process because she was not getting clear-cut answers about what good mentoring is all about.

Orit, whose comment embedded a prominently 'problem-solving discourse,' was not learning from the experience, and probably others too.

Disturbed by the incident, I used it as 'a loop' for analyzing the ways in which professional conversations in mentoring structured around a constructivist approach can, on the one hand, facilitate and enhance learning but, on the other hand, block certain participants, as in Orit's case.

The incident highlighted for me the voices that are claimed and those that are silenced when the course mentor professor tries to promote a 'dilemmatic' kind of discourse with a 'problem-solving' type of audience-participants. Orit's persistence in seeking clear-cut answers, as opposed to my persistence in documenting clear-cut questions, created a situation in which two competing discourses, the 'dilemmatic-knowing that' discourse (conveying the hegemony of abstraction of the academic world) and the 'problem-solving-knowing how' discourse (representing the concrete world of practice), were struggling to gain prominence on the conversational floor.

As mentioned at the outset of this section, constructivist pedagogy in academic mentoring contexts is not an easy endeavor and can often 'go wrong.' The lessons learned remind us about the importance of raising the mentor's awareness of his/her various positionings and construals in relation to the discursive practices that he/she appreciates and participates in and through which he/she improvises.

Chapter 12
Epilogue: Putting It All Together

Quoting Richardson (1997) in *Fields of Play: Constructing an Academic Life*, Miller-Marsh (2002) reminds us that each of us sees from 'somewhere,' and because we are always on some corner, standing somewhere, each of us harbors an ideological preference and political program. The important thing, she suggests, is to examine the corners on which each of us stand by, identifying the ideologies embedded in the discourse that predominate in our speech and actions (p. 106). Learning to mentor as a discursive practice is about examining those corners and making them transparent to others. And, in the writing of this book, I also hope to have made my own corners transparent.

Writing a book about learning to mentor-as-praxis marks, without doubt, the contours of a personal, professional, and academic journey. As Peshkin (2000) reminds us '. . . by looking at what problems interest us and at what questions we ask, we may discover an avenue that leads us to a better understanding of what is important and of meaning to each of us . . . [One's] research is autobiographical in that some aspect of yourself is mirrored in the work you choose to pursue. . .' (p. 178). The journey that I decided to undertake is rooted in a strong ideological, educational, and pedagogical standpoint toward how the practice of mentoring should be conceptualized. Such a standpoint, embedded in the discourse of my speech and actions, is grounded in the complex webs of my lived and researched experiences as a mentor, as a mentor of mentors, as a teacher educator, and as a researcher. Yet, in writing, as in speaking, we come to know (Goodall, 2000, p. 127) and, indeed, the journey revealed itself [every time anew] at the point of my pen (Malquais in Mailer, 1997), constantly challenging me to construct and reconstruct emergent understandings of how discursive, dialogical processes of appreciation, participation, and improvisation play out in 'real-life' mentoring situations. The process grounded in hermeneutic cycles of close interpretative readings of multiple data sources. Gadamer (1975) entailed constant dialogue between the parts and the whole by zooming in and out of the experience, while attending to the whole as being '*more* than the sum of its parts.' Pamela Lomax (2000) refers to this process as an intra-subjective dialect through which one's own understanding is transformed, as one engages in the struggle to represent what one means (p. 43). Hence, the process of writing became in itself a method of inquiry (Connelly & Clandinin, 1990; Denzin & Lincoln, 1994). The new

L. Orland-Barak, *Learning to Mentor-as-Praxis*, Professional Learning and Development in Schools and Higher Education 4, DOI 10.1007/978-1-4419-0582-6_12,
© Springer Science+Business Media, LLC 2010

interpretative journey I engaged in has engendered, I hope, a new body of knowledge which can inform thinking and acting in the practice, and which is open to scrutiny and reexamination.

I return to the initial incentive that guided the writing of this book – that teacher education be more concerned with the question of which educational, moral, and political commitments ought to guide our work in the field rather than with solely dwelling on procedures and organizational arrangements (Zeichner, 1983; Cochran-Smith, 2004; Villegas & Lucas, 2002). The various chapters in the book have, I hope, attended to this call by foregrounding how ideologies, rituals, values, belief systems, and behaviors play out to shape mentors' attributions, reasoning, and actions in a variety of mentoring contexts and interactions.

The stories, reflecting multicultural and multidisciplinary ideologies, values, belief systems, and behaviors provide authentic, situated scenarios of modes of appreciation, participation, and improvisation in praxis. As such, they underscore an extended view of learning to mentor, one which goes beyond the initial vision of Mentor as a guide, instructor, and protector of his protégé Telemachus. As in the words of Athens while appearing to Telemachus in the form of Mentor:

> Then this journey will not be vain or fruitless … And the journey that you have set your heart on shall not elude you long. I am too good of a friend for that – to your father first and now for you; I will rig a fast-sailing ship for you and will sail with you myself pp. 18–19 (Homer, 1998)

Mentoring is a joint venture that requires both parties (mentor and mentee) the moral commitment and responsibility to take an active part in the learning process of growth, development, and change. In a similar spirit, writing a book engages writer and reader; god and men; and creation, the created and those for whom it is created, in a shared journey of change and development. I see my humble duty to attempt framing a new conceptual trajectory. I am led by the certainty that each reader will responsibly direct its further evolution as guided by the values and moral commitments to the profession.

References

Achinstein, B., & Athanases, S. Z. (Eds.). (2006). *Mentors in the making*. New York: Teachers College Press.

Adler, P., Lovaas, K., & Milner, N. (1988). The ideologies of mediation: The movement's own story. *Law and Policy*, 10(4), 317–319.

Anderson, E. A., & Shannon, A. L. (1988). Toward a conceptualization of mentoring. *Journal of Teacher Education*, > January–February, 38–42.

Argyris, C., & Schon, D. A. (1996). *Organizational learning II: Theory, method, and practice*. Reading, MA: Addison-Wesley.

Aristotle. (1985). *Nicomachean ethics*, (T. Irwin, Trans.). Indianapolis: Hackett Publ. Co.

Athanases, S. Z., & Achinstein, B. (2003). Focusing new teachers on individual and low performing students: The centrality of formative assessment in the mentor's repertoire of practice. *Teachers College Record*, 105(8), 1486–1520.

Austin, J. L. (1962). *How to do things with words*. In J. O. Urmson (Ed.). Oxford: Clarendon Press.

Bailey, D. B. (1996). Preparing early intervention professionals for the twenty-first century. In M. Brambring, H. Rauh, & A. Beelman (Eds.), *Early childhood intervention: Theory, evaluation, and practice* (pp. 488–503). New York: Walter DeGryter.

Bakhtin, M. (1981). *The dialogic imagination: Four essays by M.M. Bakhtin*. In M. Holquist & C. Emerson (Trans. and Ed.). Austin: University of Texas Press.

Bakhtin, M. (1984). *Problems of Dostoevsky's poetics*. C. Emerson(Ed. and Trans.). Minneapolis: University of Michigan Press.

Bakhtin, M. (1986). *Speech genre and other essays*. Austin: University of Texas.

Baldwin, C. (1977). *One to one: Self understanding through journal writing*. New York: M. Evans.

Ball, D. L. (2000). Bridging practices: Intertwining content and pedagogy in teaching and learning to teach. *Journal of Teacher Education*, 51, 241–247.

Ball, D. L., & Wilson, S. M. (1996). Integrity in teaching: Recognizing the fusion of the moral and intellectual. *American Educational Research Journal*, 33, 155–192.

Bar-On, R. (2000). Emotional and social intelligence: Insights from the Emotional Quotient Inventory. In R. Bar-On & J. D. A. Parker (Eds.), *The handbook of emotional intelligence* (pp. 363–388). San Francisco: Jossey-Bass.

Bardram, J. (1998). Designing for the dynamics of cooperative work activities. *Proceedings of the 1998 ACM conference on computer supported cooperative work* (pp. 89–98). November, 14–18, 1998. Washington, United States, Seattle.

Bass, B. M. (1985). *Leadership and performance beyond expectation*. New York: Free Press.

Beauchamp, C., & Thomas, L. (2006). *Imagination and reflection in teacher education: The development of professional identity from student teaching to beginning practice*. Symposium Proceedings of the 4th International Conference on Imagination and Education, Opening Doors to Imaginative Education: Connecting Theory to Practice, Vancouver, British Columbia, July, 2006.

L. Orland-Barak, *Learning to Mentor-as-Praxis*, Professional Learning and Development in Schools and Higher Education 4, DOI 10.1007/978-1-4419-0582-6, © Springer Science+Business Media, LLC 2010

Behar, L. S. (1994). An empirical analysis of curriculum domains: Implications for program development and evaluation. *Peabody Journal of Education*, 69(4), 100–112.

Beijaard, D., Van Driel, J., & Verloop, N. (1999). Evaluation of story-line methodology in research on teachers' practical knowledge. *Studies in Educational Evaluation*, 25(1), 47–62.

Ben-Peretz, M., Mendelson, N., & Kron, F. W. (2003). How teachers in different educational contexts view their roles. *Teaching and Teacher Education*, 19(2), 277–290.

Bengtsson, J. (1995). What is reflection? On reflection in the teaching profession and teacher education. *Teacher and Teaching: Theory and Practice*, 1(1), 23–32.

Benner, P. (1982). Issues in competency-based nursing. *Nursing Outlook*, 30(5), 303–309.

Benner, P. (1984). *From novice to expert: Excellence and power in clinical nursing practice.* California: Addison-Wesley.

Bereiter, C. (2002). *Education and mind in the knowledge society.* Mahwah: Lawrence Erlbaum Associates Publishers.

Berger, P., & Luckmann, T. (1966). *The social construction of reality.* Garden City, New York: Doubleday.

Berliner, D. C. (1987). Ways of thinking about students and classrooms by more and less experienced teachers. In J. Calderhead (Ed.), *Exploring teachers' thinking* (pp. 60–83). London: Cassell Education Limited.

Berliner, D. C. (2001). Learning about and learning from expert teachers. *International Journal of Educational Research*, 35(5), 463–482.

Berschfield, E. (1994). Interpersonal relationships. *Annual Review of Psychology*, 45, 79–92.

Blau, P. M. (1964). *Exchange and power in social life.* New York: Wiley.

Bloom, B. S. (1953). Thought processes in lectures and discussions. *Journal of General Education*, 7, 160–169.

Blumenthal, D. (1999). Representing the divided self. *Qualitative Inquiry*, 5(3), 377–393.

Borko, H., & Livingston, C. (1989). Cognition and improvisation: Differences in mathematics instruction by expert and novice teachers. *American Educational Research Journal*, 26(4), 473–498.

Bornstein, M. H., & Bruner, J. S. (Eds.). (1989). *Interaction in human development.* Hillsdale, NJ: Lawrence Erlbaum Associates Publishers.

Boshhuizen, H. P. A., Bromme, R., & Gruber, H. (Eds.). (2004). *Professional learning: Gaps and transitions on the way from novice to expert.* Netherlands: Kluwer Academic Publishers.

Bourdieu, P. (1977). *Outline of a theory of practice.* Cambridge: Cambridge University Press. (First published in French, 1973). (R. Nice, Trans.).

Bradbury, L. U., & Koballa, T. R., Jr. (2008). Borders to cross: Identifying sources of tension in mentor–intern relationships. *Teaching and Teacher Education*, 24, 2132–2145.

Brown, M., & Edelson, D. C. (2001, April). *Teaching by design: Curriculum design as a lens on instructional practice.* Paper presented at the Annual meeting of the American Educational Research Association. Seattle, WA.

Brown, S., & Glasner, A. (Eds.). (1999). *Assessment matters in higher education: Choosing and using diverse approaches.* Buckingham, UK: SRHE & Open University Press.

Burke, K. (1989). *Symbols and society.* Chicago: University of Chicago Press.

Brundage, D. H., & Mackerarcher, D. (1980). *Adult learning principles and their application to program planning.* Toronto: Ontario Institute for Studies in Education.

Bruner, J. (1986). *Actual minds, possible worlds.* Massachusetts: Harvard University Press.

Bruner, J. (1990). *Acts of mind.* Cambridge, MA: Harvard University Press.

Buber, M. (2000). *I and thou.* (R. Gregor Smith, Trans.). New York: Scribner Classics.

Buber, M. (2002). *Between man and man.* London, New York: Routledge. (First presented at the National conference of Jewish Teachers of Palestine, Tel Aviv, 1939). (R. Gregor-Smith, Trans.).

Bullough, R. V. (1989). *First-year teacher.* New York: Teachers College Press.

Bullough, R. V., Jr. (2005). Being and becoming a school-based mentor: School-based teacher educators and teacher educator identity. *Teaching and Teacher Education*, 21, 143–155.

Bulterman-Bos, J. A. (2008). Will a clinical approach make education research more relevant for practice? *Educational Researcher*, 37(7), 412–420.

Burns, J. M. (1978). *Leadership*. New York: Harper and Row.

Butt, R., & Raymond, D. (1988). Studying the nature and development of teachers' knowledge using collaborative biography. *International Journal of Educational Research*, 13, 403–419.

Byham, W. C. (1996). *What is an assessment center; method, application and technologies?* Los Angeles: Development Dimensions International.

Calderhead, J., & Shorrock, S. B. (1997). *Understanding teacher education*. London: The Falmer Press.

Candlin, C. N., & Maley, Y. (1997). Intertextuality and interdiscursivity in the discourse of alternative dispute resolution. In B. L. Gunnarsson, P. Linell, & B. Nordberg (Eds.), *The construction of professional discourse*. London: Longman.

Carr, D. (1999). Is teaching a skill? In: R. Curren (Ed.), *Philosophy of education yearbook* (pp. 204–12). Urbana, Ill. Philosophy of Education Society.

Carr, W., & Kemmis, S. (1986). *Becoming critical: Education, knowledge and action research*. London: Palmer.

Carson, T. R. (1997). Reflection and its resistances: Teacher education as a living practice. In T. R. Carson & D. J. Sumara (Eds.), *Action research as living practice* (pp. 77–93). New York: Peter Lang Publishing Inc.

Carter, K. (1988). Using cases to frame novice–mentor conversations about teaching. *Theory into Practice*, 27, 214–222.

Carter, K. (1990). Teachers' knowledge and learning to teach. In W. R. Houston (Ed.), *Handbook of research on teacher education* (pp. 291–310). New York: Macmillan.

Carter, M., & Francis, R. (2001). Mentoring and beginning teachers' workplace learning. *Asia-Pacific Journal of Teacher Education*, 29(3), 249–262.

Chambers, A. (1983). *Introducing books to children* (2nd ed.). Boston: The Horn Book Inc.

Clandinin, J. (2001). Foreword. In C. M. Clark (Ed.), *Talking shop* (pp. vi, vii). New York: Columbia University; Teachers College Press.

Clandinin, J., & Connelly, F. M. (1987). Teachers personal knowledge: What counts "personal" in studies of the personal. *Journal of Curriculum Studies*, 19, 487–500.

Clark, C. M. (1995). *Thoughtful teaching*. New York: Teachers College Press.

Clark, C. M. (2001). *Talking shop: Authentic conversation and teachers learning*. New York: Teachers College Press.

Clark, K., & Holquist, M. (1984). *Mikhail bakhtin*. Cambridge, MA: Harvard University Press.

Cobb, S. (1976). Social support as a moderator of life stress. *Psychosomatic Medicine*, 38, 300–314.

Cobb, P. (1994). Where is the mind? Constructivist and sociocultural perspectives on mathematical development. *Educational Researcher*, 23(7), 13–20.

Cochran-Smith, M. (2004). The problem of teacher education. *Journal of Teacher Education*, 55(4), 295–299.

Cochran-Smith, M., & Demers, K. (2008). Teacher education as a bridge? Unpacking curriculum controversies. In F. M. Connelly (Ed.), *The sage handbook of curriculum and instruction* (pp. 263–281). California: Sage Publications.

Cochran-Smith, M., & Fries, M. K. (2002). The discourse of reform in teacher education: Extending the dialogue. *Educational Researcher*, 31(6), 26–28.

Cochran-Smith, M., & Lytle, S. (1991). Research on teaching and teacher research: The issues that divide. *Educational Researcher*, 19(2), 2–10.

Cochran-Smith, M., & Lytle, S. (1993). *Inside/outside: Teacher research and knowledge*. New York: Teacher's College Press.

Conle, C. (2001). The rationality of narrative inquiry in research and professional development. *European Journal of Teacher Education*, 24(1), 21–33.

Conle, C. (2006). Moral qualities of experiential narratives. *Journal of Curriculum Studies*, 6, 1–20.

Connelly, F. M., & Clandinin, D. J. (1986). Rythms in teaching: The narrative study of teachers' personal practical knowledge of classrooms. *Teaching and Teacher Education*, 2(4), 377–387.

Connelly, F. M., & Clandinin, D. J. (1990). Stories of experience and narrative inquiry. *Educational Researcher*, 19(5), 2–14.

Connelly, F. M., & Clandinin, D. J. (1995). Narrative and education. *Teachers and Teaching: Theory and Practice*, 1(1), 73–85.

Connelly, F. M., & Clandinin, D. J. (1999). *Shaping a professional identity: Stories of educational practice*. New York: Teachers College Press.

Convery, A. (1999). Listening to teachers' stories: Are we sitting too comfortably? *International Journal of Qualitative Studies in Education*, 12(2), 131–146.

Conway, P. F. (2001). Anticipatory reflection while learning to teach: From a temporally truncated to a temporally distributed model of reflection in teacher education. *Teaching and Teacher Education*, 17(2), 89–106.

Conway, P. F., & Clark, C. M. (2003). The journey inward and outward: A re-examination of Fuller's concerns-based model of teacher development. *Teaching and Teacher Education*, 19, 465–482.

Cooper, J. E. (1991). Tell our own stories: The reading and writing of journals and diaries. In C. Witherell & N. Noddings (Eds.), *Stories lives tell: Narrative and dialogue in education* (pp. 91–112). New York: Teachers College Press.

Craig, C. J. (2009). Research in the midst of organized school reform: Versions of teacher community in tension. *American Educational Research Journal*, 46(2), 598–619.

Craig, C. J., & Deretchin, L. F. (Eds.). (2009). *Teacher learning in small-group settings. Teacher education yearbook xvii*. U.K.: Rowman & Littlefield Education.

Daloz, K. (1983). Mentors: Teacher who make a difference. *Change*, 15(6), 7–24.

Darling-Hammond, L. (1988). Policy and professionalism. In A. Lieberman (Ed.), *Building a professional culture in schools* (pp. 55–77). New York: Teachers College Press.

Darling-Hammond, L. (2000). Authentic assessment of teaching in context. *Teaching and Teacher Education*, 16, 523–545.

Darling–Hammond, L., & McLaughlin, M. W. (1996). Policies that support professional development in an era of reform. In M. W. Mc. Laughlin, & I. Oberman (Eds.), *Teacher learning: New policies, new practices* (pp. 202–218). New York: Teachers College Press.

Day, C. (1998). Working with the different selves of teachers: Beyond comfortable collaboration. *Educational Action Research*, 6(2), 255–272.

Day, C. (1999). *Developing teachers: Developing teachers: The challenges of lifelong learning*. London, New York: Routledge.

Day, C., Kington, A., Stobart, G., & Sammons, P. (2006). The personal and professional selves of teachers: Stable and unstable identities. *British Educational Research Journal*, 32(4), 601–616.

DeCoster, D. A., & Brown, R. D. (1982). Mentoring relationships and the educational process. In R. D. Brown & D. A. DeCoster (Eds.), *Mentoring-transcript systems for promoting student growth. New directions for student services* (pp. 5–18, No. 19). San Francisco: Jossey-Bass.

Denicolo, P., & Pope, M. (1990). Adults learning – teacher thinking. In C. Day, M. Pope & P. Denicolo (Eds.), *Insight into teachers' thinking and practice* (pp. 155–170). London: The Falmer Press.

Denzin, N. K., & Lincon, Y. S. (1994). The fifth moment. In N. K. Denzin, & Y. S. Lincon, (Eds.), *Handbook of qualitative research* (pp. 575–587). London: Sage Publications.

Dewey, J. (1933). *How we think*. Buffalo, NY: Prometheus Books (Original work published in 1910).

Diamond, C. (1994). Writing to reclaim the self: The use of narrative in teacher education. *Teaching and Teacher Education*, 9(5/6), 511–517.

Diamond, C. T. P., & Mullen, C. A. (1997). Alternative perspectives on mentoring in higher education: Demography as collaborative relationship and inquiry. *Journal of Applied Social Behavior*, 3(2), 49–64.

Edwards, A., & Collison, J. (1996). *Mentoring and developing practice in primary schools supporting student teacher learning in schools*. Buckingham: Open University Press.

Edwards, A., Gilroy, P., & Hartley, D. (2002). *Rethinking teacher education, collaborative responses to uncertainty*. London: Routledge Falmer Press.

Eisner, E., & Powell, K. (2002). Art in science? *Curriculum Inquiry*, 32(2), 131–159.

Elbaz, F. (1983). *Teacher thinking: A study of practical knowledge*. New York: Nichols.

Elbaz-Luwisch, F., Moen, T., & Gudmundsdottir, S. (2002). *Narrativity and biographical research: Stories of teachers and philosophers*. Sophy Press: University of Jyvafkyla.

Elbaz-Luwisch, F. (2001). Personal story as passport: Story telling in border pedagogy. *Teaching Education*, 12(1), 81–101.

Elliott, B., & Calderhead, J. (1993). Mentoring for teacher development: Possibilities and caveats. In D. McIntyre, H. Hagger, & M. Wilkin, *Mentoring: Perspectives on school-based teacher education* (pp. 166–189). London: Kogan Page.

Elnir, P. (2005). *The interpersonal and the professional in group mentoring*. M.A. Thesis, University of Haifa.

Engeström, Y. (1994). Teachers as collaborative thinkers: Activity theoretical study of an innovative teacher team. In I. Carlgren, (Ed.), *Teachers' minds and actions* (pp. 43–46). London: The Falmer Press.

Engeström, Y. (1995). Voice as communicative action. *Mind, Culture, and Activity*, 2(3), 192–214.

Engeström, Y. (2001). Expansive learning at work: Toward activity theoretical reconceptualization. *Journal of Education and Work*, 14(1), 133–156.

Eraut, M. (1995). Schön Shock: A case for reframing reflection-in-action? *Teacher and Teaching: Theory and Practice*, 1(1), 9–22.

Eraut, M. (2004). Practice-based evidence. In G. Thomas, & R. Pring, (Eds.), *Evidence-based practice in education* (pp. 91–101). Maindenhead, UK: Open University Press.

Erickson, F. (1982). Classroom discourse as improvisation: Relationships between academic task structure and social participation structure in lessons. In L. C. Wilkinson (Ed.), *Communicating in the classroom* (pp. 153–181). New York: Academic Press.

Erikson, E. H. (1989). *Identity and the life cycle*. New York: International Universities Press.

Evans, T. W. (2000). The new mentors. *Teachers College Record*, 102(1), 244–263.

Evertson, C. M., & Smithey, M. W. (2000). Mentoring effects on protégés' classroom practice: An experimental field study. *Journal of Educational Research*, 93(5), 294–304.

Fairclough, N. (1989). *Language and power*. London: Longman.

Fairclough, N. (1992). *Discourse and social change*. London: Polity.

Farr Darling, L. (2001). Portfolio as practice: The narratives of emerging teachers. *Teaching and Teacher Education*, 17, 107–121.

Feiman-Nemser, S. (2001). From preparation to practice: Designing a continuum to strengthen and sustain teaching. *Teachers College Record*, 103(6), 1013–1055.

Feiman-Nemser, S. (1994). *Teacher socialization*. National Center for Research on Teacher Learning, Michigan State University.

Feiman-Nemser, S. (2001). From preparation to practice: Designing a continuum to strengthen and sustain teaching. *Teachers College Record*, 103(6), 1013–1055.

Feiman-Nemser, S., & Parker, M. B. (1993). Mentoring in context: A comparison of two U.S. programs for beginning teachers. *International Journal of Educational Research*, 19(8), 699–718.

Feiman-Nemser, S., & Remillard, J. (1996). Perspectives on learning to teach. In F. Murray (Ed.), *The teacher educator's handbook: Building a knowledge base for the preparation of teachers* (pp. 63–91). San Francisco: Jossey-Bass.

Fendler, L. (2003). Teacher reflection in a hall of mirrors: Historical influences and political reverberations. *Educational Researcher*, 32(3), 16–25.

Fenstermacher, G. D. (1990). Some moral considerations of teaching as a profession. In J. I. Goodlad, R. Sodler, & K. Sirotnik (Eds.), *The moral dimensions of teaching* (pp. 130–154). San Francisco: Jossey-Bass.

Fineman, M. (1988). Dominant discourse, professional languages and legal change in child custody decision making. *Harvard Law Review*, 101(4), 727–774.

Fish, D. (1998). *Appreciating practice in the caring professions: Refocusing professional development & practitioner research*. Oxford: Butterworth Heinemann.

Fiske, J. (1987). *Television culture*. London: Methuen.

Fiske, J. (1989). *Understanding copular culture*. Boston: Unwin Hyman.

Flanagan, J. C. (1954). The critical incident technique. *Psychological Bulletin*, 51(4), 327–358.

Fleming, J., & Benedek, T. F. (1983). *Psychoanalytic supervision*. New York: International Universities Press.

Flores, M. A., & Day, C. (2006). Contexts which shape and reshape new teachers' identities: A multi-perspective study. *Teaching and Teacher Education*, 22(2), 219–232.

Florio-Ruane, S. (1991). Conversation and narrative in collaborative research: An ethnography of the written literary forum. In C. Witherell, & N. Noddings, (Eds.), *Stories lives tell: Narrative and dialogue in education* (pp. 234–256). New York: Teachers College Press.

Florio-Ruane, S., & Clark, C. M. (1993, August). *Authentic conversation: A medium for research on teachers' knowledge and a context for professional development*. Paper presented to the international study association on teacher thinking. Gothenburg, Sweden.

Foucault, M. (1990). *Politics, philosophy, culture: Interviews and other writings, 1997–1984*. New York: Routledge.

Foucault, M. (1997). Subjectivity and truth. In P. Rabinow, (Series Ed. & Vol. Ed.). *The essential works of Michel Foucault 1954–1984: Vol. 1. Ethics: Subjectivity and truth* (pp. 87–92). New York: The New Press.

Fox, R. (2001). Constructivism examined. *Oxford Review of Education*, 27(1), 23–35.

Franke, A., & Dahlgren, L. O. (1996). Conceptions of mentoring: An empirical study of conceptions of mentoring during the school-based teacher education. *Teaching and Teacher Education*, 12(6), 627–641.

Freeman, D. (1993). Renaming experience/reconstructing practice: Developing new understanding of teaching. *Teaching and Teacher Education*, 9(5–6), 485–497.

Freire, P. (1970). *Pedagogy of the oppressed*. New York: Seabury.

Frost, A., & Yarrow, R. (1989). *Improvisation in drama*. New York: St. Martin's Press.

Fullan, M. (1991). *The new meaning of educational change*. New York: Teachers College Press.

Fuller, F., & Bown, O. H. (1975). Becoming a teacher. In K. Ryan (Ed.), *Teacher education, 74th yearbook of the national society for the study of education* (pp.25–52, Part 2). Chicago IL: University of Chicago Press.

Gadamer, H. G. (1975). *Truth and method*. New York: Seabury Press.

Gadotti, M. (1996). *Pedagogy of praxis: A dialectical philosophy of education*. Albany: State University of New York Press.

Garman, N. B. (1986). Reflection, the heart of clinical supervision: A modern rationale for professional practice. *Journal of Curriculum and Supervision*, 2(1), 23–41.

Gee, J. (1996). *Social linguistics and literacies: Ideology in discourses* (2nd ed.). London: Taylor & Francis.

Gee, J. (1999). *An introduction to discourse analysis: Theory and method*. New York: Routledge.

Gee, J. (2001). Identity as an analytic lens for research in education. *Review of Research in Education*, 25, 99–125.

Georgakopoulou, A. (2006). The other side of the story: Towards a narrative analysis of narrative-in-interaction. *Discourse and Studies*, 8(2), 235–257.

Gergen, K. J. (1985). The social constructionist movement in modern psychology. *The American Psychologist*, 40(3), 266–275.

Gergen, K. J. (1994). *Realities and relationships: Soundings in social construction*. Cambridge, London: Harvard University Press.

Giddens, A. (2000). *Runaway world: How globalization is reshaping our lives*. New York: Routledge Falmer.

Giroux, H. A. (1996). Educational visions: What are schools for and what should we be doing in the name of education? In J. L. Kincheloe, & S. R. Steinberg (Eds.), *Thirteen questions* (pp. 295–303). New York: Peter Lang.

Giroux, H. A. (2005). The terror of neoliberalism: Rethinking the significance of cultural politics. *College Literature*, 32(1), 1–19.

Glaser, R. (1987). Thoughts on expertise. In C. Schooler, & W. Schaie, (Eds.), *Cognitive functioning and social structure over the life course*. Norwood, NJ: Ablex.

Glass, R. D. (2001). On Paulo Freire's Philosophy of Praxis and the Foundations of Liberation Education. *Educational Researcher*, 30(2), 15–25.

Glazer, J. L. (2008). Educational professionalism: An inside-out view. *American Journal of Education*, 114(2), 168–189.

Goldberg, T., Porat, D., & Schwartz, B. B. (2006). Here started the rift we see today: Student and textbook narratives between official and countermemory. *Narrative Inquiry*, 16(2), 319–347.

Goodall, H. L. (2000). *Writing the new ethnography*. New York: Altamira Press.

Goodfellow, J. (2003). Practical wisdom in professional practice: The person in the process. *Contemporary Issues in Early Childhood*, 4(1), 48–63.

Goodlad, J. I., Soder, R., & Sirotnik, K. (1990). *The moral dimensions of teaching*. San Francisco: Jossey-Bass.

Goodson, I. (1992). *Studying teachers' lives*. London: Routledge.

Goodson, I. F., & Hargreaves, A. (1996). *Teachers professional lives*. London: Falmer Press.

Goolishian, H. A. (1990). *Therapy as a co-created conversation*. Workshop in Sidney, Australia, May 21–22.

Gore, J. M., & Zeichner, K. M. (1991). Action Research and reflective teaching in preservice teacher education: A case study from the United States. *Teaching and Teacher Education*, 7(2), 119–136.

Gratch, A. (1998). Beginning teacher and mentor relationships. *Journal of Teacher Education*, 49(3), 220–227.

Green, K. (2002). Defining the field of literature in action research: A personal approach. In C. Day, J. Elliott, B. Somekh, & R. Winter, (Eds.), *Theory and practice in action research* (pp. 121–140). United Kingdom: Symposium Books.

Greeno, J. G. (1997). On claims that answer the wrong question. *Educational Researcher*, 26(1), 5–17.

Greeno, J. G., Collins, A., & Resnick, L. (1996). Cognition and learning. In D. Berliner & R. Calfee (Eds.), *Handbook of educational psychology* (pp. 15–46). New York: Simon and Schuster Macmillan.

Greenwood, J. (2003). The role of reflection in single and double loop learning. *Journal of Advanced Nursing*, 27(5), 1048–1053.

Griffiths, M. (1995). *Feminisms and the self*. New York: Routledge.

Grimmett, P. P., & Grehan, E. P. (1992). The nature of collegiality in teacher development: The case of clinical supervision. In A. Fullan, & A. Hargreaves, (Eds.), *Teacher development and educational change* (pp. 56–85). London: Falmer Press.

Grossman, P. L. (1991). Overcoming the apprenticeship of observation. *Teaching and Teacher Education*, 7, 345–357.

Grossman, P. L., Smagorinsky, P., & Valencia, S. (1999). Appropriating tools for teaching English: A theoretical framework for research on learning to teach. *American Journal of Education*, 108, 1–29.

Grossman, P., Wineburg, S., & Woolworth, S. (2001). Toward a theory of teacher community. *Teachers College Record*, 103, 942–1012.

Grumet, M. (1988). *Bitter milk: Women and teaching*. Amherst, MA: University of Massachusetts Press.

Gudmunsdottir, S. (1991). Story maker, story teller: Narrative structures in the curriculum. *Journal of Curriculum Studies*, 23(3), 207–218.

Guyton, E., & McIntyre, D. J. (1990). Student teaching and school experiences. In R. Houston (Ed.), *Handbook of research on teacher education* (pp. 329–348). New York, London: Macmillan.

Habermas, J. (1973). *Theory and practice*. (J. Viertel, Trans.). Boston: Beacon Press.

Halley, J. (Ed.). (1967). *Advanced techniques of hypnosis and therapy: The selected papers of Milton H. Erickson*. New York: Grune & Stratton.

Hammer, D. (2000). Teacher inquiry. In J. Minstrell, & E. van Zee (Eds.), *Inquiring into inquiry learning and teaching in science* (pp. 184–215). Washington DC: American Association for the Advancement of Science.

Hansen, D. T. (1994). Teaching and the sense of vocation [electronic version]. *Educational Theory*, 44(3), 276–279 (Retrieved from: http://www.ed.uiuc.edu/EPS/Educational-Theory/Contents/44_3_Hansen.asp).

Hansen, D. T. (1998). The moral is in the practice. *Teaching and Teacher Education*, 14, 643–655.

Hanson, N. R. (1958). *Patterns of discovery*. Cambridge: Cambridge University Press.

Hargreaves, A. (1982). *The challenge for the comprehensive school*. London: Routledge and Kegan Paul.

Hargreaves, A. (1992). Cultures of teaching: A focus for change. In A. Hargreaves, & M. Fullan (Eds.), *Understanding teacher development*. London: Cassell and New York: Teachers College Press.

Hargreaves, A. (2001). Emotional geographies of teaching. *Teachers College Record*, 103(6), 1056–1080.

Hargreaves, A., & Dawe, R. (1990). Paths of professional development: Contrived collegiality, collaborative culture, and the case of peer coaching. *Teaching and Teacher Education*, 6(3), 227–241.

Harre, R., & Gillett, G. (1994). *The Discursive mind*. USA: Sage publications.

Harrington, H. L., & Garrison, J. W. (1992). Cases as shared inquiry: A dialogical model of teacher preparation. *American Educational Research Journal*, 29(4), 715–735.

Hatton, N., & Smith, D. (1995). Reflection in teacher education: Towards definition and implementation. *Teaching and Teacher Education*, 11(1), 33–49.

Hawkey, K. (1997). Roles, responsibilities, and relationships in mentoring: A literature review and agenda for research. *Journal of Teacher Education*, 48(5), 325–335.

Heikkinen, H. (1998). Becoming yourself through narrative: Autobiographical approach in teacher education. In A. Erkkila, L. Willman, & L. Syrjala, U. P. Oulu (Eds.), *Promoting teachers' personal and professional growth* (pp. 111–131). Oulu: Oulu University Press.

Heron, J. (2001). *Helping the client – a creative practical guide* (5th ed). London: Sage publications.

Hicks, D. (1996). Discourse, learning, and teaching. In M. Apple (Ed.), *Review of research in education* (21, 49–95). Washington, DC: American Educational Research Association.

Higgs, J., & Titchen, A. (2001). Towards professional artistry and creativity in practice. In J. Higgs, & A. Titchen, (Eds.), *Professional practice in health, education and the creative arts* (pp. 273–290). Oxford: Blackwell Science.

Hofer, B., & Pintrich, P. R. (2002). *Personal epistemology, the psychology of beliefs about knowledge and knowing*. Mahwah: Lawrence Erlbaum Associates Publishers.

Holland, D., Lachicotte, W., Skinner, D., & Cain, C. (1998). *Identity and agency in cultural worlds*. Cambridge, MA: Harvard University Press.

Homer. (1998). *The odyssey*, (W. Shewring, Trans.). Oxford: Oxford University Press.

House, J. S. (1981). *Work stress and social support*. Reading, MA: Addison-Wesley.

Hunt, D. E. (1978). In-service training for persons in relation. *Theory into Practice*, 17, 239–244.

Hunt, D. M., & Michael, C. (1983). Mentorship: A career training and development tool. *Academy of Management Review*, 8, 475–485.

Hutchins, E. (1995). *Cognition in the wild*. Cambridge: The MIT Press.

Johnson, G. C. (2002). Using visual narrative and poststructuralism to (re)read a student teacher's professional practice. *Teaching and Teacher Education*, 18(4), 387–404.

R. Josselson (Ed.). (1996). *Ethics and process in narrative study of lives*. Newbury Park, California: Sage Publications.

Kagan, D. M. (1992). Professional growth among pre service and beginning teachers. *Review of Educational Research*, 62(2), 129–169.

Kagan, D. M. (1993). Contexts for the use of classroom cases. *American Educational Research Journal*, 30(4), 703–723.

Kagan, N., Krathwohl, D. R., & Miller, R. (1963). Stimulated recall in therapy using video tape: A case study. *Journal of Counseling Psychology*, 10(3), 237–243.

Kahn, C. N. (2001). *Pythagoras and the Pythagoreans: A brief history*. Indianapolis, IN: Hackett Publ. Co.

Kelchtermans, G., & Vandenberghe, R. (1994). Teachers' professional development: A biographical perspective. *Journal of Curriculum Studies*, 26(1), 45–62.

Kelly, G. A. (1955). *The psychology of personal construct*. New York: Norton.

Kerry, T., & Mayes, A. S. (1995). *Issues in mentoring*. London: Routledge.

Kessels, J. P. A. M., & Korthagen, F. A. J. (1996). The relationship between theory and practice: Back to the Classics. *Educational Researcher*, April, 19–22.

Kimberly, J. C. (1984). Cognitive balance, inequality, and consensus: Interrelations among fundamental processes in groups. In E. J. Lawler (Ed.), *Advances in group processes* (1, pp. 95–103).

Kitchener, K. S., & Brenner, H. G. (2003). Wisdom and reflective judgment: Knowing in the face of uncertainty. In: R. J. Sterberg (Ed.), *Wisdom: Its nature, origins and development*. New York: Cambridge University Press.

Kivinen, O., & Ristela, P. (2003). From constructivism to a pragmatist conception of learning. *Oxford Review of Education*, 29(3), 363–375.

Kizel, A. (2008). *Subservient history: A critical analysis of history curricula and textbooks in Israel 1948–2006*. Tel Aviv: Mofet (Hebrew).

Knowles, M. S. (1978). *The adult learner: A neglected species*. Houston, TX: Gulf.

F. Kochan, & D. Pascarelli (Eds.). (2003). *Global perspectives on mentoring*. Connecticut: Information Publishing Age.

Kooy, M. (2006). The telling stories of novice teachers: Constructing teacher knowledge in book clubs. *Teaching and Teacher Education*, 22, 661–674.

Korthagen, F. A. J. (1995). Characteristics of reflective practitioners: Towards an operationalization of the concept of reflection. *Teacher and Teaching: Theory and practice*, 1(1), 51–72.

Korthagen, F. A. J., & Kessels, J. P. A. M. (1999). Linking theory and practice: Changing the pedagogy of teacher education. *Educational Researcher*, 28(4), 4–17.

Korthagen, F. A. J., & Vasalos, A. (2005). Levels in reflection: Core reflection as a means to enhance professional growth. *Teachers and Teaching*, 11(1), 47–71.

Korthagen, F. A. J., & Wubbles, T. (1995). Characteristics of reflective practitioners: Towards an operationaliztion of the concept of reflection. *Teachers and Teaching: Theory and practice*, 1(1), 51–72.

Kram, K. E. (1985). *Mentoring at work: Developmental relationships in organizational life*. Glenviwe, IL: Scott Foresman.

Kristeva, J. (1986). *The Kristeva reader*. T. Moi (Ed.). Oxford, UK. Blackwell Science.

Kristjánsson, K. (2005). Smoothing IT: Some Aristotelian misgivings about the phronesis-praxis perspective on education. *Educational Philosophy and Theory*, 37(4), 455–473.

Kulavkova, K. (2004). *Intertextual options and modifications*. (Z. Anchevski, Trans.). (Retrieved from: http://www.kulavkova.org.mk/theory/intertxt.htm).

Kuutti, K. (1994). Information systems, cooperative work and active subjects: The activity-theoretical perspective. *Research papers, Ser A23*, Department of Information Processing Science, University of Oulu.

Kvale, S. (1995). The social construction of validity. *Qualitative Inquiry*, 1, 19–40.

Kvernbekk, T. (2000). Seeing in practice: A conceptual analysis. *Scandinavian Journal of Educational Research*, 44(4), 358–370.

Kwo, O. (1996). Learning to teach english in Hong-Kong classrooms: Patterns of reflection. In D. Freeman, & J. C. Richards, (Eds.), *Teacher learning in language teaching* (pp. 295–320). United Kingdom: Cambridge University Press.

Laboskey, V. K. (1994). A conceptual framework for reflection in preservice teacher education. In
   J. Calderhead, & P. Gates, (Eds), *Conceptualizing reflection in teacher development*. London:
   The Falmer Press.

Lantolf, J. P. (1994). Sociocultural theory and second language learning: Introduction to the special
   issue. *The Modern Language Journal*, 78(4), 418–420.

Lather, P. (1992). Ideology and methodological attitude. In W. Pinar (Ed.), *Contemporary
   curriculum discourses* (pp. 246–262). New York: Peter Lang.

Lave, J., & Wenger, E. (1991). *Situated learning, legitimate peripheral participation*. Cambridge:
   Cambridge University Press.

Leikin, R. & Dinvr, S. (2003). Patterns of flexability: Teachers' behaviour in mathematical discussion. *Electronic proceedings of the third conference of the European Society
   for Research in Mathematics Education*. (Retrieved from http://www.dm.unipi.it/~didattical/
   GERME3/WE11).

Leinhardt, G., & Greeno, J. G. (1986). The cognitive skill of teaching. *Journal of Educational
   Psychology*, 78(2), 75–95.

Leinhardt, G., McCarthy Young, K., & Merriman, J. (1995). Integrating professional knowledge:
   The theory of practice and the practice of theory. *Learning and Instruction*, 5(4), 401–408.

Lewis, C., & Ketter, J. (2004). Learning as social interaction: Interdiscursivity in a teacher and
   researcher study group. In R. Rogers (Ed.), *An introduction to critical discourse analysis in
   education* (pp. 117–146). New Jersey: Lawrence Erlbaum Associates Publishers.

Lickona, T. (1980). Preparing teachers to be moral educators: A neglected duty. *New Directions
   for Higher Education*, 8(3), 51–64.

Lieberman, A. (1995). Practices that support teacher development. *Phi Delta Kappan*, 76(8),
   591–596.

Lieberman, A., & Miller, L. (1999). *Teachers: Transforming their world and their work*. New York:
   Teachers College Press.

Lieberman, A., & Miller, L. (2004). *Teacher leadership*. San Fransisco: Jossey-Bass.

Linell, P. (1998). *Approaching dialogue: Talk, interaction, and contexts in dialogical perspectives*.
   Amsterdam: John Benjamins.

Linton, M. (1979). I remember it well. *Psychology Today*, July, 81–87.

Little, J. W. (1990). The mentor phenomenon and the social organisation of teaching. In C. B.
   Cazden (Ed.), *Review of research in education* (16, pp. 297–350). Washington, DC: AERA.

Little, J. W. (1993). Professional community in comprehensive high schools: The two worlds
   of academic and vocational teachers. In J. W. Little & M. W. McLaughlin (Eds.), *Teachers'
   work: Individuals, colleagues and contexts* (pp. 137–163). New York: Teacher College Press,
   Columbia University.

Little, J. W., & McLaughlin, M. W. (1993). Introduction: Perspectives on cultures and contexts of
   teaching. In J. W. Little & M. W. McLaughlin (Eds.), *Teachers' work: Individuals, colleagues
   and contexts* (pp. 1–8). New York: Teacher College Press, Columbia University.

Lomax, P. (2000). Coming to a better understanding of educative relations through learning from
   individual's representations of their action research. *Reflective Practice*, 1(1), 43–57.

Loughran, J. J. (2002). Effective reflective practice. In search of meaning in learning about
   teaching. *Journal of Teacher Education*, 53(1), 33–43.

Loughran, J. (2003) Knowledge construction and learning to teach about teaching. Keynote address
   presented at the ISATT biennial conference, Leiden, June 27–July 1.

Loughran, J., & Corrigan, D. (1995). Teaching Portfolios: A strategy for developing learning and
   teaching in pre-service education. *Teaching and Teacher Education*, 11(6), 565–577.

Luria, A. R. (1973). *The working brain: An introduction to neuropsychology*. New York: Basic.

MacIntyre, A. C. (1981). *After virtue: A study in moral theory*. Notre Dame, IN: University of
   Notre Dame Press.

McMillan, J. H. (Ed.). (2007). *Formative classroom assessment: Theory into practice*. New York:
   Teachers College Press.

Mailer, N. (1997, December). Man at his best. *Esquire*, p. 122.

Mason, L. (2005). *On warm conceptual change, the role of personal epistemology in knowledge
   restructuring*. Key note address. EARLI 2005 conference, Aug 23–27. Nicosia, Cyprus.

Mayeroff, M. (1971). *On caring.* New York: Harper and Row.

Maynard, T., & Furlong, J. (1993). Learning to teach and models of mentoring. In D. McIntyre, H. Hagger and M. Wilkin (Eds.), *Mentoring: Perspectives on school-based teacher education* (pp. 69–85). London: Kegan.

Mazor, E. (2003). *Druze student teachers in Jewish schools: Strangers in practice teaching placements learning to teach English.* Thesis submitted for the Degree of Doctor of Philosophy. Israel: Hebrew University.

McIntyre, D., & Hagger, H. (1993). Teachers' expertise and models of mentoring. In D. McIntyre, H. Hagger & M. Wilkin (Eds.), *Mentoring: Perspectives on school-based teacher education.* London: Kogan Page.

McIntyre, D., Hagger, H., & Wilkin, M. (Eds.). (1993). *Mentoring: Perspectives on school-based teacher education.* London: Kegan.

McIntyre, D., & Hagger, H. (1996). Mentoring: Challenges for the future. In: D. McIntyre & H. Hagger (Eds), *Mentors in schools* (pp. 144–165). London: David Fulton.

McLaren, P. (1986). *Schooling as a ritual performance: Towards a political economy of educational symbols and gestures.* London: Routledge and Kegan Paul.

McLaren, P. (1988). The liminal servant and the ritual roots of critical pedagogy. *Language Arts,* 65(2), 164–179.

McLaughlin, M. W., & Talbert, J. E. (2001). *Professional communities and the world of high school teaching.* Chicago: University of Chicago Press.

McNally, J., Cope, P., Inglis, B., & Stronach, I. (1994). Current realities in the student teaching experience: A preliminary inquiry. *Teaching and Teacher Education,* 10(2), 219–230.

Miles, M., Saxl, E., & Lieberman, A. (1988). What skills do educational 'change agents' need? An empirical view. *Curriculum Inquiry,* 18(2), 157–193.

Miller-Marsh, M. (2002). The influence of discourses on the precarious nature of mentoring. *Reflective Practice,* 3, 103–115.

Miller-Marsh, M. (2002b). The shaping of Ms. Nicholi: The discursive fashioning of teacher identities. *International Journal of Qualitative Studies In Education,* 15(3), 333–347.

Mitchell, C., & Weber, S. (1996). Drawing ourselves into teaching: Studying the images that shape and distort teacher education. *Teaching and Teacher Education,* 12, 303–313.

Moje, E. B., & Wade, S. E. (1997). What case discussions reveal about teacher thinking. *Teaching and Teacher Education,* 13(7), 691–712.

Mullen, C. A. (1997). Breaking the circle of one through mentorship. In C. A. Mullen, M. D. Cox, C. K. Boettcher, & D. S. Adoue, (Eds.), *Breaking the circle of one: Redefining mentorship in the lives and writings of educators* (pp. xv–xxv). New York: Peter Lang (Counterpoints series).

Mullen, C. A., Cox, M. D., Boettcher, C. K., & Adoue, D. S. (Eds.). (1997). *Breaking the circle of one. Redefining mentorship in the lives and writings of educators.* New York: Peter Lang.

Mullen, C. A., Kochan, F. K., & Funk, F. F. (1999). Adventures in Mentoring: Moving from Individual Sojourners to Traveling Companions. In C. A. Mullen & D. W. Lick (Eds.), *New directions in mentoring: Creating a synergy of culture* (pp. 18–34). New York: Falmer Press.

Mullen, C. A., & Lick, D. W. (Eds.). (1999). *New directions in mentoring: Creating a culture of synergy.* London: Falmer Press.

Newman, J. (Ed.). (1990). *Finding our own way.* Portsmouth, NH: Heinemann.

Noddings, N. (1988). An ethic of caring and its implications for instructional arrangements. *American Journal of Education,* 96(2), 215–230.

Noddings, N. (1991). Stories in dialogue: Caring and interpersonal reasoning. In C. Witherell & N. Noddings (eds.), *Stories lives tell: Narrative and dialogue in education.* New York: Teachers College Press.

Norman, P. J., & Feiman-Nemser, S. (2005). Mind activity in teaching and mentoring. *Teaching and Teacher Education,* 21(6), 679–697.

Olsen, B. (2008). *Teaching what they learn, learning what they live.* Boulder, CO: Paradigm Publishers.

Olson, P. M., & Carter, K. (1989). The capabilities of cooperating teachers in USA schools for communicating knowledge about teaching. *Journal of Education for Teaching,* 15(2), 113–131.

Olson, M. R., & Craig, C. J. (2001). Opportunities and challenges in the development of teachers' knowledge: The development of narrative authority through knowledge communities. *Teaching and Teacher Education*, 17, 667–684.

Orland-Barak, L., & Klein, S. (2005). The expressed and the realized: Mentors' representations of a mentoring conversation and its realization in practice. *Teaching and Teacher Education*, 21(4), 379–402.

Orland, L. (1997). *Becoming a mentor: A study of the learning of novice mentors*. Unpublished doctoral dissertation. Faculty of Education. Israel: The University of Haifa.

Orland, L. (2000). What's in a line? Exploration of a research and reflection tool. *Teachers and Teaching: Theory and Practice*, 6(2), 197–213.

Orland-Barak, L., & Hasin, R. (2009). Star Mentors. *Teaching and Teacher Education*.

Orland-Barak, L. (2001a). Learning to mentor as learning a second language of teaching. *Cambridge Journal of Education*, 31(1), 53–68.

Orland-Barak, L. (2001b). Reading a Mentoring Situation: One aspect of learning to mentor. *Teaching and Teacher Education*, 17(1), 75–88.

Orland-Barak, L. (2002). What's in a case? What mentors' cases reveal about the practice of mentoring. *Journal of Curriculum Studies*, 34(4), 451–468.

Orland-Barak, L. (2003a). In between worlds: The tensions of in-service mentoring in Israel. In F. Kochan & J. T. Pascarelli (Eds.), *Global perspectives on mentoring: transforming contexts, communities, and cultures* (pp. 191–211). Connecticut: Information Age Publishing.

Orland-Barak, L. (2003b). Emergency room (ER) stories: Mentors at the intersection between the moral and the pedagogical. *Journal of In-Service Education*, 29, 489–512.

Orland-Barak, L. (2004). What have I learned from all this? Four years of teaching an action research course: Insights of a second order. *Educational Action Research*, 1, 33–59.

Orland-Barak, L. (2005a). Lost on translation: Mentors learning participate in competing discourses of practice. *Journal of Teacher Education*, 56(4), 355–367.

Orland-Barak., L. (2005b). Portfolios as evidence of mentors' learning: What remains 'untold'. *Educational Research*, 47(1), 25–44.

Orland-Barak, L. (2005c). Cracks in the Iceberg: Surfacing the tensions of constructivist pedagogy in the context of mentoring. *Teachers and Teaching: Theory and Practice*, 11(3), 293–313.

Orland-Barak, L. (2006). Convergent, divergent, and parallel dialogues: Knowledge construction in professional conversations. *Teachers and Teaching: Theory and Practice*, 12(1), 13–31.

Orland-Barak, L., & Leshem, S. (2009). Making sense of one of observation in practice teaching. *Teacher Education Quarterly*, 36 (3), 21–37.

Orland-Barak, L., & Wilheim, D. (2005). Novices in clinical practice settings: Student nurses stories of learning the practice of nursing. *Nurse Education Today*, 25(6), 455–464.

Orland-Barak, L., & Yinon, H. (2005). Sometimes a novice and sometimes an expert: Mentors' expertise as revealed through their stories of critical incidents. *Oxford Review of Education*, 31(4), 557–579.

Orr, J. (1990). Talking about Machines: An Ethnography of a Modern Job, Ph.D. Thesis, Cornell University.

Parkison, P. (2008). Space for performing teacher identity: Through the lens of Kafka and Hegel. *Teachers and Teaching: Theory and Practice*, 14(1), 51–60.

Peshkin, A. (2000). The nature of interpretation in qualitative research. *Educational Researcher*, 29(9), 5–10.

Pfeiffer, L., Featherstone, H., & Smith, S. P. (1993, April). *"Do You Really Mean All When You Say All?", A Close Look at the Ecology of Pushing in Talk about Mathematics Teaching*. National Center for Research on Teacher Learning, Michigan State University.

Polkinghorne, D. (1988). *Narrative knowing and the human sciences*. Albany: Sunny Press.

Pope, M., & Denicolo, P. (1986). Intuitive theories-a researcher's dilemma. *British Educational Research Journal*, 12(2), 153–165.

Popper, M. (2001). *Hypnotic leadership: Leaders, followers and the loss of self*. Westport, CT: Praeger.

Popper, M., Mayseless, O., & Castelnovo, O. (2000). Transformational leadership and attachment. *Leadership Quarterly*, 11, 267–289.

Proctor, E. (1982). Defining the worker–client relationship. *Social Work*, 27, Spring, 430–435.

Pultorak, E. G. (1993). Facilitating reflective thought in novice teachers. *Journal of Teacher Education*, 44(4), 288–295.

Radnowsky, M. L. (1996). *Models as Visual Methaphors: Image/text balance in representing qualitative data*. Paper presented at the Annual Meeting of the American Educational Research Association, April, New York.

Rice, L. A. (1980). A client-centered approach to the supervision of psychotherapy. In A. K. Hess (Ed.), *Psychotherapy supervision: Theory, research and practice*. New York: John Wiley & Sons.

Richardson., V. (1990). The evolution of reflective teaching and teacher education. In R. T. Clift, W. R. Houston, & M. C. Pugach (Eds.), *Encouraging reflective practice in education: An analysis of issues and program* (pp. 3–19). New York, London: Teacher College Press, Columbia University.

Richardson, V., & Kile, R. S. (1999). Learning from videocases. In M. A. Lundeberg, B. B. Levin, & H. L. Harrington (Eds.), *Who learned what from cases and how? The research base for teaching and learning with cases* (pp. 121–136). Hillsdale, NJ: Erlbaum.

Roberts, A. (2000). Mentoring revisited: A phenomenological reading of the literature. *Mentoring and Tutoring*, 8(2), 145–170.

Rodgers, C. R. (2001). "It's elementary": The central role of subject matter in learning, teaching, and learning to teach. *American Journal of Education*, 109, pp. 472–480.

Rodgers, C. (2002). Defining reflection: Another look at John Dewey and reflective thinking. *Teachers College Record*, 104(4), 842–866.

Rodgers, C., & Scott, K. (2008). The development of the personal self and professional identity in learning to teach. In M. Cochran-Smith, S. Feiman-Nemser, D. J. McIntyre & K. E. Demers (Eds.), *Handbook of research on teacher education: Enduring questions and changing contexts* (pp. 732–755). New York: Routledge.

Rogers, R. (2004). An introduction to critical discourse analysis in education. In R. Rogers (Ed.), *An introduction to critical discourse analysis in education* (pp. 1–18). Mahwah, NJ: Lawrence Erlbaum Associates Publishers.

Rorty, R. (1980). *Philosophy and the mirror of nature*. Oxford: Blackwell Science.

Rowe, S. (2004). Discourse in activity and activity in discourse. In R. Rogers (Ed.), *An introduction to critical discourse analysis in education* (pp. 79–96). Mahwah, NJ: Lawrence Erlbaum Associates Publishers.

Rust, F. O. (1994). The first year of teaching: It's not what I expected. *Teaching and Teacher Education*, 10(2), 205–217.

Rust, F. O., & Dreifus, H. (Eds.). (2001). *Guiding school change: The role and work of change agents*. New York: Teachers College Press.

Rust, F., & Orland, L. (2000). Learning the discourse of teaching: Conversation as professional development. In C. M. Clark (Ed.), *Talking shop*. New York: Teachers College Press.

Sachs, J. (2005). Teacher education and the development of professional identity: Learning to be a teacher. In P. Denicolo & M. Kompf (Eds.), *Connecting policy and practice: Challenges for teaching and learning in schools and universities* (pp. 5–21). Oxford: Routledge.

Sawyer, R. K. (2003). *Improvised dialogues: Emergence and creativity in conversation*. Westport, CT: Greenwood.

Schatz Oppenheimer, O. (2005). *What can be learnt from beginning teachers' narratives*. Paper presented at the EARLI 11th Biennial Conference, August. Nicosia, Cyprus.

Schommer, M. (2002). An evolving theoretical framework for an epistemological belief system. In B. K. Hofer, & P. Pintrich (Eds.), *Personal epistemology: The psychology of beliefs about knowledge and knowing* (pp. 103–119). Mahwah: Lawrence Erlbaum Associates Publishers.

Schutz, A. (1970). *On phenomenology and social relations*. Chicago and London: The University of Chicago Press.

Schön, D. A. (1987). *Educating the reflective practitioner: Toward a new design for teaching and learning in the professions*. San Fransisco: Jossey-Bass.

Searle, J. R. (1995). *The construction of social reality*. London, Allen Pane: Penguin Group.

Semeniuk, A., & Worrall, A. M. (2000). Rereading the dominant narrative of mentoring. *Curriculum Inquiry*, 30(4), 406–428.

Seng, J. S. (1998). Praxis as a conceptual framework for participatory research in nursing. *Advanced Nursing Science*, 20(4), 37–48.

Sfard, A., & Prusak, A. (2005). Telling identities: In search of an analytic tool for investigating learning as a culturally shaped activity. *Educational Researcher*, 34(4), 14–22.

Shank, M. J. (2006). Teacher story telling: A means for creating and learning within a collaborative space. *Teaching and Teacher Education*, 22, 711–721.

Shapira, O., Orland-Barak, L. (2009, accepted). The multifaceted character of ethical dilemma in teaching: The Israeli Case. *Educational Practice and Theory*, 31(2).

Sherin, M. G. (2002). When teaching becomes learning. *Cognition and Instruction*, 20(2), 119–150.

Sherin, M. G., & Ham, S. Y. (2004). Teacher learning in the context of a video club. *Teaching and Teacher Education*, 20, 163–183.

Shulman, L. S. (1986). Those who understand: Knowledge growth in teaching. *Educational Researcher*, 15(2), 4–14.

Shulman, L. S. (1992). Toward a pedagogy of cases. In J. Shulman (Ed.), *Case methods in teacher education* (pp. 1–30). New York: Teachers College Press.

Shulman, L. S. (2004). *The wisdom of practice: Essays on teaching, learning, and learning to teach*. San Francisco: Jossey-Bass.

Shulman, J. H., & Sato, M. (Eds.). (2006). *Mentoring teachers toward excellence: Supporting and developing highly qualified teachers*. San Francisco: Jossey-Bass.

Sidorkin, A. M. (1999). *Beyond discourse: Education, the self and dialogue*. Albany: State University of New York Press.

Silva, D. Y., Gimbert, B., & Nolan, J. (2000). Sliding the doors: Locking and unlocking possibilities for teacher leadership. *Teachers College Record*, 102, 779–804.

Sleeter, C. E. (1998). Teaching whites about racism. In E. Lee, D. Menkart, & M. Okazawa-Rey (Eds.), *Beyond heroes and holidays: A practical guide to K-12 anti-racist. Multicultural education and staff development* (pp. 36–44). Washington, DC: Teaching for Change.

Smagorinsky, P., Cook, L. S., Moore, C., Jackson, A. Y., & Fry, P. G. (2004). Tensions in learning to teach: Accommodation and the development of a teacher identity. *Journal of Teacher Education*, 55(1), 8–24.

Smith, M. B. (1991). *Values, self, and society: Toward a humanist social psychology*. London: Transaction Publishers.

Smith, T. W., & Strahan, D. (2004). Toward a prototype of expertise in teaching. *Journal of Teacher Education*, 55(4), 357–371.

Soltis, J. F. (1984). On the nature of educational research. *Educational Researcher*, 13(5), 5–10.

Stake, R. E. (1988). Case study methods in educational research: Seeking sweet water. In R. M. Jaeger (Ed.), *Complementary methods for research in education* (pp. 253–265). Washington D.C: AERA.

Stanulis, R. N., & Russell, D. (2000). "Jumping in": Trust and communication in mentoring student teachers. *Teaching and Teacher Education*, 16(1), 65–80.

Steinman, J. F. (1971). Santayana and croce: An aesthetic reconciliation. *The Journal of Aesthetics and Art Criticism*, 30(2), 251–253.

Strahovsky, R., Marbach, A., & Hertz-Lazarowitz, R. (1998). *Six stages of the beginning teacher's hurdle race*. Paper presented at the annual meeting of the American Educational Research Association (AERA). San Diego, CA, USA.

Straker, A., & Hall, E. (1999). From clarity to chaos and back: Some reflections on the research process. *Educational Action Research*, 7(3), pp. 419–432.

Stromquist, N., & Monkman, K. (2000). Defining globalization and assessing its implications on knowledge and education. In N. Stromquist & K. Monkman (Eds.), *Globalization and education* (pp. 3–25). Lanham: Rowman & Littlefield Education.

Suchman, L. (1987). *Plans and situated actions: The problem of human–machine communication.* New York: Cambridge University Press.

Sundli, L. (2007). Mentoring – A new mantra for education? *Teaching and Teacher Education,* 23(2), 201–214.

Suppe, F. (Ed.). (1977). *The structure of scientific theories.* Urbana IL: University of Illinois Press.

Søreide, G. E. (2006). Narrative construction of teacher identity: Positioning and negotiation. *Teachers and Teaching: Theory and Practice,* 12(5), 527–547.

Tajfel, H. (1978). *The Social psychology of minorities.* London: Minority Right Group Report, 38.

Tharp, R., & Gallimore, R. (1988). *Rousing minds to life.* New York: Cambridge University Press.

Thorne, S. L. (2004). Cultural historical activity theory and the object of innovation. In O. St. John, K. van Esch, & E. Schalkwijk (Eds.), *New insights into foreign language learning and teaching* (pp. 51–70). Frankfurt: Peter Lang Verlag.

Tillema, H. H. (1998). Design and validity of a portfolio instrument for professional training. *Studies in Educational Evaluation,* 24(3), 263–278.

Tillema, H. H. (2005). Collaborative knowledge construction in study teams of professionals. *Human Resource Development International,* 8(1), 47–65.

Tillema, H. H. (2009). Assessment for learning to teach: Appraisal of practice teaching lessons by mentors, supervisors, and student teachers. *Journal of Teacher Education,* 60(2), 155–167.

Tillema, H. H., & Orland-Barak, L. (2006). Constructing knowledge in professional conversations: The role of beliefs on knowledge and knowing. *Learning and Instruction,* 16(6), 1–17.

Tillema, H. H., & Smith, K. (2000). Learning from portfolios: Differential use of feedback in portfolio construction. *Studies in Educational Evaluation,* 26(1), 193–210.

Tirri, K. (1999). Teachers' perceptions of moral dilemmas at school. *Journal of Moral Education.,* 28(1), 31–47.

Tom, A. R. (1984). *Teaching as a moral craft.* New York: Longman.

Tomlinson, P. (1995). *Understanding mentoring. Reflective strategies for school-based teacher preparation.* Buckingham: Open University Press.

Tripp, D. (1993). *Critical incidents in teaching: Developing professional judgment.* London: Routledge.

Valli, L. (1990). Moral approaches to reflective practice. In R. T. Clift, W. R. Houston, & M. C. Pugach (Eds.), *Encouraging reflective practice in education* (pp. 39–56). New York: Teachers College Press.

Van Manen, M. (1991). *The tact of teaching: The meaning of pedagogical thoughtfulness.* Albany: State University of New York Press.

Van Manen, M. (1995). On the epistemology of reflective practice. *Teachers and Teaching: Theory and Practice,* 1(1), pp. 33–50.

Van Veen, K., & Sleegers, P. (2006). How does it feel? Teachers' emotions in a context of change. *Journal of Curriculum Studies,* 38(1), pp. 85–111.

Villegas, A. M., & Lucas, T. (2002). *Educating culturally responsive teachers: A coherent approach.* Albany: State University of New York Press.

Von Glasserfeld, E. (1996). Introduction: Aspects of constructivism. In C. T. Fosnot (Ed.), *Constructivism: Theory, perspectives and practice* (pp. 3–7). New York: Teachers College Press.

Vygotsky, L. (1962). *Thought and Language.* Cambridge, MA: MIT Press.

Vygotsky, L. (1978). *Mind in Society: The development of higher psychological processes.* Cambridge, MA: Harvard University Press.

Wade, R., & Yarbrough, D. (1996). Portfolios as a tool for reflective thinking in teacher education? *Teaching and Teacher Education,* 12(1), 63–79.

Wang, J. (2001). Contexts of mentoring and opportunities for learning to teach: A comparative study of mentoring practice. *Teaching and Teacher Education*, 17, 51–73.

Webb, K., & Blond, J. (1995). Teacher knowledge: The relationship between caring and knowing. *Teaching and Teacher Education*, 11(6), 611–625.

Wenger, E. (1998). *Communities of practice: Learning, meaning and identity*. Cambridge: Cambridge University Press.

Wenger, E., Dermott, Mc., & Snyder, B. (2002). *Cultivating communities of practice*. Cambridge: Harvard University Press.

Wertsch, J. V. (1991). *Voices of the Mind: A sociocultural approach to mediated action*. Cambridge, MA: Harvard University Press.

Whitehead, J. (2000). How do I improve my practice? Creating and legitimating an epistemology of practice. *Reflective Practice*, 1(1), pp. 91–105.

Wiggins, G. (1989). A true test: Toward more authentic and equitable assessment. *Phi Delta Kappan*, 70(9), 703–713.

Wildman, T. M., Magliaro, S. G., Niles, R. A., & Niles, J. A. (1992). Teacher mentoring: An analysis of roles, activities, and conditions. *Journal of Teacher Education*, 43(3), 205–213.

Wilkin, M. (Ed.). (1992). *Mentoring in schools*. London: Kogan Page.

Witherell, C., & Noddings, N. (1991). Prologue: An invitation to our readers. In C. Witherell, & N. Noddings (Eds.), *Stories lives tell: Narrative and dialogue in education* (pp. 1–12). New York: Teachers College Press.

Yeomans, R., & Sampson, J. (1994). *Mentorship in the primary school*. London: Falmer Press.

Yerushalmi, H., & Karon, T. (1999). *Between supervisor and supervisee*. Jerusalem (Hebrew): The Hebrew University Magnes Press.

Yinger, R. J. (1987). *By the seat of your pants: An inquiry into improvisation and teaching*. Paper presented as the annual meeting of the American Educational Research Association, April, 1987, Washington, DC.

Yinger, R. J. (1990). The conversation of practice. In R. T. Clift, W. R. Houston & M. C. Pugach (Eds.), *Encouraging reflective practice in education: An analysis of issues and program* (pp. 73–94). New York, London: Teacher College Press, Columbia University.

Zanting, A., Verloop, J. D., Vermunt, J. D., & Van Driel, J. H. (1998). Explicating practical knowledge: An extension of mentor teachers' roles. *European Journal of Teacher Education*, 21(1), 11–28.

Zeichner, K. (1983). Alternative paradigms of teacher education. *Journal of Teacher Education*, XXXIV(3), 3–9.

Zeichner, K. M., & Tabachnick, B. R. (1985). The development of teacher perspectives: Social strategies and institutional control in the socialization of beginning teacher. *Journal of Education for Teaching*, 11, 1–25.

Zeichner, K., & Wray, S. (2001). The teaching portfolio in US teacher education programs: What we know and what we need to know. *Teaching and Teacher Education*, 17, 613–621.

Zellermayer, M., & Munthe, E. (Eds). (2007). *Teachers learning in communities*. Rotterdam: Sense Publishers.

Zembylas, M. (2003). Caring for teacher emotion: Reflections on teacher self development. *Studies in Philosophy and Education*, 22, 103–125.

Zilberstrom, S., Schatz Oppenheimer, & O. (Eds). (2005). *Novices in story*. Israel (In Hebrew): Ministry of Education.

Index

Note: The letters 't' and 'f' following the locators refer to tables and figures respectively.

LaVergne, TN USA
02 March 2010
174715LV00001B/95/P

9 781441 905819